# ŚŪNYA AND NOTHINGNESS

# India's Scientific Heritage

Founder Editor : Late Dr L M Singhvi



# 10

# ŚŪNYA AND NOTHINGNESS

*in Science, Philosophy and Religion*

JAYANT BURDE

MOTILAL BANARSIDASS PUBLISHERS
PRIVATE LIMITED • DELHI

*First Edition: Delhi, 2009*



ISBN: 978-81-208-3343-2

MOTILAL BANARSIDASS

41 U.A. Bungalow Road, Jawahar Nagar, Delhi 110 007
8 Mahalaxmi Chamber, 22 Bhulabhai Desai Road, Mumbai 400 026
236, 9th Main III Block, Jayanagar, Bangalore 560 011
203 Royapettah High Road, Mylapore, Chennai 600 004
Sanas Plaza, 1302 Baji Rao Road, Pune 411 002
8 Camac Street, Kolkata 700 017
Ashok Rajpath, Patna 800 004
Chowk, Varanasi 221 001

*Printed in India*

BY JAINENDRA PRAKASH JAIN AT SHRI JAINENDRA PRESS,
A-45 NARAINA, PHASE-I, NEW DELHI 110 028
AND PUBLISHED BY NARENDRA PRAKASH JAIN FOR
MOTILAL BANARSIDASS PUBLISHERS PRIVATE LIMITED,
BUNGALOW ROAD, DELHI 110 007

*In memory of*
*my father (Baba)*
*Dattatreya*

# Contents

# Preface

"You have been standing there, gazing at the empty glass for half an hour. What's the matter?"

"The glass is not empty, it's full of air. Even if you remove the air you will find an electromagnetic field in the glass".

The answer may appear facetious, but it need not be. It is quite possible that the glass-gazer is a physicist who is wondering what will happen if by some means even the electromagnetic field is removed. Will the glass be empty? In fact he/she may be thinking of the metaphysical riddle of *nothing* which science has led him/her to the puzzle humankind may never be able to solve.

In our day-to-day life we frequently use such words as zero, śūnya, nothing, nihil, nonbeing, nonexistence, void and emptiness. We know they are not synonyms, but believe that there is a common kernel which conveys the sense of "no thing". We are aware that these words differ from one another in meaning, and also that a given word has different connotations depending on the context. What we do not know is that the entire range of their meanings is almost infinite.

We usually treat mathematics as an exact science. But if a mathematician tells you that there are infinitely many zeros, and adds that the *integer* zero is not the same as the *fraction* "zero upon one", which differs from the *rational* zero which in turn is different from the *real* zero, you are bound to be shocked. You will be equally stunned if a student of *tantra* tells you that there is little difference between śūnya (zero) and infinity.

This book analyzes the notions of śūnya, nothing and other similar concepts found in various fields: mysticism, religion, philosophy, science and mathematics. This exploration reveals a strange but fascinating world of *nothingness*: a weird world with its mind-boggling contradictions and irrationalism conveying the same central message of *nihil*, a world where one finds prophets and philosophers trying to harmonize the contraries, *non sequiturs* and irreconcilables.

The book is aimed at the general reader who is assumed to have the knowledge of school mathematics. Most of the new mathematical concepts can be appreciated intuitively. The proofs of most results are not given, since the work is not addressed specifically to the students of mathematics.

I hope that apart from the general audience, the serious students of religion, philosophy and science, too, will find the work interesting. To them the book will present new dimensions: it will enable them to see how the idea of *nothing* in their field is connected with similar concepts in other disciplines.

The tortuous journey of this work right from the stage of its conception was beset by many hurdles which could only be overcome with the help of my friends and the staff of MLBD. I am grateful to all those who were helpful one way or another. I must particularly mention Mr. Rajendra P. Jain of MLBD without whose perseverance and suggestions, the book may not have seen the light. Dr. Sambhaji Bhavsar's excellent guidance was of great help. My sister, Meena, went through the entire manuscript and offered many suggestions. Mr. Yashwant Dusane prepared the manuscript and designed the figures.

Nasik
March 2006

Jayant Burde

# Abbreviations

| | | |
|---|---|---|
| AG | - | Avadhūta Gītā |
| AV | - | Atharvaveda |
| BG | - | Bhagavad Gītā |
| E | - | Examples or Illustrations numbered as E1, E2, ... etc. separately in each chapter. |
| RV | - | Rigveda (Ṛgveda) |
| SV | - | Sāmaveda |
| YV | - | Yajurveda |

# The Pronunciation of Sanskrit / Indic Letters and Words

1. Sanskrit vowels are pure such as are as found in French, Italian and Spanish. (a, i, u, ṛ, ḷ) are short while ( ā, ī, ū, ṝ, ḹ, e, o, ai, au) are long.
2. A dental consonant is one in which the tip of the tongue presses against the upper teeth.
3. A retroflex sound is pronounced with the tongue-tip curled back.
4. An aspirate is a consonant followed by the sound of 'h' e.g. gh in doghouse.
5. It is necessary to know the sounds only to recognize their basic differences. It is not necessary to pronounce the words exactly as Indians do, unless one is learning Sanskrit or an Indic language.
6. Some Indic languages have also borrowed certain sounds from Dravidian languages. These are omitted to avoid complications.

a p*u*n
ā f*a*rm
ai *ai*sle (approximate)
au c*ow* (approximate)
b *b*ear
bh aspirated b as in a*bh*or
c *ch*est
ch aspirated as in chur*chh*ill
ḍ *d*en, but retroflex
d *d*en but dental similar to th in *th*en

| | |
|---|---|
| ḍh | aspirated ḍ resembling dh in a*dh*ere |
| dh | aspirated d |
| e | pl*ay* |
| g | *g*o |
| gh | aspirated g, as in do*gh*ouse |
| ḥ | (slight aspiration of the preceding vowel) |
| h | *h*im |
| i | *i*n |
| ī | s*ee* |
| j | *j*et |
| jh | aspirated j as in lo*dgeh*ouse (approx) |
| k | *k*ill |
| kh | aspirated k similar to kh in wor*kh*ouse |
| ḷ | a short vowel resembling lry in reve*lry* |
| ḹ | similar to l, but longer. Usually not found in the text |
| l | *l*ip |
| ṃ | (nasalization of the preceding vowel) |
| m | *m*eet |
| ṅ | si*ng* |
| ṇ | a*n*d |
| ñ | ni*n*a (girl child) as in Spanish |
| n | *n*ever |
| o | n*o* |
| p | *p*en |
| ph | aspirated p similar to ph in u*ph*ill |
| ṛ | short retroflex vowel slightly resembling short ' i ' in the third syllable in *ability* |
| ṝ | similar to ṛ, but longer |
| r | *r*un, but more audible than in English resembling that in Italian |
| ś | *sh*e |
| ṣ | as in *sh*e but retroflex |
| s | *s*it |
| ṭ | *t*ip, but retroflex |

t wa*te*r, but dental

ṭh aspirated ṭ similar to th in an*th*ill

th aspirated t similar to th in *Th*ailand

u p*u*t

ū r*u*de

v *v*ery

y *y*es

# Introduction

Zero, śūnya, nihil, nonbeing, non-existence, void, emptiness, nothing. All these words seem to convey some common meaning. They certainly have a common core, "no thing". However, we are aware that they are not synonyms. There are many differences which appear in their usage. Moreover, any one of these given words can have different meanings depending on the context.

In this book we shall analyze these concepts to find out how they are inter-related. The analysis will reveal the entire range of possible meanings. To our astonishment we will find that some of these meanings are diametrically opposite to one another.

All of us study zero in school mathematics. There is a perception that mathematics is an exact science. It will surprise you to know that the word "zero" has different meanings in modern arithmetic — a fact we were not aware of when we struggled with numbers in school. For most of us zero is a number which roughly means "nothing", and which has specific properties. When added to another number we get the same number; when multiplied by any number we get back zero.

Mathematicians develop a system of numbers logically with some assumptions or axioms which need not be proved. The natural numbers consists of 0,1,2,... or 1,2,3... etc. There is no unanimity about whether 0 should be considered a natural number. There are many methods of "designing" the natural numbers. In most of these methods, the mumbers can be interpreted in infinitely many ways. Consequently, zero when considered as a natural number has countless meanings.

Mathematicians "derive" the integers on the basis of the natural numbers. They then proceed to construct the rational numbers with the help of the integers. Finally, the real numbers are built using the rationals as raw material. This leads to a hierarchy of numbers. The natural numbers 0,1,2... are not the same as integers 0,1,2,... The real numbers, again, are not the same as the rational numbers. For example, the real 5/3 is different from the rational 5/3. Consequently, we also have a hierarchy of zeros: natural, integral, rational and real. Fortunately, in practice we can forget the different avatars of zeros (or for that matter any other number) and work out our calculations ignoring their existential status as we did when we were in school. How this is possible will be clear later.

In our daily life we use many of the words such as *zero* and *void* metaphorically. "From hero to zero" is a common expression in which zero means worthless. When a great person dies, his obituary usually contains the words "the void created by his death cannot be filled". When we have a severe setback in our life, we feel that we are reduced to nothing. Elderly people, especially those who have lost their spouse, feel that there is nothing left in life. They feel a void and often wish they were dead.

Some psychiatric patients who suffer from severe psychosis have many delusions. One of them is that of nihilism. Life or the world appears strange or meaningless to them. However, the word "nihilism" is often used in social sciences to indicate the attitude which denies all authority.

In law, the words "null" and "void" are quite common. A void contract is a dead contract or no contract in the eyes of law. However, the phrase "null and void" is ubiquitous in legal parlance. When a lawyer tells you that a particular section of a legal Act is null and void, he means that the provisions of that section are not valid. Many lawyers appear to think that "null" and "void" have no independent existence, and unless they use the emphatic "null and void" their argument may not carry weight with the judiciary.

In the Eastern mysicism and philosophy, śūnya (zero, nothing) and Ākāśa (sky, ether, void) have great importance. But śūnya can mean many things. Some theologians have interpreted it as infinity. For example, Kṛtsnam sukhaṃ śūnyam means wholeness, brightness and infinity, though śūnya literally means zero. A school of Buddhism is called śūnyavada (literally "zeroism"). Its adherents will tell you that śūnya does not connote "nothing", but implies "indescribable". *Nirvāṇa* etymologically conveys nothingness, but to the śūnyavadins it means the state of enlightenment which cannot be verbalized.

Śūnya can also mean Brahman or the Ultimate Reality in the philosophy of Vedānta. Many Indian philosophers believe that emptiness is not nothing, it has its own fullness. It is also believed that in order to be free or liberated we have to empty our mind or whatever humankind has learnt for millions of years. This alone can lead us to insight and the universal Mind.

In Tantra, śūnya is the Great Void which exists below the sahasrāra, and is the Parama Śiva's (who is identified with Brahman) abode. In fact the Great Void is Śiva himself. Ākāśa (space, void, ether) is also identified with Brahman.

The word śūnya is often used to denote a mystical experience that is indescribable. Along with śūnya, mysticism and religion often use contradictions: "Brahman is finite as well as infinite", "In that state the yogi feels neither happiness nor misery"

In fact contradictions go hand in hand with zero and nothing. A corollary of this thought is the assertion that in any creation or substance there are male/female or positive/negative aspects. The conscious Puruṣa (male principle) and unconscious Prakṛti (female principle) provide an illustration from Sāṃkhya philosophy.

In Taoism one finds the principle of yang (male) and yin (female). Both Taosim and Zen appear quaint or bizarre in which opposites are involved. The Zen trainee is exposed to weird experiences: apparently meaningless riddles, merciless humiliation, ostensible blasphemy and so on. The Zennists, however, maintain that the training is calculated to expose the student to apparent contradiction and nothingness which ultimately leads to unity in emptiness. Taosim contends that it teaches "action in inaction" thus reconciling contradictions.

It is interesting to compare the concepts of zero and infinity in Eastern mysticism and modern mathematics. In both, zero (śūnya) and infinity are closely related. In mathematics they are opposites but go hand in hand. If a quantity x is made smaller and smaller, its reciprocal 1/x becomes larger and larger, and "tends to infinity" when "x tends to zero". This has made some mathematicians posit that $a/o$ is infinity when $a$ is not equal to 0. But while in mathematics there is only an association of these extreme concepts, in mysticism one finds their fusion: the void has an infinite potential for creativity, and the *bindu* which is a dimensionless point is an endless source of enormous power.

The Western philosophers, too, are aware of contradictions in life. Their reaction is usually confusion and pessimism which leads to the philosophy of nothingness. This is reflected in sophism, cynicism, skepticism and stoicism. A few philosophers like Hegel try to synthesize the opposites, by eliminating what is unnecessary and absorbing what is constructive so that the encounter between thesis and antithesis takes us to a higher level of knowledge viz. synthesis.

The Western philosophers also consider such concepts as being and nonbeing, becoming, existence, and nonexistence. However, all these ideas appear to be controversial.

The existential philosophy is centered around human existence, limitations of rationality and primacy of feelings. Many existentialists treat nonbeing as an entity. Some of them like Sartre perceive a confrontation between being and nonbeing. Nonbeing is identified with consciousness which continually desires *to be,* but its pursuit of being is futile. Some existentialists view nonbeing as a threat to being and a source of different types of anxieties. In existentialism one finds subjectivism, abstruseness, yearning for freedom, all expressing a multiplicity of reactions to contradictions. Many existentialists deal with the problem of nothingness of human existence and assert that existential predicament should be accepted through authentic living. The existentialists are more like creative artists than the cogitating philosophers.

In science we usually find two types of zero: the zero of the scale which is relative, and the quantitative zero. The origin of coordinate axes in geometry, the instant with respect to which the time of an event is measured, the zero of the temperature scales (Celsius or Fahrenheit) are a few examples of the relative zeros. These zeros can be shifted and are fixed according to our convenience. On the other hand, we have quantitative zeros which imply "nothing": zero gram, zero meter etc. A question which is philosophically important is whether all quantitative zeros constitute only one zero or whether their description is complete only when the physical units of measurement are specified. You will recall that your physics instructor insisted that when you write a magnitude you should also state the units: grams per cc, meters per sec. etc.

Logical and epistemological approach to zero, *nothing* and *null class* reveal interesting facts. "Not" appears almost equivalent to "false". Negative statements lead to contradictions and we resolve them only when we assume a hierarchy of words. The null class and zero are closely related: the cardinal number of the null class is zero.

The concepts of "nothing" and "void" have become extremely nebulous. Relativity and quantum theories have left scientists utterly confused. According to relativity theory, the world of phenomena can be completely described without any reference to absolute space and absolute time. What matters is the relations between different events. What we call "void" is not really void even if there is no air in it. There is always electromagnetic radiation in any given region of space. What's more, mass can be converted into energy and *vice versa* under suitable conditions.

At the subatomic level the world appears weird due to quantum phenomena. In what seems to be void "virtual particles" may suddenly appear as if by sleight of hand, and soon vanish.

Another quantum phenomenon that baffles scientists is the dual nature of subatomic existents which may behave either as waves or particles. "Interference" is a well known phenomenon displayed by interacting waves. A stream of electrons also can produce interference. What is astonishing is that a single electron can produce this effect. This apparently leads to the conclusion that an electron can be at two places at the same time.

The subatomic world often involves the "pairs of opposites" which are either created from nothing or annihilate each other. Many scientists have been fascinated by these phenomena which have parallels in Eastern mysticism which not only finds the pairs of opposites everywhere but attempts to reconcile them. The puzzled scientists hope to find answers to the riddles of modern science in Eastern mysticism.

Conceptually they appear to believe that both mysticism and modern science contain some such general law as

$$a + a' \Leftrightarrow 0$$

where *a'* is a negative of the phenomenon *a*, and the double arrow shows the two — way possibility. Whether this apparent parallelism in such diverse fields is really significant will be discussed in the last Chapter.

# Part I

## Elementary Concepts

1

# Zero in Arithmetic

## Zero and the Decimal System

The decimal system of numbers we use today, including zero or *śūnya* was invented by Indian mathematicians. In the beginning, the denary system of numbers did not have 'zero', but the symbol was added later. There was a misconception in the West that Arabs invented the denary system as well as zero, due to the fact that the West learnt the system through Arabs who picked up the system from Indians. They called mathematics "the Indian (art)" or *hindisat.*

The Roman and Greek systems of numbers appear primitive compared to the Indo-Arabic system and had it not been for the Indian numerals along with zero, progress in higher mathematics and science would not have been possible. Some other civilizations had numeral systems similar to ours, and included zero. This will be considered in Part II.

The sophisticated decimal system which we use today was not invented by one person. It has evolved over several centuries, and has undergone many stages of development.

One of the reasons why the Indian system took such a long time to reach the present stage is that it has several characteristics. During the intervening period of growth several systems came into existence, but were gradually replaced by revised systems which incorporated newer features not contained in the earlier ones. These features will be discussed in detail in chapter 7, but a brief account may be given here. (i) *The additive principle:* For example, 12 = 10 plus 2. (ii) *Multiple symbols* such as 0,1,2,..(iii) Zero as "nothing" as in 01, and zero as a place-holder as in case of 103 (iv) *Multiple functions* including place-value. For instance, in 11, the first 1 has the value ten, while the second has the value one. (v) *Base-symbol compatibility.* The base or radix in our system is ten and there are exactly ten symbols from 0 to 9. The following is an overview of the development of the decimal system in India.

## Vedic Literature

The rudiments of the decimal system are found even in the Vedas. The primary numbers from 1 to 9 are expressed in words: *eka, dvi, tri, catur, pañca, ṣaṭ, sapta, aṣṭa* and *nava.* The decuple (tenfold) terms were *daśa, viṃśati, trimśat, catvāriṃśat, pañcaśat, ṣaṣtī, saptatī, asiti* and *navatī* represented 10,20,30....90 in which one finds the numbers obtained by multiplying 1,2,..9 by 10. There was a third subsystem which was used to express powers: *daśa*(10), *śata* ($10^2$), *sahasra* ($10^3$) and so on upto *parārdha* ($10^{12}$). You will notice that this is a three-tier system based on ten, but there was no zero. Compound numbers were stated using a descending scale except for the last two denominations. For example,

1. *Sapta śatāni viṃśatiḥ* for seven hundreds and twenty (RV 1.164.11)
2. *Ṣaṣṭīṃ sahasra navatīṁ nava* for sixty thousands ninety and nine. (RV 1.53.9)

A number greater than sahasra was often expressed in the centesimal system. For example, *pañcāśat sahasram* for $50 \times 10^3$ (RV 1V.6.13)

While the principle of addition was common, the subtraction principle appears to have been used alternately with the addition principle in *Taittirīya Saṃhitā.* Thus *ekān-na-viṃśati* would mean. 20–1=19 (*nava-daśa*)

## Object - Numerals

Object-numerals (*Bhūta-saṅkhyā*) which are also called word-numerals seem to have been used even in Vedic times. To use modern language, object-numerals were based on the well-known "classes" or "sets". There are four Vedas. Hence the word Veda is used to denote four. Later, when we study modern views on "number" you will find that a cardinal number is defined in terms of classes containing the same number of elements. "Four" was also denoted by the words *varṇa, āśrama* and *yuga. Rūdra* represented 11 since there were 11 gods called Rūdra. *Nakṣatra* (asterisms) would denote 27.

A few fractions have also been expressed in the Vedas in object-numerals. For instance *kalā* (1/16) and *kuṣtha* (1/12).[1] Word-numbers were first used without place value which came into vogue later. A variant of word-numbers is the verbal representation of a number as it is pronounced: *eka*(1), *dvi* (2) etc. With or without place-value.

Word-numerals were also used in verse and were subject to various grammatical rules relating to gender, affixation and so on. Long numbers were constructed by juxtaposing word-numbers and using place value according to the rule: "*aṅkānām vāmato gatiḥ*" i.e. "the way of placing the numerals is from right to left".[2] For example, the words "*kha-rāma-guṇa-candraiḥ guṇāyet*" would mean "multiply by 1330". The word-numbers involved here are kha(0), rāma(3), guṇa(3) candra(1).

Word-numbers have been extremely popular and have been used extensively in mathematical and astronomical works by Bhāskara I, Brahmagupta, Śrīdhara, Bhāskara II and many other scholars. They were also used in texts relating to music, tantra and in the colophons of texts. Their use is found even in Sanskrit inscriptions dated *śaka* 526 (604 C E) and 547 (625 CE). These inscriptions were found in Jāvā and belong to the period when the island was an Indian colony.

## Alphabetic Numerals

Many systems based on the letters of the alphabet were invented. Perhaps the most famous system is Kaṭapayādi I that originated in Kerala. Āryabhaṭa I (b. 476 CE) was familiar with it, and hence it must have come into existence much earlier.

In this system one or more letters of the alphabet represented each of the ten numbers from 0 to 9 and the elements were written from right to left. There were a number of rules such as all vowels are treated as zero and those attached to consonants are ignored. Ten letters in Malayalam alphabet *ka* to *ña* represented numbers 1 to 9 and zero. The same numbers were represented by the letters from *ṭa* to *na*. The letters from *ya* to *la* again represented numbers from 1 to 9. The fact that there was no one-one correspondence between the letters and the numbers from zero to nine should make the system ambiguous. Nevertheless this very feature presented an opportunity to scholars to express numbers laconically. The system was so popular that it is used even today for certain purposes. In astronomy and mathematics it was used as late as in sixteenth century.

Āryabhaṭa I of Kusumapur (Patna) devised his own system based on the Sanskrit alphabet but it does not seem to have been accepted widely.

Āryabhaṭa II revised the Kerala system. His version is called Kaṭapayādi II. In this system the digits are presented from left to right. For example, *manana* indicates 500. In the older version it would indicate 005. However, it had some defects and did not survive long.[3] It is necessary to realize that both Kaṭapayādi I and II recognized the place-value.

## Quasi-decimal and Decimal Systems

The history of zero and decimal system in India cannot be expressed as a single sequence. One finds several strands each having its own evolutionary development. One of the reasons for this situation is that there were a number of languages and cultures which came into contact with one another. The Buddhist text *Lalitavistara* (100 BCE) maintains that there were about sixty four scripts (*lipis*), the prominent among them being Brāhmī and Kharoṣṭī. However, the latter disappeared gradually and Brāhmī and its derivative alphabets became common.

Scholars believe that apart from word-numbers, there were also twenty basic signs in Brāhmī for numbers from 1 to 9, 10, 20, 30... upto 90 and for 100 and 1000. Mixed numbers were formed by adding to these signs, strokes and ligatures. There was neither zero nor place-value. This assumption is contested by those who maintain that some of these so-called numerals were adaptations of Brāhmī letters. However, these arguments have been refuted by G.H. Ojha.[4] Be that as it may, unlike Kaṭapayādi systems, there seems to be a one-one correspondence between the basic numbers and their symbols. The oldest evidence is found in the edicts of emperor Aśoka, early third century BCE. However, many scholars believe that the numerals must have existed much before this period.

While the concept of zero as "nothing" is ancient we do not know exactly when it was incorporated into the system of numbers.

The earliest document is a mathematical tract written on birch-barks retrieved from under the ground in a village called Bakhshālī in Yusufzai district of Pakistan. This is generally known as Bakhshālī manuscript. According to many scholars including A.F.R. Hoernle it dates from third or fourth century CE. It not only uses the place-value and zero but employs the well-known symbol dot (*bindu*) for zero. However, the manuscript is in Śāradā script and some scholars feel that the putative date is not authentic.

Curiously, some of the earliest records are found in South-East Asia. Inscriptions dated 605, 606 and 608 according to śaka calendar (683, 684, 685 CE) have been found in Sambor, Palembang and Banka. Since the records are in Sanskrit, most scholars believe that the system was transported there by Indian immigrants.

In India the system appears in Ragholī charter of king Jayavardhana II dating from about eighth century. In Kaman (Rajasthan) an inscription dated 220 believed to be of Harṣa era which commenced in 606, has been found.

While śūnya appears in epigraphy much later there is no doubt that it was known and used much earlier. The word śūnya is mentioned in *Chandaḥsūtra* of Piṅgala (ca 400-200 BCE) in connection with verse meters.[5] Subandhu, a Sanskrit fictionist, (ca fourth century CE) compares the stars in the cloudless night to zero-dots (*śūnyabindavaḥ*).[6] The Jaina author Siddhasenagaṇi (sixth century CE) in one of his commentaries "makes an interesting observation about the inherent decimal property of śūnya".[7]

An early epigraphic evidence of place-value is found in Maṅkaṇi plates of Taralasvāmin of the Kalachuri year 346 (594-595 or 595-596 CE). Maṅkaṇi is a place in Vadodara district of the State of Gujarat. This style accords with the modern way of expressing a number. In the earlier quasi-decimal method the number would have appeared as 300 (+) 40 (+) 6.

A few remarks are in order. In general there is considerable resistance to any new ideas in an intellectual discipline and it takes some time before innovations are fully accepted by intellectuals as well as the public. The history of the denary system with zero reflects this attitude admirably. While the first epigraphs in the full-fledged system appeared much later, there is enough evidence in astrological and astronomical treatises and other literary sources to suggest that several variants of quasi-decimal and decimal systems were used concurrently before the full-blown system as we know today was universally accepted.

Varāhamihira (early sixth century CE) was familiar with the place-value. In his Pañcasiddhāntikā the number 1050 is expressed as *kha-indriya-diśaḥ*: *kha* for zero, *indriya* for five and *diśaḥ* for ten. While some of his expressions use *Bhūta-saṅkhyā* as in the above case, we find a singular example of an advance towards modern system in his *Bṛhat-Saṃhitā.* The number 8589 is written as *nava-aṣṭa-pañca-aṣṭa.* Note that nava, aṣṭa and pañca are the correct names for nine, eight and five unlike the metaphors kha (sky), indriya (senses) and diśaḥ (directions) in the previous example.

A few interesting illustrations are mentioned below. These are inscriptions of the Eastern Gangas and are dated in Ganga Era (G.E.)[8]

| No. | Year G.E | CE (Approx) | Inscription (transliterated) | | |
|---|---|---|---|---|---|
| 1. | 185 | 681-683 | 100 | 8 | 5 |
| 2. | 192 | 688-690 | 100 | 9 | 2 |
| 3. | 195 | 691-693 | 1 | 9 | 5 |
| 4. | 204 | 700-702 | 2 | 0 | 4 |

Note that 1-2 are in quasi-decimal form while 3-4 are in the modern style. The dates are so close to one another that one feels that both systems prevailed concurrently for some time. In 4 one finds the symbol 0, the way we write it today.

According to David Pingree, Indians borrowed the symbol 0 from Greeks who frequented India at the beginning of the common era. Before that Indians used "empty pit" or wrote "śūnya" to indicate zero.[9]

Mention must be made of Pāṇini (ca 350-250 BCE) a great Indian grammarian who used the concept of *lopa* (zero) in his grammar. This zero has close resemblance with mathematical zero.[10]

According to Prof. Ginsburg, the Indian numerical notation was carried to Arabia around 770 CE by a scholar Kaṅka who lived in Ujjain. He was invited to the court of Baghadad by Abbaside Khalif Al-Mansur. Kaṅka taught Indian (Hindu) astronomy to Arabian scholars. With his help Brahmagupta's text *Brahmasphuṭa-Siddhānta* was translated into Arabic.

While zero has several functions, in arithmetic we shall confine ourselves to its connotation of *nothing* in this chapter.

## Properties of Zero

Zero has the following main properties which all of us have studied in school.

1. If *a* is any number and "+" indicates addition, then
   a + 0 = a = 0 + a
2. If 'x' denotes multiplication,
   a x 0 = 0 = 0 x a
3. If a/b denotes 'a is divided by b' where *a* and *b* are numbers, then 0/a = 0 provided *a* is not zero.
4. The cases 0/0, a/0 (*a* not equal to zero) appeaı perplexing. Most modern mathematicians prefer not to define these divisions. However, the second ratio is often termed infinity (∞), a "number" which exceeds all numbers. The rationale for this is as follows: Suppose 5 is divided by 2, 1, 1/10, 1/100, .... we get the values 5/2, 5, 50, 500,.... As the denominator decreases, the ratio 5/b increases, and can be made as large as we want. It is, therefore, reasoned that when b becomes zero the ratio must reach the highest number. This notional entity is called "infinity" to distinguish it from finite numbers like 1, 20,000, 20,000,00 etc. However, this logic leads to ambiguities. For example in 5/0 the denominator can be approached through negative values -2, -1, -1/10, -1/100 which will give us -5/2, -5, -50, -500 etc. This ultimately should lead us to the "largest number" having the negative sign or -∞. This shows that it is difficult to define a/0. We have not defined addition and multiplication in a formal way. For the present we assign to them the same meaning as a school student intuitively attaches.

In the arithmetic which we study in school, zero *by itself* has the implication of "nothing". However this is not the only system of numbers mathematicians know. In fact, as we shall see later, those mathematicians who deal with "abstract mathematics" have constructed a formal system, in which *their* zero obeys the same laws as the zero mentioned above, but their zero need not necessarily mean "nothing".

2

# Commonsense Zero and Relative Zero

## Quantitative Zero

In the last chapter we considered the type of zero which could be used to indicate "nothing". This concept of zero can be appreciated even by those who have not been exposed to higher arithmetic. If you are familiar with counting and quantity, if you can understand that 5 mangoes are more than 3 mangoes and 3 mangoes are more than one mango or if you can assert that 1 kg of rice is less than 7 kgs of rice which in turn is less than 10 kgs of rice, it is only a small step to know that "zero mango" or "zero kg of rice" means no mangoes or no rice. This is an easy concept because it is intimately connected with our external world in which we count or measure something. There is not much of abstraction. In a+0=a, one only has to understand "+" which in practice means "and". For example, 5 bananas and zero bananas make 5 bananas. This sort of operation which has a real counterpart in what we do in practice is sometimes called "addition of individuals" by logicians. For the time being, however, we shall only confine ourselves to commonsense which implies intuition as well as our experience with the world in which we live. We might designate this zero indicating nothing as *commonsense zero or quantitative zero.* It may be argued that zero is zero, a number in mathematics and when we speak of "quantitative zero" we are unnecessarily confusing the number zero with its function of measurement. There is some substance in this argument. However, we shall see later that even in arithmetic, "zero" can have infinitely many meanings. Hence the term "commonsense zero", which certainly indicates a definite meaning may be used by us tentatively without any ambiguity.

## Relative Zero

Suppose there is a line on which three objects are situated at different points. In order to specify their relative positions we usually choose an origin O which is designated as "the zero of the line". All of us have learnt how to specify the locations of A, B, C with respect to O. All points on the right of O are given positive values and all points on the left are given negative values. What's more there is a one-to-one correspondence with respect to the points on the line and the real numbers. When we say that the "coordinate" of B is 2 we simply mean B is on the right hand side of O and OB = 2, and there is no other point whose coordinate is 2. In the figure below A(-1), B(2), C(3) indicate the position of A, B, C.

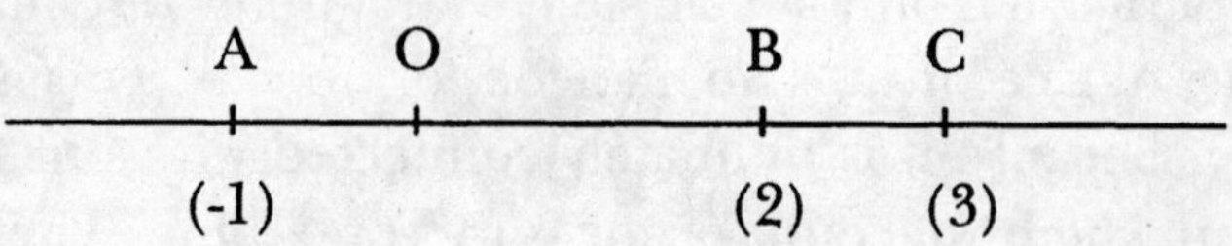


It is necessary to realize that O whose coordinate is zero, is arbitrarily chosen. We could have chosen A as the origin in which case A(0), O(1), B(3), C(4) would be the description of the locations of A, O, B, C. This zero is sometimes called the "zero of the scale" It is a shifting zero and not a constant.

You will recall the relationship between the Celsius (C) and Fahrenheit (F) scales of temperature given by

$F = 32 + 9/5\ C$

The temperature of ice is $0^{0}$C. If you let C = 0 in the above formula we get F = 32, which is the temperature of ice on the Fahrenheit scale. However, this case is more complicated: not only the zeroes of C and F are different, one unit of the Centigrade

is 5/9 that of the Fahrenheit. You are also aware that there is another scale — Absolute scale or Kelvin scale in which the zero coincides with $-273^0$C. C and K are related by
C = K-273

Let us recall Boyle's law of perfect gas
$V = V_0(1 + at)$

at constant pressure, where V, $V_0$ are the volumes of the gas at temperatures $t^0$ and $0^0$ in Celsius, and a is a constant which equals 1/273. If you substitute $t = -273^0$C, i.e. when the temperature is 0 on Absolute scale, you will find V = 0. Of course it is assumed that Boyle's law holds good at all temperatures. This may not be true — nobody has reached the Absolute zero in practice. But this illustration succinctly explains the difference between the relative zero ($0^0$C, $0^0$F) and Absolute zero or what we have termed the quantitative zero or commonsense zero.

## Cartesian Coordinates

Let us go back to geometry and the shifting zero on the line. Let P and Q be two points whose coordinates are p and q with respect to the origin O. The "distance" between P and Q is defined as

$PQ = |p - q|$, the absolute value of p-q. When P and Q coincide this distance is zero. This zero is certainly the commonsense zero showing "no distance" between P and Q. We shall later consider the generalized distance called *metric.*

In three dimensions, the position of a point is denoted by three coordinates: (x, y, z). The origin which can be arbitrarily chosen is given by the triple (0,0,0) which is a relative 'zero'. The distance between two points P (x,y,z), and Q (a,b,c) is given by

$$d = \sqrt{(x-a)^2 + (y-b)^2 + (z-c)^2}$$

Again, when P and Q coincide x = a, y = b, and z = c, which gives d = 0. This is the real quantitative zero.

Incidentally (0,0,0), the relative zero, is an example of zero which is not a number in the usual sense of the term. We shall encounter many such zeros as we proceed.

It would be interesting to consider in what way the quantitative zero differs from the relative zero or the "zero of the scale". The difference, of course, arises on account of the fact that the zero of the scale can be arbitrarily chosen.

Strictly speaking, to build a scale or locate a point on a line the only apparatus we need is "order". If we have a spatial order, say, A precedes B, B precedes C and so on and forth, ... on a line, what we need to indicate the position of these points is a correlation of real numbers (positive, negative and zero) with each point on the line. This is the minimum apparatus we need. Of course with the help of addition, multiplication and division we can construct advanced geometry, but "order" is the minimum "requirement" for building a scale. In a way we may call the relative zero *ordinal zero* which may be used in counting. Suppose there are twenty people in a room. Each of them can be assigned a number starting with 1 and ending with 20. We normally do not start with 0 but there is no harm if we label the first person as 0, the next as 1 and so on upto 19. I know at least one author who has started his book with "Chapter 0"[1].

The relative zero is extremely useful in any variable that is 'bipolar'. If we want to construct a scale to reflect such social or psychological parameters as poor-rich, dull-intelligent, malevolent-benevolent etc. we can arbitrarily choose a zero. For convenience the average can be taken as zero. The quantities exceeding this average can be assigned positive values and the ones falling short can be assigned negative values. On all such scales the "order" is a pre-requisite.

Like the points on a line, events can be correlated with real numbers. We can select any arbitrary event as zero. All the relatively future events occurring at a specific time will have positive values and the relatively past events will have negative values — all events with respect to an observer can thus be arranged in order on a time-scale.

3

# The Null Class

A concept closely related to quantitative zero in mathematics appears in logic and modern mathematics. At one place Russell calls it *logical zero.* To understand this concept, we should know something about *sets.*

## Set

A set is a collection of things or objects. For example,

{1, 2, 5}, {Paul, Abraham} are sets. An equivalent word "class" is used to denote a set. Logicians are more at home with "class" while mathematicians prefer "set". Sometimes the words "class" and "set" are reserved for specific collections. We shall, however use them interchangeably in this chapter.

It is unfortunate that mathematicians do not define what an object or a thing is. Some authors, in fact, treat the existence of sets as an axiom.[1]

Russell defines an object or an element of a class as anything that can be called a unit or a term which is the subject of counting. A major problem of this definition is handling the borderline cases. If two objects close to each other are viewed with naked eye they might appear as 'one' and the collection will be indicated only by one object. However, if they are viewed through a microscope they will appear distinct ... and the "set" will be said to consist of two objects. In such cases a line will have to be drawn to properly define an object. In any case, this shows that *spatial discontinuity* plays a role in counting. If a void is perceptible between two objects they will be reckoned as distinct terms, else the whole shall be treated as a single object. Discontinuity in time or *temporal discontinuity* plays a similar role. Suppose three notes are played in rapid succession. To the human ear they might appear as one note. But we may have an instrument which can indicate the time gap between the successive notes. We emphasize that perceived discontinuity is a factor that decides how many objects are there at one place.

Apart from discontinuity, there may be practical problems. A lady passenger carrying an infant who does not need a ticket, may have to be counted as one object for certain purposes. These problems can usually be resolved by custom and convention as well as the purpose for which a set is considered.

The objects which constitute a set are called the elements of the set. A set is usually denoted as follows:

A = {0, 5, 100}

B = {London, Paris, Mumbai}

0, 5, 100 are the elements of A and London, Paris, Mumbai belong to the set B.

There are a few misconceptions about a set, for which some textbooks are primarily responsible. First, the set need not be homogeneous. A collection {2, Rama, Ganges } is a legitimate set, though its elements are disparate. Second, the objects constituting a set need not be close to each other either spatially or temporally. {Caeser, North Pole, 5} is a valid set. Third, one should get rid of the idea that a set is a heap, though in certain cases its elements may be, say, stones forming a heap.

It is not necessary that an element should have "existence". It is sufficient if it has a being, by which we mean mythological or imaginary objects can be members of a set. For example, {chimera, Krishna, Apollo} is a legitimate set. The first is a mythical element and the second and third are gods in Hindu and Greek mythology.

Usually, verbs, adjectives and predicates are not treated as fit to be elements of a set. For example, {blue, jumped} is not a set, unless, perhaps when they are treated as examples of words.

You cannot repeat an element in a set. For example,

{5, 3, 3} is the same set as {5, 3}.

Similarly, the order in which the elements are written is immaterial. Thus

{7,8,9} = {9,7,8}

This implies that two sets are equal if they contain the same elements.

## Null Set

A null set or an empty set is a notional set which contains no elements. We can have an endless discussion on whether such a set can exist in the first place. Undoubtedly it resembles the quantitative zero in mathematics, but it looks more like an empty container, the container itself being not detectable. The null set is denoted by { } or $\phi$

Suppose you have a set {2,3,5}. If you remove the element 2, you get ... the set {3,5} . Remove 3, and you have the one-element set {5}. If 5 is also removed, nothing remains and strictly speaking there is no set because the collection ceases to exist. Nevertheless the null set is of practical utility. Though not as important as the commonsense arithmetical zero, it serves many purposes, as we shall see later. To circumvent the difficulty of defining it, many mathematicians treat the existence of the null set as an axiom.

## Extension and Intension

A set can be defined in different ways. When it is enumerated as in case of {2,0,5}, the method is called specification by *extension.* As pointed out above, this method appears awkward when we define a null set. Another difficulty lies in the enumeration of an infinite set or the set containing an infinite number of elements. Suppose we have to define the set of natural numbers

{1,2,3...}, the process is endless and we have to use "dots" to indicate the implication. But if the set is heterogeneous, its representation is impossible.

In the *intensional* method a class is specified by description
"All natural numbers"
"All inhabitants of New York"
"All rivers in North China"

These are examples of the intensional definition of a set. Though extension is a favourite method used by mathematicians, they employ intension to describe infinite sets or when intensional definition is precise. For example,

$A = \{x^3: x \text{ is a natural number}\}$
is a set $\{1,8,27....\}$

Needless to say the intensional method is laconic. Moreover, infinite sets can be expressed only intensionally. Russell also found a solution to the embarrassing problem of non-existence in case of the null set. We shall discuss it in a later chapter.

## Algebra of Sets

We can briefly discuss a few operations in the set theory. This will help you understand the utility of the null set.

### *Subsets*

A is called a subset of B if every element of A is also an element of B. For example,

$\{2,5\}$ is subset of $\{2,5,3\}$. Symbolically, we write $A \subset B$. Note that A is a subset of itself i.e. $A \subset A$; $\subset$ is called the inclusion relation. We also introduce a symbol '$\in$'. This indicates the relationship between an element and the set to which it belongs.

For example, $2 \in \{2,5\}$

It is easy to see that for any set A
$\phi \subset A$
i.e. the null set is a subset of every set.

The union of two sets A and B is the set consisting of elements which belong to A or to B or to both ("or" is used in the inclusive sense in logic)

Thus if $A = \{0,5,2\}$ , $B \{-1,0\}$

$A \cup B = \{0,5,2,-1\}$

$\cup$ is the symbol for union.

The intersection of two sets A and B is the set of elements common to A and B. In the above example,

$A \cap B = \{0\}$

$\{0\}$ is a one-element set and should not be confused with either '0' or the null set.

The formal way of defining these sets is

$A \cup B = \{x: x \in A \text{ or } x \in B\}$

$A \cap B = \{x: x \in A \text{ and } x \in B\}$

The union and intersection of more than two sets are similarly defined.

The following properties of the null class are obvious.

$A \cup \phi = A$

$A \cap \phi = \phi$

whatever the set A may be.

It is easy to verify the following results. Where A, B, C, D ....are any sets

1. $A \subset A \cup B$
2. $A \cap B \subset A$
3. $(A \cup B) \cup C = A \cup (B \cup C)$ Associative Law
4. $A \cup B = B \cup A$ Commutative Law
5. $(A \cap B) \cap C = (A \cap B) \cap C$ Associative Law
6. $A \cap B = B \cap A$ Commutative Law
7. $A \cup (B \cap C) = (A \cup B) \cap (A \cup C)$ Distributive Law
8. $A \cap (B \cup C) = (A \cap B) \cup (A \cap C)$ Distributive Law

You will notice rules 3 through 6 are similar to those of addition and multiplication in arithmetic.

For example, $2 + (3+5) = (2+3) + 5$

$2+3 = 3+2$ etc.

7-8 are distributive laws of (1) the union over intersection and (2) the intersection over union. In arithmetic multiplication is distributive over addition. For example,

$2 \times (3+7) = 2\times3 + 2\times7$.

However, you can easily verify that addition is not distributive over multiplication.

If A is a subset of B, B is called the superset of A, and we write $B \supset A$.

## Geometrical Representation

When we discuss sets, sometimes it is convenient to think of the *universal set U*.

If we are discussing the integers and rational numbers, we may think of the real numbers as the universal set. For convenience, a set is shown by a circle whose area is proportional to the number of elements they contain. Fig 3.1 shows sets A and B.

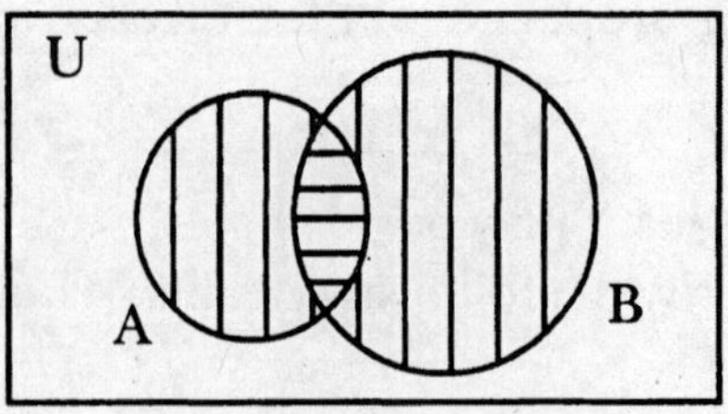


Fig. 3.1

and the universal set by U. Note that the horizontally shaded portion contains elements common to A and B, and is $A \cap B$. The portion shaded horizontally or vertically is $A \cup B$.

If two sets A, B have no common elements, obviously

$A \cap B = \phi$ or the null set.

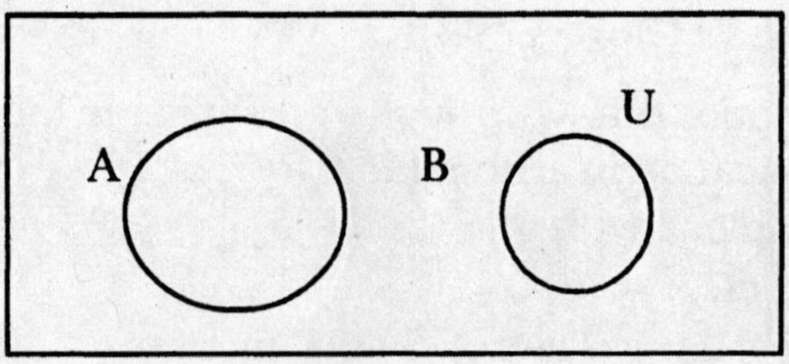


Fig. 3.2

Such sets are called disjoint sets. For instance {2,3} and {5,0} are disjoint. Fig. 3.2 shows two disjoint sets $A \cap B = \phi$ .Where is the null set? Since it is empty, it cannot appear on the diagram though we may denote it by $\phi$ . This will convince you that the null set is similar to the quantitative or commonsense zero.

## The Complement

The complement of a set A is defined as the set of elements which belong to the universal set but not to A.

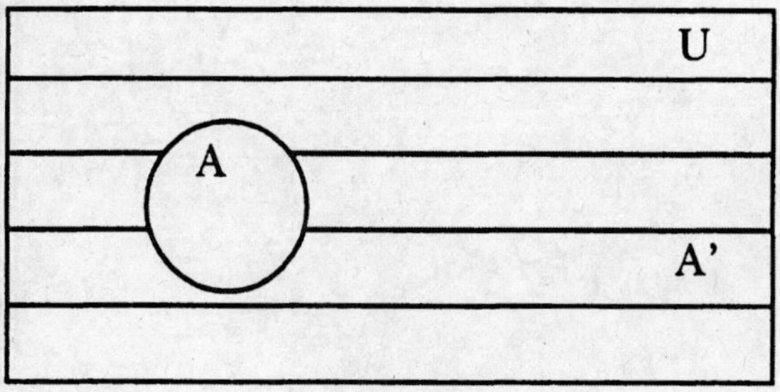


Fig. 3.3

We shall denote it by A'. In fig. 3.3 A' is represented by the shaded region.

The following results can be easily proved.

1. $(A')' = A$
2. $\phi' = U$
3. $U' = \phi$
4. $(A \cup B)' = A' \cap B'$
5. $(A \cap B)' = A' \cup B'$

# 4

# The Void and Science

## Atomism

We saw in chapter 2 that there exists a commonsense zero in geometry viz. zero distance. Distance relates to space, and there is another concept, *void*, in connection with space. It connotes emptiness, nothing etc. Unlike the zero distance, which implies space of zero dimensions, void can be large and in fact, we can conceive of an infinite void. The void implies the existence of space which does not contain any material things. Of course, this leads to a paradox: since the void exists it is not nothing.

A philosophy called *atomism* prevailed in ancient Greece. The philosophy is closely related to what is called realism. A distinguishing feature of atomism is that its adherents had a scientific approach to the world unlike many other Greek philosophers who were attracted to mysticism.

The word atom in Greek means that which is indestructible or indivisible ("a" for *not* "tomos" for *cut.*)

Three philosophers are closely associated with atomism; Leucippus (ca 440 BCE), Democritus (460- 370 BCE) and his follower Epicurus (341-270 BCE). Leucippus came from Melitus, a city associated with rationalism. He was influenced by the philosophers Parmenides and Zeno. Unfortunately very little is known about this personage and Epicurus is believed to have denied his existence.

Atomists believed that everything is composed of atoms which were physically, though not geometrically, indivisible. Atoms differed in colour, size and shape, and were infinite in number. They were also constantly in motion.

In order to accommodate the motion of atoms, the philosophers reasoned that there had to be a void between any two atoms. If there was only plenum, motion could not be conceived since plenum could not be penetrated. However, they were not entirely correct in their argument because in the plenum, there can be a cyclical motion, provided it has ever been there.[1] The atomists' approach is considered scientific in the same sense as the word "scientific" is used today. There was great emphasis on empiricism rather than speculation.

Atomists did not seek the "final cause" or teleological explanation for their universe. Hence, they did not need the concept of God or Creator. They did not try to explain how the motion of atoms started in the first place: this was taken as a basic premise.

Leucippus tried to reconcile atomism with apparently contradictory theories of the earlier philosophers and tried to mediate between monism and pluralism.

## Void as Non-being

According to Leucippus, the void is a non-being, and part of what *is* can be non-being. What *is* is in the strictest sense absolute plenum. But this plenum is not *one* but many and infinitely many. When the individual atoms come into contact with one another they interact with one other.

Unfortunately, there were two arguments to be countered. The first is related to the arguments of the earlier philosopher Parmenides (515-440 BCE) who is usually called an adherent of idealism. A hypothetical argument of Parmenides would appear as follows: You say that there *is* the void. If the void *is*, it cannot be nothing. If the void is nothing, there cannot be the void. The atomists were aware of this kind of rebuttal of the existence of the void, but they simply ignored it because the void was *sine qua non* for their philosophy of moving atoms. The other argument against the void came from the empirical evidence: though we feel there is a void, say, in a vessel, we know that there is air in it.

One method of avoiding the first argument is to distinguish between *matter* and *space*. We may say that space is not nothing but has the nature of a container or receptacle. The receptacle may or may not contain matter. According to Aristotle, " the theory that void exists involves the existence of place: for one defines void as place bereft of body."[2]

## Descartes and Newton

Rene Descartes (1596-1650 CE) regarded extension as the essence of matter. Hence matter existed everywhere. He treated "extension" as an adjective, not a substantive. This adjective qualified matter which is substantive. Hence extension or void cannot exist without matter. According to him empty space is absurd as happiness is without a sentient human being who is happy.

Issac Newton suspected that there was no absolute space, but the existence of the absolute void was implicit in his theory.

He distinguished between absolute and relative motions. The discovery by Copernicus (1473-1543) of the earth's rotation around the sun has interesting implications. His theory demolished the long-established Heliocentric theory of Ptolemy, and as we know the Church was on the side of the orthodox thinkers. However, if relative motion was accepted, then " the sun rising in the east and moving to the west" and "the earth moving from the west to the east" would imply that both sides accepted the empty space.

If all motion is relative, then these statements above are merely two different ways of saying the same thing like "John is the father of James" and "James is the son of John".[3]

Empirically, it is difficult to define a void. If we do not perceive anything in space, we know there is air. Even if we create a vacuum in an enclosed space, it will continue to show some properties it had when it was filled with air. Light will continue to travel through the 'void' and magnetic effects will not cease merely because the jar is emptied of air.

Newton conceived light as consisting of corpuscles having material properties. However, light showed many wave-like properties. It was James Maxwell who in 1865 propounded his theory of the propagation of light. Maxwell's equations integrated magnetic and electric fields. The solution of his equations showed that there could exist in space electromagnetic field which travelled with a fixed speed. The electromagnetic waves or radiation which travelled like ripples in a pond has a wide range of wavelengths.

What we call the visible light has a wavelength between 40 and 80 millionth of a centimeter. This is only a small portion of the entire range from the shorter wave lengths of the gamma and cosmic rays to the longer lengths of the radio waves.

There was, however, one problem about these waves. The sound waves, for example, need some medium, they cannot travel in vacuum. It was therefore assumed that space was filled with a substance called ether which facilitated the transmission of electromagnetic fields including visible light. Since there are hundreds of stars like the sun emitting energy in the form electromagnetic radiation, it is reasonable to assume that the major part of the universe which we think is void contains electromagnetic waves and hence the ether. But ether is an elusive medium that cannot be detected. Since it does not contain ordinary material atoms, its detection is impossible. Its omnipresence in the void can only be treated as a premise.

However, it was shown later by Einstein that the concept of ether was not at all necessary and the propagation of electromagnetic field did not need a medium. The modern view on this aspect will be discussed later.

For the time being we can only conclude that even what we call void contains electromagnetic fields; and hence it is no void at all.

Before we end this chapter, we must mention the views of Leibnitz (1646-1716), a contemporary of Newton's, on space. He was a renowned mathematician and philosopher. He believed in plenum, but maintained that space is merely a system of relations. He was strongly opposed by Newton and Clerke. It was Einstein who put an end to the controversy by showing that it is relations between several events that describe the universe, thus apparently vindicating Leibnitz.

5

# The Void in Darśanas

## The Schools of Indian Philosophy

*Darśana* in Sanskrit means "direct vision", but is the closest translation of the word "philosophy" in English. While philosophy is an intellectual pursuit, darśana connotes the personal experience of the philosopher who not only *thinks* but also *feels* the teachings of darśanas. Despite this difference darśanas, like western philosophy include logic, physics, epistemology and metaphysics.

There are two broad streams of Indian philosophy. The most important category accepts the Vedic authority and ... the respective schools (darśanas) are called orthodox. The schools which are heterodox include Buddhism, Jainism and Cārvāka. The last school is believed to be founded by Bṛhaspati. It is usually regarded as the "lowest" school because of its materialistic teachings. We shall discuss Buddhism and Jainism later.

The orthodox schools are: (1) *Nyāya* (2) *Vaiśeṣika* (3) *Sāṃkhya* (4) *Yoga* (5) *Mimāṃsā* and (6) *Vedānta.*

Of these, Nyāya and Vaiśeṣika are important for us at the moment. They discuss what may be called the physical "void". In this chapter we shall concentrate on the physical void or *nothing.* The spiritual void will be discussed later.

## Nyāya

This school was founded by Gotama who was also called Akṣapāda. Logic is the backbone of the Nyāya which is sometimes called *Nyāya Vidyā* or *Tarka Śāstra*, "the science of logic and reasoning."

Nyāya divides Reality into sixteen divisions of knowledge.[1] It also considers twelve categories of all the "objects" of the world. They are the soul, body, senses, objects of the senses, cognition (*buddhi*), mind (*manas*), activity, mental modifications, rebirth, pain-pleasure, regarded as the results of action, suffering and total freedom from suffering. However, it considers physical world as consisting of earth, fire, water and air. It regards space and time as nonmaterial though they belong to the physical world.

This has led to their ambiguous attitude towards space or *Ākāśa* or ether. Though *Ākāśa* is a physical substance, it is not the material or productive cause; in other words it is totally inert. While the earth, water, air and fire consist of eternal unchanging atoms, Ākāśa and time are treated as "wholes" though they, too, are eternal and infinite. Since Ākāśa has no constituents, it can be treated as a void. Nevertheless its treatment as a substance, though inert, gives it a double role — it can be treated as an inert plenum which cannot cause any changes.

## Vaiśeṣika

This school was founded by Kaṇāda also known as Ulūka. It is similar to the Nyāya. However, it recognizes seven categories (padārthas) of Reality. They are substance (dravya), quality (guṇas), action (karma), generality (sāmānya), uniqueness (viśeṣa), inherence (samavāya) and non-existence (abhāva).

The nine substances are the earth, water, fire, air, Ākāśa (ether), time, direction, soul and mind.

This school believes that the earth, water, fire and air consist of *paramāṇus*, or atoms which are indivisible and eternal. Atoms can neither be created nor destroyed. Each of these substances has distinct types of atoms.

The attitude of Vaiśeṣika towards Ākāśa is a bit strange. Ākāśa does not consist of atoms, but it is the substratum of sound.

Sound can be heard but Ākāśa cannot be perceived. Ākāśa is eternal and has no parts, and is all-pervading and infinite.

The description of Ākāśa brings about the following facts: the adherents of this philosophy were aware that for the propagation of sound a material medium such as air is needed. In all probability the philosophers considered Ākāśa as a void necessary for the propagation of sound. But like the Nyāya, this school treated Ākāśa as a "whole" and "substance". Hence from one viewpoint it can be treated as a plenum. Its status, therefore, seems to be ambiguous.

Ākāśa cannot be perceived because (1) it lacks any form and is colourless. (2) It has no perceptible dimensions. The relationship between sound and Ākāśa is quaint. We cannot say "sound travels in Ākāśa" rather, "sound is the quality of Ākāśa" would be more appropriate.

Time and direction have similar properties as space. They are infinite and indivisible. Like space, time and direction can be inferred, not directly perceived. However, they have a peculiar property due to certain limiting conditions called *upādhi*: in a vessel the space *appears* to be limited. Similarly time and direction may appear "multiples" (20 minutes, 2 hours, east, west). But this is only an appearance. In reality, space, time and direction, each should be treated as "one".

*Abhāva* - Vaiśeṣika recognizes a category called abhāva or non-existence. We have to remember that according to this philosophy "non-existence" is as much real as any other category.

The philosophy recognizes two types of abhāvas: (1) The absence of something in something else. This is called *saṃsārgābhāva,* (2) mutual non-existence or *anyonyābhāva.* The first non-existence has three sub-categories. Suppose you are going to paint a newly constructed house. The paint-on-the house comes into existence only when you actually paint the house. Before that the painting is a mere idea. Such non-existence has no beginning but has an end. This type is called "antecedent non-existence" (*prāgbhāva*). The second type of non-existence is *pradhvaṃsābhāva* in which non-existence appears after destruction. When fuel is burnt it ceases to exist as fuel. In this case the non-existence has a beginning, but no end, because the non-being (burnt fuel) cannot become being (fuel). The third type of saṃsārgābhāva is "absolute non-existence" (*atyantābhāva*). It has neither the beginning nor the end. "The horn of a man" would fall into such a category.

Mutual non-existence or anyonyābhāva is an assertion of diversity. A cat and a dog are different. We may say there is non-existence of cat in a dog and the absence of dog in a cat. This conception appears closely related with the notion of individuation in the western philosophy.

To see how "mutual non-existence" leads to endless classification and individuation, suppose there are 20 persons in a group. First, seggregate the two groups into men and women because "man does not exist in woman and woman does not exist in man." Suppose there are 8 men and 12 women. We find, among men, three dark and five fair men. Since on account of non-existence of certain pigmentation (dark or fair) we have a subdivision of say 5 fair men and 2 dark men. Of the dark men one is old, the other is a teenager. The old cannot exist in the young and there is non-existence of youth in the old age. Hence the dark men are divided into two categories each containing only an individual. If this process is continued, the entire group can be thus divided on the basis of non-existence into 20 categories, each category containing only one individual. Incidentally we have found a criterion for individuation to some extent. This is not surprising. For example, if A, B, C.... are the individuals, taking any two of them, say, B and C we can say that B does not exist in C and C has non-existence in B.

Individuation has other dimensions such as spatial or temporal discontinuity which are ignored for the time being.

One of the seven categories according to Vaiśeṣika are uniqueness (Viśeṣa) from which the school derives its name.

Viśeṣa is the unique characteristic of a thing which distinguishes it from other things. It is easy to see how uniqueness and mutual non-existence are connected. Suppose we have two things, *A* and *B*. Anyonyābhāva implies that A is non-existent in B. This argument holds good for all pairs A, B. In other words this is equivalent to saying that A, B, C etc., each has a unique characteristic which makes it non-existent in other things. This is how Viśeṣa and anyonyābhāva are connected. This also explains that by analysis either on the basis of uniqueness or mutual non-existence we can arrive at the conception of 'individuation' a term which implies that we can distinguish between 'this individual' and 'that individual'.

6

# Nihilism

## The Origins of Nihilism

The word *nihil* in Latin means "nothing". The word "nihilism" is a derivative which is used to indicate negative attitude. Unfortunately nihilism can be interpreted in several ways.

In the extreme sense nihilism means total and absolute denial of any positive ideals. Friedrich Heinrich Jacobi (1743-1819) is believed to be the first philosopher to have used this term. Jacobi was a German idealist philosopher and believed in feelings and faith rather than reason. Rationalism cannot explain religious feelings, which according to him, is the foundation of philosophy. His conclusion was that rationalism was atheism.

A closely connected philosophy which arose in Germany at the turn of the 19th century was called the *philosophy of life* which was a subjective-idealist philosophy. It was a reaction to the progress of science. The philosophy centered around life which cannot be understood by reason or senses. This philosophy may have contributed to nihilism, irrationalism and existentialism.

Nihilism became very popular in Russia after the famous writer Ivan Sergeyevich Turgenev (1818-1883) published his novel, *Fathers and Sons.* It is believed to depict the clash of two generations or the consequences of what we today call the "generation gap". However, it is much more than the defiance of authority. A synopsis of the novel is absolutely necessary to understand what its hero Bazarov thought about nihilism.

## The Nihilist

Bazarov was a doctor whose father, too, was a physician who once served in the army. The family considered itself as inferior to the country aristocrats. Bazarov had a friend, Arkady who belonged to such an aristocratic family. The germs of Bazarov's nihilism possibly lay in his own perceived social inferiority. At one place his family is described as "plebeians". Bazarov thus adopted unconventional ways, called himself nihilist and his friend Arkady was greatly influenced by his thoughts.

To understand what Bazarov's concept of nihilism was we will have to consider some sentiments expressed by the characters of the novel.

When Arkady refers to Bazarov as a nihilist, his father Nikolai Petrovitch understands by that word as the one who does not accept anything. Arkady's uncle Paul Petrovitch feels that a Nihilist respects nothing, which implies that a nihilist is against any authority.

Arkady, the pupil of Bazarov provides a definition of a nihilist: a person who regards things solely from the critical point of view.

Bazarov seems to be interested in dissection for which he captures a few frogs. Uncle Paul considers himself a perfect gentleman of his generation, and English culture and etiquettes are his ideals. His contempt for the revolutionary Bazarov is captured in his sarcastic remark: Bazarov believes more in frogs than in principles.

Bazarov considers a man who stakes his whole upon a woman's love a fool. He detests anyone who blames his environment for his plight. There is no reason why man should depend on a certain "period", he himself should be its creator. He hates romanticism and treats the relationship between man and woman purely in physiological terms. Arkady's father falls in love with a teenager and the girl has a child from him, and she continues to live with Arkady's family. Arkady's conscience tells him that his father should marry the girl. Bazarov's reaction to these sentiments is that it is a pity that Arkady attaches so much importance to the institution of marriage. The girl begins to like Bazarov because he has cured her child of a minor malady. Uncle Paul who hates the nihilist, one day finds the nihilist kissing this girl. Bazarov may not believe in love, but he seems to take the attraction between the opposite sexes in his stride. Moreover he is not bound by the contemptible conventions. Social conventions are for ordinary people, not for the nihilist.

Is nihilism a meaningless word? Consider what Bazarov has to say when Uncle Paul praises aristocracy. "The aristocratic idea, forsooth! Liberalism, progress, principles! Why, have you considered the vanity of these terms? The Russian of today does not need them."

At one point it appears Bazarov and his pupil Arkady believe only in denial. They do not recognize authority. Nevertheless Bazarov admits that he recognizes no basis for action except the useful, and given the prevailing conditions, denial is the best course. Their philosophy is: deny everything including poetry and art.

When Arkady's father asks Bazarov whether his philosophy implies that everything should be consigned to destruction, Bazarov's opinion is that the site must be totally cleared before reconstruction is undertaken. This suggests that the world must be totally destroyed and then rebuilt. This is the spirit of the revolutionary. But Bazarov does not seem to expatiate on which positive world he wants to build.

Once Uncle Paul remarks that the doctrine which Bazarov "preached" is nothing new. Materialism has been advocated before, and each time it failed. Bazarov replies that Paul is unnecessarily using foreign terms. "We nihilists don't preach at all. It is not our custom." He adds that the nihilists merely proclaim such facts as the bribery prevailing among civil servants, lack of highways and bridges and paucity of ethics in the judiciary. They feel that the question of bread is the most important. They find leaders unnecessarily discussing Parliamentary and legal points of no importance. They find it unbearable that the peasants are allowed to indulge in drinking while the leaders have futile discussions.

Paul taunts Bazarov that the nihilist's true *forte* is to apply seriously to *nothing*. Bazarov agrees and adds that Nihilism is denying everything.

Later, Bazarov meets an aristocratic and a beautiful widow, Madame Odinstove to whom Bazarov is attracted. He tries to kiss her, but that seems to express only a physiological reaction and not love.

It would be interesting to know what Bazarov has to say about his own profession. "Let me tell you that we ridicule all medicine and render reverence to no one." Bazarov feels that being a doctor and deriding medicine are compatible.

Some of his other views are:

1. There are no such things as principles. It is the instincts that alone exist; everything else depends on instincts.
2. Bazarov does not care whether he is young or old. He, however, confesses that he is a lonely man and wishes that someone pitied him. However, in another statement he contradicts himself. He recalls his childhood when he felt that an aspen tree and the depression near it was like a talisman for him. He never found time hang heavy upon him. Now that he is grown up, that talisman is lost. He realizes that his immunity from boredom in olden days was due to the fact that he was a boy.

His friend and the pupil Arkady falls in love with Madame Odinstove's sister, Katia. He accepts his own feelings and decides to marry her. Though he believes he stands for truth, he is no more a nihilist. Bazarov tells his friend that in the decision to marry, he has acted well because a true nihilist lives in battle and bloodshed constantly, and Arkady's nature is not meant for such hard life.

When Bazarov is on the deathbed suffering from pyaemia, he sends for Madame Odinstove. It is difficult to describe the struggle between Man Bazarov and Nihilist Bazarov. He calls her beautiful and a woman of kind heart. He recalls how he had kissed her. However, the nihilist warns her: if "I love" had no meaning for him earlier, now it has yet less meaning. He has seen that love is a form and his particular embodiment of it is about to dissolve.

## Bazarov and Nihilism

Can we truly believe that Bazarov was a nihilist who believed in nothing? It is doubtful. The novel depicts the confrontation between two generations in which the younger generation appears defiant, unconventional and revolting. This conflict can be partly attributed to the dynamics of social change. Partly it can be described as the manifestation of the child's natural rebellion against authority. Bazarov, though he is a tougher nihilist than Arkady, could never be a nihilist *in toto.* His behaviour appears to contradict his own principles at times, though he tries to keep the facade of the nihilist. In fact, denial of everything and acceptance of nothing is neither theoretically logical nor practically possible. Despite his ostensible nihilism Bazarov's human qualities could not be concealed. He loved his parents though he may not openly admit, and he had a close friend like Arkady. How can a nihilist who believes in nothing can believe in friendship? Bazarov, though he did not "believe" in medicine, administered it and was aware of its benefits.

Ivan Turgenev's *Fathers and Sons* was published in 1862. It attempted to depict the conflict between the generations after the Crimean war: the younger intellectuals and the older generation committed to the ideals of western civilization. Unfortunately, the novelist was criticized both by conservatives and radicals for his portrayal of Bazarov. Frustration led Turgenev to leave the country in 1863.

## Russian Revolutionaries and Nihilism

Russian revolutionists stoutly deny that they are nihilists. They asserted that the revolutionaries were democrats who had put forward concrete programs for progress. This did not amount to nihilism or acceptance of *nothing*. Lenin differentiates (1) revolutionary nihilism which was a natural negative attitude or response to reactionary social order and (2) nihilism which had roots in anarchic philosophy he imputed to Nietzsche.

Evidently, neither the older generation nor the younger intellectuals of Russia wanted to be identified with Turgenev's version of nihilism depicted in *Fathers and Sons.*

We will now briefly discuss two topics, negation and relativism, which are closely connected with nihilism.

## Negation

Negation does not mean denial of everything. For example, for socialists negation is selective, a condition for qualitative change and this negative component is regarded as a necessary moment of development.

In Hegelian philosophy or dialectics, in negation an object is transformed into another; the former is destroyed, but the transformation leads to an object at a higher level. Many philosophers believe that every object contains its negative aspect. Unity cannot exist without the opposites. In other words two contradictions form a unity. When these two "antitheses" are not mutually exclusive but penetrate each other, it is possible for us to "negate the negative". A third negative emerges which preserves what was "good" and eliminates what was unnecessary. This process is called *sublation.* The intrinsic negative of an object or a process takes us to the higher level. This process of inner contradictions and progressive sublation may continue till the entire unnecessary portion is thrown out.

This thinking shows that negativism *per se* need not lead to either anarchy or nihilism.

## Relativism

When we inspect different societies and their conventions and mores we find that they widely vary. Even within the same society there are cultural subgroups which have different ethical rules. These conventions also change over time.

Polygamy was prevalent in Hinduism but is now banned. Homosexuality is an offence in many countries like India, but is permitted in some others.

What I call a crime may be an innocuous act for you. Non-vegetarianism is not only tolerated in many countries, but is a necessity, while some sects like Jainas consider eating of flesh a sin.

This shows that what we call positive and negative thoughts or behaviour are relative words. This cultural relativity therefore is one of the causes of "apparent" negativism which, when the societal conditions are appropriate, may lead to conflict, anarchy and nihilism.

## Anekāntavāda and Syādavāda

In Jainism we find a philosophy connected with the mutual negativism as well as relativism. The renowned *tirthaṅkāra* Mahāvīra taught against absolutism. His thought that reality is relative and multi-faceted and is called *anekāntavāda* (*anekānta* for "not one end")

Relativism appears in different forms. For example, if A is a person, all the statements ; A is a lawyer; A is B's father; A is C's son; A is D's brother-in-law etc. may be true. Anekāntavāda may also appear in other forms: our views on a moral tenet or natural phenomenon may change with time: different societies may have different views. There is no room for the Absolute. This could be one of the reasons why the conception of God, the Absolute Truth or Ultimate Reality is absent in Jainism.

Anekāntavāda also recognizes that opposites exist simultaneously. We should endeavour to see that they are not mutual negatives which lead to cancellation or destruction, but they complement each other to produce the healthy unity. From this philosophy arises the Jaina maxim: *paraspara apagraho jīvanam* or "the function of living beings is to help one another." *Anekāntavāda* is vision or thought process. Jaina thinkers use another word *Syādavāda* which implies the manner in which this wisdom is given expression to.

Non-violence is the cornerstone of Jainism. Anekāntavāda and Syādavāda reflect how the inner as well as outer violence resulting from "double negatives" can be used for human growth. It may be mentioned that the mutual negatives can lead to anarchy, nihilism and destruction when not properly handled.

# Part II

## Zero in Mathematics

7

# Zero and the Grammar of Numerals

## Characteristics of the Decimal System

In order to appreciate the functions of the numeral 0, we need to discuss the decimal system which we use. The Indian system of numerals which we use has the following main characteristics: (1) Additive principle, (2) Multiple symbols, (3) Multiple functions, (4) Zero and (5) Base-symbol compatibility. Each of these will be discussed in brief.

We must remember that the numeral system is a sign system like a script, but differs from the Roman script which we employ in expressing non-mathematical thoughts. For example, we write a number as, say, 105 and not as "one hundred and five" though the latter mode may be used on certain occasions, say, in legal documents or in writing a check. Hence, the numeral system has its own rules. We shall avoid niceties and use the simple word *grammar* to indicate collectively all these rules.

## Additive Principle

This principle or the *principle of conjunction* is used not only in the Hindu-Arabic system but in most other numeral systems. For example, when we use the Roman numerals, 12 is indicated by XII in which 10(X), 1(I) and 1(I) are added to get XII. Our system too uses this principle.

Thus

$12 = 1 \times 10 + 2$

"1" in our system has a positional value 1 x 10 and not just 1. For example,

$5555 = 5 \times 10^3 + 5 \times 10^2 + 5 \times 10 + 5$

The additive principle appears here along with the positional values of "5". The unit's place has the value 5, the ten's place 5 x 10, the hundred's place 5 x 100 and so forth.

Sometimes a subsidiary rule of subtraction appears in some systems. For example IX in Roman means 9 = 10(X) - 1(I), but the use of this principle is limited.

## Multiple Symbols

At one extreme, a numeral system can use only one symbol. For example, if we use the symbol /, for "one", the successive numbers with additive principle would appear as

2 = //
3 = ///
4 = ////
5 = /////

Such devices are still used in statistics and charts. We may use points or bars to indicate population, each point or bar showing a certain number of persons. However, the one-symbol system would be extremely cumbersome and would require inordinate space to write large numbers. The arithmetical operations also would appear unwieldy. For instance,

7 + 9 = 16
would appear as /////// + ///////// = ////////////////

Most numeral systems use multiple symbols. The ancient Egyptians using hieroglyphics employed a stroke for one, an inverted arch for 10, a coiled rope for 100 and so on. The Roman numerals have seven key symbols:

I(1), V(5), X (10), L (50), C (100), D (500), M(1000)

With the additive principle and a subsidiary principle of subtraction it expresses numbers such as

7 = VII
20 = XX
24 = XXIV
(IV) = 5 (V) - 1 (I)
2322 = MMCCCXXII

At the other extreme we can conceive of a system in which each number has a separate symbol. Without doubt, such a system will be extremely clumsy and of no practical use.

## Multiple Functions

The Roman numerals do not use the principle of "positional value" which we mentioned earlier. This severely restricts the utility of the system. Suppose we have to add 624 and 758, the operations in the Indian and Roman systems would appear as follows:

| | |
|---|---|
| 624 | DCXXIV |
| + 758 | + DCCLVIII |
| 1382 | MCCCLXXXII |

We are so much used to our decimal system, that we would not understand how unwieldy the Roman numerals are unless we worked out such operations as addition and multiplication in this system.

Some other systems did use the concept of positional value. For example, the Babylonians used a positional system, but it was based on sixty and not ten (like ours). For instance, the wedge 𒁹 indicates "one".

Hence

𒁹 𒁹 𒁹 𒁹

would be interpreted as

$60^2 \times 1 + 60^1 \times 2 + 1$

= 3600 + 120 + 1
= 3721

Note that since the system did not have a placeholder such as zero as in our case, gaps were used to indicate successive positions. However, such systems often create ambiguities when it comes to writing fractions, and the value has to be interpreted contextually.

I have used the term *multiple functions* instead of positional value for this section. The reason will be clear from the following examples.

(A) 125, (B) 5/2, (C) $5^2$, (D) $5^0$

In (A) 2 has a positional value which equals 20. In (B) and (C) we cannot speak of the positional value of "2" which has the function of an operator. This is especially clear in (C) and (D) where 2 is 2, and 0 is 0, but 5 becomes 25 in (C) and 1 in (D). We should therefore, talk of the multiple functions, of a single symbol.

## Zero

The arithmetical zero was incorporated into the decimal system at a later date. Before it was introduced, the Indians combined numerals with linguistic expressions. Thus 132 was written as "1 *śata* 3 *daśan* 2" (*śata* = 100, *daśan* = 10). The invention of zero made the Indian numeral system more sophisticated.

It is interesting to compare our decimal system with that used by the Mayans in Central America (ca 400 CE). It used both the concepts viz. place value and zero. They had only three symbols; a dot for 1, a vertical bar for five and an ellipse for zero. Their system is called *vigesimal* (based on 20) which is not entirely correct. The place values were dependent on 20 and 18.

Thus 22 = 2 x 20 + 2 = 42
222 = 2.20.18 + 2.20 + 2
= 762
2222 = 2.20.20.18 + 2.20.18 + 2.20+2

= 14400 + 720 + 40 + 2

= 15162

The use of 18 was related to the Mayan calendar which we need not consider. The Mayans wrote the numbers from top to bottom.

For example,

•|| = 11 x 360 + 0 x 20 + 7

= 3967

**Base - Symbol Compatibility**

Our numerical system has the base or radix 10, and we also have 10 symbols. Mathematicians usually do not seem to realize that it is not just a coincidence but a principle which may be called *base-symbol compatibility.*

To understand this principle, let us compare the Mayan system, which is called a positional system, with our system.

In our system we write all digits horizontally. The Mayan system has to use two directions: one (horizontal) for fixing the digit and another (vertical) for fixing the position. The reason is obvious: the Mayan system has only four symbols and if they wrote them in one direction ambiguities would arise with principle of addition. For instance,

•| = 6 or 25

The Chinese "commercial" numeral system provides an interesting comparison. It lacked the base-symbol compatibility. For example, only one symbol | would be used to denote 1 ( | ), 2 ( || ), 3 ( ||| ). Nonetheless, the Chinese indicated the "digital position" by another symbol (pictogram). For example, ||+ = 20. The symbol + stands for *ten* (*shi*). The earlier system did not use zero. The pictogram ensured unambiguity despite the system being non-positional. For example, 215 was written as || followed by the pictogram for hundred followed by | which in turn was followed by the pictogram for ten, followed by the symbol for 5. In fact, this system was a mixture of numeral and alphabetical systems.[1]

## Fractions

The extension of the decimal to fractions in our system is facilitated by using a decimal point. However, the system has one disadvantage. For example, 1/3 = .333... which involves infinite number of the digits on the right hand side of decimal point, and a device like a superscript ($.\dot{3}$) has to be used.

## Other Numerical Systems

Instead of the denary system having the base 10, other systems having different bases but all other characteristics of our systems are also used in modern times. Computer scientists find it is useful to use the binary system in which only two symbols 0, 1 are used. In this system, a number, say 1101 is equal to $1 \times 2^3 + 1 \times 2^2 + 0 \times 2^1 + 1$
$= 8 + 4 + 0 + 1 = 13$

Computer scientists also use the hexadecimal system in which the base is 16 and the base symbol compatibility is achieved by having sixteen different symbols.

| Hexa-decimal | 0 | 1 | 2 | 3 | 4 | 5 | 6 | 7 | 8 | 9 | A | B | C | D | E | F |
|---|---|---|---|---|---|---|---|---|---|---|---|---|---|---|---|---|
| Decimal | 0 | 1 | 2 | 3 | 4 | 5 | 6 | 7 | 8 | 9 | 10 | 11 | 12 | 13 | 14 | 15 |

In this system $(13)_{16}$ would men $1 \times 16 + 3 = 19$

Table 7.1 shows different numeral systems and their characteristics.[1]

**Table 7.1**

| System | Additive Principle | Type | Positional | Zero | Base-symbol compatibility |
|---|---|---|---|---|---|
| Indian (Hindu-Arabic) | Yes | Decimal | Yes | Yes | Yes |
| Maya | Yes | Vigesimal (20 and 18) | Yes | Yes | No |
| Inca (Knotted strings) | Yes | Decimal | Yes | (Blank space) | No |
| Sumerians (Early) | Yes | Sexagesimal | No | No | No |
| Babylonian | Yes | Sexagesimal | Yes | No | No |
| Egyptian (Hieroglyphics) | Yes | Decimal | No | No | No |
| Early Chinese (Commercial) | Yes | Decimal | No | No (but unambiguous) | No |
| Greek (Ionic) | Yes | — | No | No | No |
| Greek (Attic) | Yes | — | No | No | No |
| Roman | Yes | — | No | No | No |
| Modern (Binary) | Yes | Binary (Base 2) | Yes | Yes | Yes |

It is interesting to see that while some systems, for example Indian and Mayan, which were invented independently had almost the same characteristics. But an independent invention is not a rarity. This is attributed to the fact that the human mind is the same and is endowed with the same logical apparatus (inside) facing the identical world (outside). However, one feature of similarity between the Mayan and our system appears startling: while our symbol for zero is a near-circle the corresponding Mayan symbol is its cousin, an ellipse.

## Power of Zero

Before we end the discussion on this topic, we may briefly mention the different powers the symbol 0 wields in our system.

1. By itself 0 is nothing or quantitative nothing.
2. As a digit its value again is nothing. For example in 1 2 3 the value of 2 is 2 x 10 while in 103 the value of 0 is 0 x 10 = 0
3. When prefixed to a number, zero does not alter the number. Thus
   0531 = 531
4. When infixed, it increases the number. Thus 17717 becomes
   10 7 7 1 7
5. When suffixed it multiplies the number tenfold
   310 = 31 x 10
6. In case of a fraction (<1) expressed with a decimal point (1) when prefixed or suffixed the fraction does not change
   .532 = 0.532 = .5320

When infixed it changes that value of the fraction. In particular if it is placed either after the decimal point or in the chain of zeros immediately following the decimal point or at the end of such a chain, the value of the original number becomes one tenth

$.012 = .12/10$
$.0\underline{0}012 = .0012/10$
$.00\underline{0}12 = .0012/10$

The infixed zero is underlined.

7. In the various operations zero behaves as follows (*a* is any number)

   (i) $a + 0 = a = 0 + a$
   (ii) $a \times 0 = 0 = 0 \times a$
   (iii) $a - 0 = a$
   (iv) $0 - a = -a$
   (v) $0/a = 0 \ (a \neq 0)$
   $0/0$ is not defined.
   (vi) $a^0 = 1 \ (a \neq 0)$
   $0^0$ is not defined.

# 8

# The Variable Zero

## Peano's System

There is no unanimity among mathematicians as to which is the first natural number: zero or one. The set of natural numbers is taken either as 0,1,2... or 1,2,3... We. shall denote the former by $\mathbf{N}^0$ and the latter by **N**.

In this chapter we shall introduce the concept of natural numbers which was suggested by mathematician Peano in his work *Formulaire* (1899, 1901). He used what may be called the serial concept in which zero appeared as the first number. We will find that this system leads to "relative numbers" or what Russell calls variable numbers. Consequently, Peano's zero is not the commonsense zero, but a relative or variable zero as we shall soon see.

Peano's concept of natural numbers is based on three primitive ideas or *indefinables* and five *primitive propositions.* The indefinables are: zero (0), number, and successor. They are called indefinables, because they can have any nature so long as they are consistent with the primitive propositions which are:

P1 0 is a number.
P2 The successor of any number is a number.
P3 No two numbers have the same successor.
P4 0 is not the successor of any number.
P5 If a property is possessed by 0 and also by the successor of

every number having this property, then every number has this property.

P5 appears a bit confusing but can be elucidated as follows: Suppose 0 has a property "x". Let n be a number which also has the property x. Then if the successor of n, too, possesses the property x, we can conclude that all numbers have the property x.

Since 0 is a number by P1, its successor, too, is a number. Call it 1. This, too, has a successor which is a number, say, 2. Repeating the argument, we have a series of (natural) numbers, viz.

(1) 0,1,2,3,....n,....

We observe the following properties of these numbers.

1. 0 is the first element because of P4.
2. A number cannot be repeated because of P3.
3. The series has a beginning but no end. If possible let "x" be the last number then its successor, say, y too is a number leading to a contradiction.
4. All numbers are included in (1) because of P5. For, if 0 belongs to $\mathbf{N}^0$ and every successor of a number n belongs to $\mathbf{N}^0$ then all numbers should belong to $\mathbf{N}^0$.

### Relativism of Numbers

Peano's system is internally consistent, but there is no way to prove that these numbers are the numbers we use in everyday life. In fact there can be infinitely many systems of numbers and hence countless zeros all obeying Peano's conditions. The following illustrations will make the point clear.

E1

1. 1,2,3,4....
2. 500,501,502,503...
3. 0,8,27...
4. 1,3,6,9...
5. 0,1,-1,2,-2...

It is easy to see that all these series are consistent with Peano's conditions. In (1) The zero is what in practice we call one.

Remember that the firsι number which is not the successor of any number is not fixed by Peano. In (2) the zero is the commensense 500, (3) is a series of the cubes of 0,1,2... Each member of these series is a number.

In (4) the "number" is the treble of the commensense number. In (5) the series starts with 0 but the successors are alternately positive and negative.

The reason for the existence of the infinitely many systems is simple: 0, number and successor are indefinables and we can assign any meaning to them so long as they are consistent with conditions P1 through P5.

With these variable numbers it would be difficult to carry on in the world where zero means *nothing*. Only the series 0,1,2,3.. where each number has the commonsense meaning can survive. However, mathematicians continue to define zero (though in a way different from Peano's) in a relative sense. They do recognize the drawback of the system, but it is the mathematicians' typical abstract approach to a problem. Of the many systems which are available they choose the system which coincides with our commonsense numbers, as the representative system to be used in practice. This is possible on account of what is called the *principle of abstraction* which we will refer to later.

Let us consider a few more examples

E2

a. .....,-2,-1,0,1,2...
b. 1,2,3,....100.
c. 0,1,2,3,3,4,4,5...
d. All points on a line segment AB, starting with point A and ending with B.

None of these examples give rise to the system of natural numbers. (a) is endless on both sides: it lacks "zero" which is not the successor of any number. If you inspect (5) of E1 you will find it contains the same elements, but (5) constitutes a valid system because it has the first term. This means that the same set arranged in one way may give rise to a system of numbers while when arranged in a different order may fail to generate a valid system. (b) does not qualify to be a system of numbers because the successor of 100 is not included, violating condition P2. (c) Suffers from the defect that "3" and "4" are repeated which means the same number can be the successor of two different numbers, which violates P3. (d) is an interesting case. No point has a "successor". Given a point on a line we cannot find the next point. In fact between any two points there are infinitely many points.

## Progression

Peano's system, in fact, can consist of any series of "numbers"

(2) $x_0$, $x_1$,$x_2$,....$x_n$, $x_{n+1}$.... provided it satisfied conditions P1 through P5.[1]

(a) The series starts with the "number" $x_0$, which is Peano's zero, and has no predecessor.

(b) We assume that all terms in the above series are different so that P3 is satisfied.

(c) The successor of $x_n$ is $x_{n+1}$

(d) We may define the words, zero, number, and successor in any way we like. The terms which appear above in (2) are in fact *numbers*, $x_0$ is a number, any number say $x_n$ which belongs to (2) has the successor $x_{n+1}$ which is also a number. P5 is automatically satisfied because we can define "property" as the property of belonging to (2). Since (2) is infinite, we can usually define it by intension. But we can also effect some changes in (2). For example, let the series be 0,1,2,....10, London, 11,12,...

calling "London" a *number*, and the successor of 10; 11 the successor of London. The above series satisfies all Peano's conditions and may be called the system of natural numbers in which the commonsense zero is 0 and the commonsense 11 is London, the commonsense 12 is 13 and so forth.

(2) is called a *progression*, a particular type of series which has a beginning and no end and whose members are all distinct. A progression may also be defined as a series satisfying Peano's five conditions.

This incidentally means that

0,1,2...

are mere labels tagged to any discrete and distinct objects arranged so that the series has a beginning but no end.

Before we end the Chapter, let us consider a few examples.

E3: The following are progressions which qualify as "natural numbers"

(a) Eiffel Tower, 1,2,3...
(b) Rasputin, Lincoln, 0,1,2....
(c) 0, The Nile,1,2,3....
(d) -1,0,1,2....
(e) Mt. Everest, Hermis,1,2,3....

You can easily identify the relative zero (the starting number) and relative one (the number next to relative zero)

However, Peano's number system is not yet complete. We have to define addition and multiplication.

Let m be any number. We define the sum as follows:

m + 0 = m. If n is any number m + (n + 1) is the successor of m + n. It can be easily verified that this operation is uniquely defined for any number m. Multiplication is similarly defined.[2] However we need not pursue the subject further, since our main purpose is to show the relativism of zero.

It must be mentioned that Peano was aware of the defect of relativism and said, "There is an infinity number of systems satisfying all primitive conditions." But he relied on what we have called the principle of abstraction.

# Relations

## Binary Relations

Before we consider other approaches to numerical zero, we need to understand the concept of relations and mapping.

The older philosophers who studied Aristotelian logic considered only one type of proposition, the subject-predicate type. This seriously hampered the progress of logic as well as mathematics. The concept of relations is extremely important in modern mathematics.

In fact we know intuitively what a relation means. "A is the husband of B", "X is Y's father", "Line L is perpendicular to line M", all indicate what are called binary relations. Suppose x, y are elements of a set S, xRy is a symbol for "x is related to y". Of course, R has to be specified.

In the set of integers, "divides" is a relation. For example 2R8 (2 divides 8), 4R8 and so forth. "Spouse" is a relation in the set of human beings. In the set of lines "parallel" is a relation; aRb means line *a* is parallel to line *b*. In xRy, x is called the *referent* and y is known as *relatum.*

It is necessary to remember that when the relation is defined two elements of a set need not be related. For example the relation "divides" is such that 3 is not related to 7. If we have aRb, a converse relation $R^{-1}$ arises such that $bR^{-1}a$. For example "divisible by" is the converse relation of "divides". Thus if 3R27 means "3 divides 27", 27 $R^{-1}$3 would mean "27 is divisible by 3".

The following examples will elucidate the concept of relations.

E1

(a) In the set of humans, aRb means *a* is the ancestor of *b*. The converse relation is $bR^{-1}a$ where $R^{-1}$ means "descendent of".

(b) In the set of real numbers "less than" is a relation whose converse is "greater than".

In E1(a) two humans need not be related, while in (b) two distinct numbers are always related either by "less than" or its converse.

(c) In the set of points on a horizontal line aRb means "point *a* is to the right of point *b*". Its converse relation is "to the left of"

## Relation and Extension

Some mathematicians prefer to define relation extensionally. Let A and B be two sets then (a,b) where $a \in A$ and $b \in B$ is called an ordered pair

(a,b) = (c, d)

if and only if a = c, b = d.

You will recall that we use ordered pairs to indicate the position of a point in plane coordinate geometry in school.

If A and B are non-empty sets, the set of all pairs (a,b) where $a \in A$ and $b \in B$ is called *Cartesian product* A x B. We can also think of the Cartesian product A x A which is sometimes denoted by $A^2$.

Extensionally, a binary relation is a subset R of a Cartesian product A x B. If A = B we call the relation R *in* A. We denote the relation as before, viz. aRb.

Let A = {0,2,1}, B = {2,3}

then the subset (0,2), (1,3), (2,2) may be called a binary relation and

R = {(0,2), (1,3), (2,2)}

Note that the extensional definition appears artificial and arbitrary while the *intensional* definition implies what our commonsense calls "relation".

## Types of Relations

(1) A relation R in a set S is called *reflexive* if for every element *a* of S, aRa.

(2) R is called *symmetric* if aRb implies bRa.

(3) R is *asymmetric* if for any a, b of S aRb implies that bRa cannot hold good.

(4) R is called *transitive* if for any a, b, c of S, aRb and bRc imply aRc.

(5) R is called *antisymmetric* if for any a, b of S, aRb and bRa imply a = b.

(6) R is a *partial order relation* if it is reflexive, transitive and antisymmetric.

(7) R satisfies the *law of trichotomy* if for any a,b of S, exactly one of the following holds good (i) aRb (ii) bRa (iii) a = b.[3]

E2

(a) S is the set of humans, R is the relation "sibling". R is symmetric and transitive, but not reflexive.

(b) In the set of real numbers R is "divides". R is reflexive and transitive.

(c) In the set of real numbers R is "equal to", R is reflexive, symmetric and transitive.

(d) In the set of real numbers R means "less than". R is transitive and asymmetric.

(e) In the set of lines R is "perpendicular to". R is symmetric.

(f) In the set of real number "is equal to or less than" is a partial order relation.

A relation is called an equivalence relation if it is reflexive symmetric and transitive. In E2 (c) exemplifies equivalence.

## Equivalence Classes

Equivalence relation is of great importance in mathematics. Suppose we conduct a survey in population statistics. In 100 couples we find the following data.

| Class | No. of Couples | No. of Children |
|---|---|---|
| A | 10 | 0 |
| B | 22 | 1 |
| C | 51 | 2 |
| D | 17 | 3 |

Consider the relation R among the set of couples, "have the same number of children as". R is reflexive, symmetric and transitive, hence an equivalence relation . The couples can be grouped in four categories A, B, C, D having 0,1,2 and 3 children respectively. They contain 10,22,51 and 17 couples respectively. These classes have the following properties.

(1) The couples in a given class have the same number of children.

(2) A couple cannot belong to more than one class.

(3) The union of sets A, B, C, D gives the surveyed population and all these classes are disjoint.

Every equivalence relation in a set S leads to such disjoint classes. For example, "earns the same salary as", "has the same height as" in humans are equivalence relations which divide humans into mutually disjoint classes. These classes are called *equivalence classes.* The "set of equivalence classes" such as {A,B,C,D} is called *quotient set* with reference to the given relation and is denoted by S/R.

## Mapping

A concept similar to relations is mapping. To understand this concept consider two non-empty sets, $X = \{x_1, x_2, x_3, x_4\}$, $Y = \{y_1, y_2, y_3, y_4\}$. (fig. 9.1)

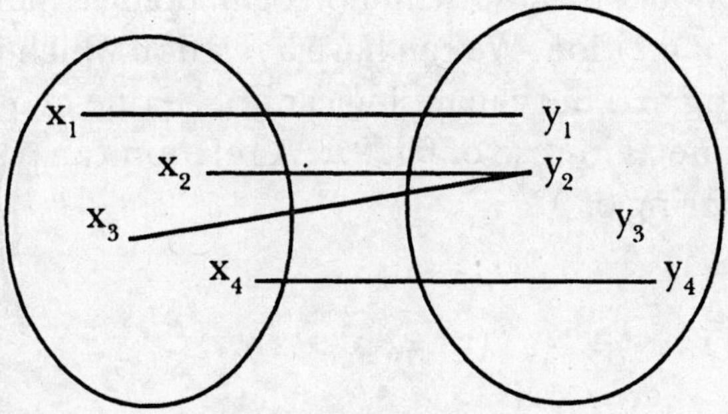


Fig. 9.1

With each element of X we associate one and only one element of Y. This correspondence is called mapping from X to Y and denoted by

$f : X \rightarrow Y$

$x_1$ is associated with $y_1$, which is indicated by $f(x_1) = y_1$. Similarly, $f(x_2) = y_2$, $f(x_3) = y_2$, $f(x_4) = y_4$

$y_1$,$y_2$... are called the images of $x_1$,$x_2$... respectively, which are termed "pre-images" of $y_1$, $y_2$ etc. X is called the domain of and Y, the co-domain.

We should particularly note the following:

1. Every element X has an image and only one image.
2. Some elements of Y need not be images. In the above figure $y_3$ is not an image.

The set of images, ($\{y_1, y_2, y_4\}$ in the above example) is called *range* of f.

## Types of Mapping

A mapping which has a single image as the range is called *constant* mapping.

A mapping is called 1-1 or *injective* if no two elements of X can have the same image. This means if $f(a) = f(b)$, then $a = b$.

A mapping is called *onto* or *surjective* if every element of Y is an image under f.

Note that in the figure 9.1, f is neither 1-1 (because $f(x_2)$, $f(x_3) = y_2$) nor onto ($y_3$ has no pre-image).

You will notice that the definition of mapping is more restrictive than that of relation. We can have a relation which is one-many (*e.g.* "sibling of") but a mapping cannot be one-many; but it can be many-one as in case of fig. 9.1. A relation can also be many-one ("offspring of")

E3

(a) **f : $N^0 \rightarrow N^0$, f(n) = 3n**
**where n $\in N^0$**
f is *one-one*, but not onto, 1, 2, 4, 5... etc. are not images.

(b) **f : R→R** (**R** is the set of real numbers)
$f(x) = x^2$
f(x) is not one-one. For example both +2 and -2 have the same image viz. 4. However, f is also not *onto* since negative numbers cannot be images under f.

(c) **f : R→R**
$f(x) = +\sqrt{x}$
This is not a mapping at all, because the negative numbers do not have images in R. We can modify f and make the domain non-negative.
f' =**$R^+$→R**
in which it is a valid mapping, one-one but not onto

(d) **f :** R→R
f(x) = 0, x ∈ **R**
This is a constant mapping.

(e) **f : X→X**
f (a) = a for all a of X, f is called *identity* mapping.
Two mappings f, g from X into Y are called *equal* if and only if
f(x) = g(x) for every element of x of X.
It is easy to see that in case of real numbers, if
$f(x) = (x+1)^3$
and $g(x) = x^3 + 3x^2 + 3x + 1$
f(x) = g(x)

## Product of Mappings

Suppose we have two mappings.

$f: X \rightarrow Y$

$g: Y \rightarrow Z$

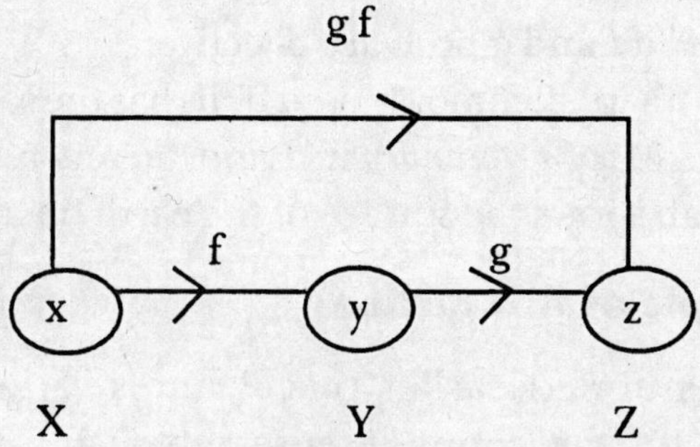


Fig. 9.2

Let the range of f be contained in the domain of g. Then we can define the *product* gf of the mappings such that

$gf(x) = g(f(x))$

In fig. (9.2) $f(x) = y$, $g(y) = z$, then $gf(x) = g(f(x)) = g(y) = z$.

In general, fg and gf (when f and g both exist) are different mappings. For example, in case of real numbers if $f(x) = x^3$ and $g(x) = x+5$

then $gf(x) = g(x^3) = x^3+5$ and

$fg(x) = f(x+5) = (x+5)^3$ Hence $fg \neq gf$

## Inverse

If $f: X \rightarrow Y$ is 1-1 and onto it is easy to see that there is one-one correspondence between the elements of X and Y (fig.9.3)

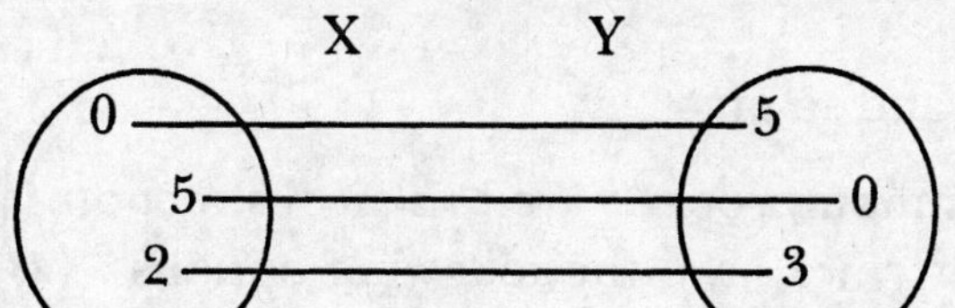


Fig. 9.3

This means that with every element X we can associate one and only one element of Y and *vice versa.* This enables us to define the inverse of f, denoted by $f^{-1}$. Thus in figure 9.3 $f(0) = 5$, $f^{-1}(5) = 0$ and so forth. It is easy to see that $f f^{-1} = f^{-1}f = i$, the *identity mapping.* Thus $i(0) = 0$. We can also prove that if f, g are two maps,

$(fg)^{-1} = g^{-1}f^{-1}$ if f and g both are bijective.

The word "map" commonly used by us has the same etymology as mapping. *Mappa* (*mundi*) in Latin means a sheet (of the world). A map shows the surface of the earth on a smaller scale.

## The Principle of Abstraction

We had mentioned earlier that Peano's variable zero was identified with the commonsense zero using the principle of abstraction.

To understand this principle, suppose we have a number of objects of different colours. We divide them into lots in such a way that each lot contains the objects of the same colour, while the objects in different lots have different colours. In fact the relation "has the same colour as" is an equivalence relation and leads to what we have called equivalence classes. Of course, there are practical problems - there may be a few border-line cases in which we may not be able to decide if a particular object should go to one lot or another. We ignore these problems for the time being.

Let us now concentrate on the lot we have labelled "red". Suppose the objects in this lot are x,y,z... etc. Then we can say

x is red
y is red
z is red, and so on.

The common property "red" is an abstraction. To designate this property, we have the following options : (a) call the lot "red" (b) identify the lot by one of the objects in it, say, y. Thus "y" will be the representative or *standard* of the lot.

The above sentences are of simple subject-predicate type. We can use the same technique when the relational sentences appear. For example, "x is as intelligent as y." Here, the sentence is not of the subject predicate type. But we know that this relation is reflexive, symmetric, and transitive. Hence it leads to equivalence classes. We can select a certain member as the standard of the class to which the member belongs. For example, if x, y.... belongs to X, Y... etc. then choose x, y.... as standards of X, Y, ... etc.

Thus our class has been abstracted. Alternatively, we may select X, Y, Z.... the classes themselves as representatives of the relation.

In fact, for abstraction what we need is not equivalence, but something less. Philosophers had realized long back that the relation which is symmetric and transitive arises from what they called "identity of content". For instance, "sibling" is a relation which is symmetric and transitive, but not reflexive, but siblings have the common property of belonging to the same parents. Suppose we have seven children who are grouped on the basis of being siblings.

| Class No. | Children | Father | Mother |
|---|---|---|---|
| 1 | A,B,C | L | M |
| 2. | D,E | P | Q |
| 3. | F,G | R | S |

These sets of children are disjoint. You can observe that this relation (sibling) can be abstracted in three ways :

(a) By the class number allotted to the set.

(b) By one representative of the class

(c) By either of the parents. For example the first can be recognized by class 1 or (say) B or L (or M). The most surprising feature of such grouping is that the group can be represented by something that is external to it (parents in this case).

## The Natural Numbers as Abstraction

Peano's method leads to infinitely many systems of natural numbers. Consider the following systems

| | | | | | |
|---|---|---|---|---|---|
| A | $a_0$ | $a_1$ | $a_2$ .......... $a_n$ | | ...... |
| B | $b_0$ | $b_1$ | $b_2$ .......... $b_n$ | | ........ |
| C | 0 | 1 | 2 ............. n | | ...... |
| D | London | New York | 3 ............. n-1 | | ..... |
| E | 1 | 4 | 9 ............. $(n-1)^2$ | | |
| F | 0 | 1 | 8 ............. $n^3$ | | ... |
| Classes | $X_0$ | $X_1$ | $X_2$ .......... $X_n$ | | |

Each of the above is assumed to be a progression and satisfies Peano's five conditions. Each system is therefore, a system of (natural) numbers. Observe that there is a one-one correspondence between the elements of the progressions. For instance $a_0$,$b_0$,0, London, 1,0 represent the first elements of A through F. This correspondence can be looked upon either as bijective mappings or one-one relations. This relation is reflexive, symmetric and transitive and leads to equivalence classes $X_0$, $X_1$... All elements in one column belong to a unique class. We adopt the following method of abstraction : choose 0 from class $X_0$,1 from class $X_1$, 2 from class $X_2$ and so on. In other words we choose the progression (C) as a representative of all progressions. Thus we select progression C : 0,1,2,...n... (where the elements are commonsense numbers) which will be the standard progression to be called the natural numbers. We choose this system to accord with Peano's conception of the numbers starting with zero.

10

# The Commonsense Zero

## Logical Approach

In the previous chapter, Peano's approach of numbers led us to infinitely many systems. From these we had to choose the "right" or commonsense system which helps us in practice, using the principle of abstraction. In this chapter we consider the *logical* approach which gives only one system. As Russell points out, the system gives us numbers that are constants and not variables. It also agrees with our commonsense and we get a zero which may be called the *commonsense zero, constant zero, absolute zero or quantitative zero of arithmetic.*

## Set of Sets

Consider a set A = {1,2,5}. Let us construct the set of all sets or class of all sets from A. This class of sets is

{ϕ, {1}, {2},{5},{1,2},{1,5},{2,5},{1,2,5}}

ϕ is the null set and there are one-element, two-element and three-element sets. The number of elements in the class of sets is 8 or $2^3$. If a set A consists of n elements, it can be proved that the set of all sets obtained from A is $2^n$. This is called the power set, and denoted by P(A).

## Similarity or Numerical Equivalence

We have already introduced the concept of 1-1 correspondence. It is believed that before numbers were invented, our ancestors used the method of 1-1 correspondence for "counting."

Suppose there are two heaps A, B of stones. With one stone from A we associate one and only one stone from B. Thus the stones from A and B are "paired". The following possibilities arise at the end of this operation.

(1) All the stones of A are paired with all the stones of B. We can then say that A and B have the same "quantity" of stones.
(2) The stones from B are exhausted, but a few stones of A remain unpaired. We can conclude that A has more stones than B.
(3) Some of the stones of B are unpaired. Our conclusion is that B has more stones than A.

The savage who did not know counting must have used this method to gauge the size of a heap.

The notion of 1-1 correspondence which appears primitive is extremely important and has revolutionized our concept of infinity.

Two sets are called similar or numerically equivalent if we can establish a 1-1 correspondence between the elements of these sets.

The relation "similar to" is reflexive, symmetric and transitive and hence an equivalence relation. This means that a class of sets can be divided into equivalence sets that are similar to one another.

The logical approach to the *number* system regards number as a characteristic of a class. The sets similar to each other have the same number. The logical approach was first incorporated in Frege's *Grundlagen der Arithmetik* in 1884, but was ignored by mathematicians, until Russell rediscovered it in 1901 and developed the concept further.

Peano has mentioned three methods of definitions: that by postulates, that by abstraction, and the nominal definition. The first method is cumbersome and ruled out in this case. Since we arrive at equivalence classes we can use a definition of number by abstraction.

(1) Since the similar sets involve symmetry and transitivity, we may assign a symbol to an equivalence class. The symbol will indicate the "common content" mentioned in the last chapter.
(2) We could take one of the sets as a standard for the equivalences class to which it belongs. For example, all "trios" form equivalence classes. We may choose a standard "trio" preserved in a laboratory. This is not practicable, since there would be countless standard sets to be preserved.

Russell has a unique method of defining a cardinal number. According to his defination called the *nominal definition,* the cardinal number of a set is the class of all sets similar to it. Thus the class of all duos *is* the number of every duo which for convenience we may call "two". Similarly, the class of all "trios" *is* the number of every trio and so on.

## Numbers as Constants

We recall that Peano's indifinables are 0, number, successor. We define them concretely as follows:

(1) A number of a set is the class of all sets similar to it. This makes a particular "number" unique. This is also called the *cardinal number.*
(2) Zero (0) is the class of all classes whose only member is the null set. The null set is empty and this concept agrees with our commonsense concept of numerical zero as "nothing".
(3) The successor of the number of a set S is the number of a new set S' which consists of all terms of S and *x* which does not belong to S. Let us see if the numbers we have created satisfy Peano's five conditions. We call the successor of 0,

1; the successor of 1, 2 and so on. If n is a number, its successor is n+1. Our numbers are:

0,1,2,.......n, n+1,....

1'. By the very definition of zero, it is a number.

2'. Zero cannot be a successor of a number. If it were, our definition of "successor" would make zero a number of nonempty set which contradicts the definition of zero.

3'. The definition of *successor* again ensures that the successor of a number is a number. There is however, an implicit axiom that there are infinite number of objects in the world. If the number of objects were finite, say fifty, we would not be able to define the successor of 50. In fact all numbers beyond fifty would lead to the null class.

4'. It is easy to prove that a number cannot be the successor of two numbers.

5'. Peano's last condition is usually modified as:

Finite numbers are those to which zero belongs and to which n+1 belongs if n belongs.

This is an assumption regarding finite numbers and is called the *axiom of mathematical induction.*

The "logical" approach leads to numbers which are constants and not variables; we may call the corresponding zero, *commonsense zero, absolute zero, constant zero or quantitative zero* of numbers.

The numbers we have obtained are also called inductive numbers. Suppose we are given a number, say, 51, we can reach by *succession* number 100. But in practice to reach $10^{27}$ from 51 would be difficult. It is the assumption regarding mathematical induction which ensures such a bridge in theory. As Russell pointed out in case of finite numbers "what can be inferred from next to next can be inferred from the first to last".[1] Infinite numbers are those to which the axiom of induction does not apply. Earlier mathematicians regarded the inductive property as a principle, but they were wrong. It is only through an axiom that the property is possessed by what we call finite numbers.

While we have defined the inductive numbers, we have not yet shown that its "zero" behaves in the same manner as the zero of the layperson. For this, we have to define two operations addition and multiplication.

## Addition

We know that a set has a unique number. Consider two sets X and Ywhose numbers are m and n respectively. We assume that X and Y are disjoint. Then the number of $X \cup Y$ is called the addition m+n. This concept can be extended to any number of sets. Let C be a class of sets, all disjoint. Then the cardinal number of the union of all sets is the sum of the numbers of individual sets.

A great advantage of this approach is that the following laws follow automatically from the properties of the union of sets.

(1) $m + n = n + m$ (Commutative law.)

(2) $m + (n + p) = (m + n) + p$ (Associative law.)

This definition is general i.e. C or its constituent sets can be finite or infinite.

In particular,

$m+0 = m = 0+m$

follows from a trivial result viz. $A \cup \phi = A$, where A is a set whose cardinal number is m, and $\phi$ is the empty set whose cardinal number is 0.

## Multiplication

We shall follow Whitehead's definition of multiplication.[2] Consider a class of two sets A and B which are disjoint. A multiplicative class of sets, M is formed as follows: each set contains one and one element only from A and B.

Suppose A = {x,y,z} and B = {a,b}. The multiplicative class consist of sets {x,a}, {x,b},{y,a}, {y,b},{z,a}, {z,b}. The number of sets is the product of the number of A and B viz. 3x2 = 6.

In general, if C is the class of any number of *disjoint* sets, we define the multiplicative class M as one whose member-sets are formed by one and only one element from each of the sets of C. The number of terms (sets) in M is the product of the numbers of all the set of C.

Since Whitehead's definition does not contain any notion of order, the following laws follow immediately.

(1) $m\,n = n\,m$ (Commutative law)
(2) $m(np) = (mn)p$ (Associative law)
(3) $m(n+p) = mn + mp$ (Left distributive law)
$(n+p)m = nm + pm$ (Right distributive law)
(4) The connection between addition and multiplication viz. if C is a class of mutually exclusive sets numbering *a* and each containing *b* elements, then the union of these sets has the number ab.

Since our attention is focussed on zero,

$m\,0 = 0 = 0\,m$

is trivial because the multiplicative set of the null set and a set whose number is m is also a null set.

There is, however, a problem in relation to multiplication. When C contains an infinite number of sets, the product cannot be defined unless we assume what is called the *multiplicative axiom*. However, if the number of sets is finite, it does not matter whether the constituent sets are finite or infinite.

## Finite and Infinite Sets

Our notion of finite and infinite sets is only intuitive. We must define these terms mathematically.

A set is called infinite if there is a one-to-one correspondence between its elements and those of its proper subset. In such a case the set is obviously similar to its own subset.

Consider the following sets

(1) 0, 1, 2,.....n,...
(2) 1, 2,.....,,,,n+1,....
(3) 51, 52,.......n+51,....
(4) 0, $1^2$, $2^2$,...$n^2$....
(5) 1, 3, 5,....2n-1....
(6) 0, $1^3$, $2^3$,...$n^3$....

The first set is our standard set of natural numbers. It is clear that there is a one-one correspondence between the elements which are in the same "column" of all these sets. Sets 2 through 6 are proper subsets of set (1). Hence the set of natural numbers is infinite. This approach is also consistent with the result we arrived at earlier viz. in abstract,

$x_1, x_2$,....

a progression without end satisfying Peano's conditions is a set of natural numbers. Sets 2 through 6, too, are infinite. You may remove some of the elements from it and show that the resulting proper subset is similar to the original set.

For example, if we omit some numbers from (2) we get a proper subset which is similar to (2)

7,8,9,....

1,2,3......

The result appears startling to our common sense. For example (4) is the set of squares of number which is similar to (1) which is the set of numbers. (5) shows that there are as many odd natural numbers as the natural numbers. (6) shows that there are as many cubes of numbers as the numbers themselves. The crux of this result lies in our definition of "infinite" as well as "number", which is based on the notion of 1-1 correspondence.

A finite set is one which is not infinite. A set, say, {1,2,...15} is finite. You may try to establish 1-1 correspondence between it and any proper subset, you will not succeed.

## Transfinite Numbers

The set $\mathbf{N}^0$ or any of the six sets mentioned above is a set of finite or inductive numbers. By that we mean that any set whose cardinal number is say, 122000, 1025, 100100 and so forth is finite and its cardinal number is a finite inductive number. But what is the status of $\mathbf{N}^0$ itself? This is an infinite set. What is its cardinal number?

We have defined the (cardinal) number of a set as the class of all sets similar to it. All six sets shown above are similar to $\mathbf{N}^0$. Hence they should have the same number. In fact all sets similar to $\mathbf{N}^0$ or $\mathbf{N}$ have the same cardinal number. Since this is not any of the finite numbers, it is called a transfinite or infinite number. The cardinal number of $\mathbf{N}^0$ is called ($\aleph_0$) which is the Hebrew letter (ℵ) *Aleph* with the suffix zero. This is believed to be the smallest transfinite number. The set $\mathbf{N}^0$ is also called denumerable or countably infinite. A subset of $\mathbf{N}^0$ which is finite is called countably finite.

# 11

# The Natural Numbers without Zero

## Mapping and the Natural Numbers

Many modern mathematicians define natural numbers using the concept of mapping.

Let **N** be a set and S a mapping from **N** into **N** . This set is called the set of natural numbers if it satisfies the following conditions.

C1 - S is injective or one-to-one.

C2- The range of S is not **N**.

C3 - If *a* is an element of **N** which is not in the range, and M is a subset of **N** such that (1) a $\in$M and (2) S(n) $\in$ M whenever n $\in$M, then M = N.

C3 is called the axiom of induction. It can be proved that *a* is the *only* element which is not in the range of S. S(n) is called the successor of n.

We call *a* "1". It has a unique successor in view of C1. Call it 2. Let S(2) = 3 and so on. Then the set of natural numbers is

1,2,3,....n,....

This definition may be compared with Peano's serial and Frege's logical definitions.

(1) The first element is 1 and not zero as in other two cases.
(2) Peano's last condition P5 is equivalent to C3 above.
(3) "Number", "*a*" and "successor" are undefined as in case of Peano's system. Hence there are theoretically infinitely many systems of natural numbers, and these numbers are

variables, not constants. However, mathematicians identify these systems with the numbers we use in practice, 1,2,......

This implicitly involves the use of the principle of abstraction.

A subset M of **N** is called an inductive set if S(n) ∈ M when n∈M. Hence the axiom of induction may be rephrased as: "if M is an inductive set containing 1, M = N"

These three approaches viz. serial, logical and that based on mapping can be shown below.

| | | | | | | |
|---|---|---|---|---|---|---|
| A. Peano | 0 | 1 | 2 | .... | n | S(n) |
| B. Frege | {} | {.} | {..} | ..... | {....} | {.....} |
| C. Mapping | | 1 | 2 | ... | n | S(n) |

It is clear in A and C, numbers are mere labels unless we identify them with commensense numbers. In B a point indicates one (distinct) element.

The systems A and C involve the concept of "order" because of the definition of "successor". This order 0,1,2,....n or 1,2,...n,... is called the *natural order.* The system C introduced here does not contain zero. Later we will see that zero is introduced as an integer.

## Operations

Though zero is not present in this system (C), we will explain operations "addition" and "multiplication" in this system.

## Addition

It can be proved that there is exactly one mapping f from **N x N** into **N** such that

f(m,1) = S(m) for all m ∈**N**

f(m,S(n)) = S(f(m,n) for all m, n.

We write f(m,n) = m+n

We can also prove the following results. For any m, n, p ∈**N**

(1) m + n = n +m (Commutative law)

(2) $m + (n+p) = (m+n)+p$ (Associative law)

(3) If $m + p = n + p$, then

$m = n$ (Law of cancellation)

(4) $m + n \neq n$

This result arises from the fact that there is no zero in this system.

## Multiplication

It can also be proved that there is exactly one mapping P from **N** x **N** into **N** such that $P(m,1) = m$ for each $m \in \mathbf{N}$

$P(m, S(n)) = P(m,n)+m$, for each $m, n \in \mathbf{N}$

We write mn or m.n or mxn for $P(m,n)$. This is the multiplication we are familiar with. This gives us

$m.1 = m$

It can also be proved that, for all $m, n, p \in \mathbf{N}$

(1) $m\,n = n\,m$ (Commutative law)

(2) $m(np) = (mn)p$ (Associative law)

(3) $m(n+p) = mn + mp$ (Left distributive law)

$(n+p)m = nm + pm$ (Right distributive law)

We say that "multiplication is distributive over addition"

We recall that the commutative and associative laws followed naturally in Frege's model.[1]

You must have noticed that we have not defined the operation of division. This is because when one natural number is divided by another we need not get a natural number. In the language of mathematics, the set of natural numbers is not *closed* for division.

## Binary Operations

Addition and multiplication are instances of what are called *binary operations*.

Formally, a binary operation is defined as follows. Let A and B be two non-empty sets then any mapping of a non empty subset of AxB into C is called a binary operation from AxB into C.

If A = B = C, we have a simple case of a mapping of a non-empty set of AxA into A, which is called a binary operation *in* A.

In a binary operation an ordered pair (a,b) of AxB is associated with a unique element of C. This is usually shown as

a o b = c

We shall normally use the multiplicative symbol viz.

ab = c to denote a binary operation unless otherwise stated.

## Semigroup

Let o be a binary operation on A, then the system (A,o) is called a *groupoid.* A groupoid is a *semi-group* if the operation is associative. A semi-group is commutative if the operation is commutative.

If in a groupoid (A,o) there is an element e such that e o a =a for every a ∈A then e is called the left identity relative to the operation. Similarly e is called right identity if a o e = a. It is called an identity if it is both the right as well as left identity.

Clearly (**N**,+), (**N**, .), ($\mathbf{N}^0$,+), ($\mathbf{N}^0$, .) are commutative semi-groups. Zero is the additive identity in ($\mathbf{N}^0$,+) .

( **N**, .) has the multiplicative identity viz. 1.

E1

(a) Those of you who are familiar with three dimensional vectors will realize that the set of such vectors with vector addition is a semigroup whose identity is the zero vector **0**

(b) If you are familiar with matrices, you can easily verify that the set of matrices of the order mxn with the operation matrix addition is a semigroup with the identity which is the zero matrix i.e. the matrix whose all elements are zero.

## Order

The order in which $\mathbf{N}^0$ and **N** appear is called the natural order.

In fact, the natural order is implicit in both the approaches, serial and mapping route.

However, the following theorem can be proved rigorously.

If T is the subset of $\mathbf{N} \times \mathbf{N}$ and $(m,n) \in \mathbf{N} \times \mathbf{N}$ such that $m+p = n$ for some $p \in \mathbf{N}$ then T is an order relation i.e. T is asymmetric and transitive.

Formally we write "$m<n$" (or "$n>m$") when $(m,n) \in T$. "$<$" stands for "less than" and "$>$" for "greater than". This will appeal to you intuitively. For example,

$7+2 = 9$

Hence $7 < 9$ or $9 > 7$

Incidentally we can also prove that the law of trichotomy exists i.e., if $m,n \in \mathbf{N}$ one of the following is true

$$m = n, m < n, n < m$$

A semigroup $(A, o, <)$ in which an order relation $<$ is defined is called an *ordered semigroup* if

$a < b$ in A implies $a \circ x < b \circ x$ for all $x \in A$.

It is easy to see that $(\mathbf{N}, +, <)$ and $(\mathbf{N}, ., <)$ are ordered semigroups.

From "$<$" and "$>$" we get the partial order relation "$\leq$" and "$\geq$" if $a \leq b$ means $a = b$ or $a<b$ and $a \geq b$ means $a = b$ or $a >b$.

## Generalized Associative and Commutative Laws

We shall assume the generalized associative and commutative laws of addition and multiplication in **N** and $\mathbf{N}^0$. What this means is that if we have numbers a, b, c.... to be added (or to be multiplied) we can arrange them in any order we like and bracket any of them together without changing the result.

For example,

$8+(2+21)+23 = (23+2)+21+8$

$= 21+23+2+8$ etc.

or $(5\text{x}8)\text{x}(21\text{x}37) = (37\text{x}8) \text{ x } (21\text{x}5)$

$= 5\text{x}21\text{x}37\text{x}8$ and so forth.

12

# The Derived Zero

## The Integers

Since the natural numbers 1,2,..... obtained by using the concept of mapping do not contain zero, the zero has to be derived. Since mathematicians are sticklers for logic, they cannot simply add zero to the existing numbers. They have to create an entirely different system of numbers called integers viz.

. . -2 -1 0 1 2 .......

in which zero will appear as an integer. Do not mistake it for the zero of the natural numbers derived by Peano or Frege. Even when we take the route of Peano and Frege we have to create non-zero integers as a different system. But we shall follow the method usually employed by the modern mathematicians.

The numbers 1,2,.... appearing above are the positive integers. Do not challange a mathematician if she tells you that the integers 1,2,... are not the same as the natural numbers 1,2,.... Logically, she is right. However, we shall see later how in *practice* we can forget this distinction.

Let (a,b) and (c,d) belong to **NxN**. Define a relation R such that

(a,b) R (c,d) if and only if a+d = c+b

Note that a,b,c,d are natural numbers. It can be proved that R is reflexive, symmetric and transitive, hence an equivalance relation which we shall denote by

(a,b)~(c,d)

As mentioned earlier, an equivalence relation leads to

mutually disjoint classes. Thus in this case an equivalence class in which (a,b) lies will be denoted by C(a,b), and is a class of ordered couples. You will find (i) (7,5) ~ (5,3) (ii) or (8,7) ~ (5,4).

In (i) 7-5 = 2 = 5-3

In (ii) 8-7 = 1 = 5-4

Thus some of our classes have a 1-1 correspondence with natural numbers. C(5,4) can be *identified* with "1" and C(7,5) with "2" and so forth.

*Inverse*

Let (G,o) be a semigroup, and *e* a right, left or unique identity. Let x, x' ∈ A then x' is called

(1) Left inverse of x relative to e if x' o x = e

(2) Right inverse of x relative to e if x o x' = e

(3) The (unique) inverse of x relative to e if x o x' = x' o x = e

It can be proved that when the identity is unique, an element has at most one (unique) inverse.

## Addition

We shall denote the integers, which are equivalence classes by **Z**. We define a binary "addition" in **Z**. Let C(a,b) = x, C(c,d) = y where x,y ∈ **Z**. Then

x + y = C(a+c, b+d)

The operation is well-defined. Strictly speaking, "+" in **Z** on the left side is not the same as "+" in **N** on the right, but we continue to use the same symbol so long as there is no confusion.

The following results can be easily proved.

(1) Addition in **Z** is associative.

(2) Addition in **Z** is commutative.

(3) There is an additive identity which is the class C(a,a) or C(1,1). This is the *zero* of the integers. We denote it by 0(z) or simply by 0. Note that this zero is an integer which is a class of natural numbers and differs from Peano's or Frege's zero qua natural number.

In what sense does it agree with "nothing"? As we mentioned earlier, positive natural numbers have a 1-1 correspondence with integers (which are classes). It can also be proved that this 0 has the property

$x+0 = x = 0 + x$, where $x \in \mathbf{Z}$

It is only in this sense of identification we can say that our new zero integer is "nothing". Because the 1-1 correspondence between **N** and **Z** helps us to use integers for counting, and in this scheme "0" fits as the zero of Peano or Frege and conveys the notion of "nothing". You must, however, observe that the class "0" is not a null class.

It can be proved that there is a unique additive inverse of any element of **Z**. Let $x = C(a,b)$ then $x' = (b,a)$ is such that

$x'+x = x+x' = (a+b, b+a) = (1,1) = 0$

$x'$ is denoted by $-x$

We have arrived at the concept of negative numbers. For example (7,5) can be identified with 7-5 = 2 and (5,7) can be identified with -2. Note, however, that negative numbers are not natural numbers. And what we naively mean by, say, -2 is not what the mathematician means by it. For her, it is a "class" or a "set".

## Multiplication

Let $x = C(a,b)$ and $y = C(c,d)$ be integers. We define their product as a mapping of **Z** x **Z** into **Z** as:

$xy = (ac + bd, ad + bc)$

We can prove the following results.

(1) Multiplication is well-defined.
(2) Multiplication is associative and commutative.

The multiplicative identity is a class $C(1+1,1)$ which we can denote by $1(z)$ or simply as 1.

Thus $x.1 = x = 1.x$

Note that the operation(·) and the identity 1 belong to the realm of integers and not the natural numbers, but we can use them so long as there is no confusion.

These properties ensure that (**Z**,.) is a commutative semi-group with identity.

We can also prove that multiplication is distributive over addition in **Z**.

i.e. $x\,(y+w) = xy + xw$

$(y+w)x = yx + wx\,;\ x,y,w \in \mathbf{Z}$

## Groups

A semigroup (G,o) with identity is called a group if every element of G has a unique inverse. We shall denote the inverse by $a^{-1}$ for convenience.

$aa^{-1} = e = a^{-1}a$ where e is the identity. A group is called abelian or commutative if ab=ba for every a, b $\in$G.

It is clear that (**Z**, + ) is a commutative group. If x $\in$**Z**, then 0 is the identity and -x is the inverse.

## Properties of Z

You can intuitively appreciate the following properties, which we use in school. We state them without proof.

Let x,y $\in$ **Z**$\in$

(1) There is a unique w $\in$ **Z** such that x= y + w. We write w = x -y

(2) If x+w = y+w then x = y which is called the *law of cancellation*.

(3) $-(-x) = x$

(4) $x+(-y) = x-y$

(5) $-(x+y) = (-x)+(-y) = -x-y$

(6) $(x-y)+(y-w) = x-w$

(7) $-(x-y) = y-x$.

## Rings

Consider a set R in which two operation called for convenience addition (+) and multiplication (.) are defined. (R, +, .) is called *ring* if

(1) (R, +) is an abelian group

(2) Multiplication is associative i.e.

$a(bc) = (ab)c$

(3) Multiplication is distributive over addition i.e.

$a(b+c) = ab + ac$

$(b+c)a = ba + ca$

We denote the identity of "+" as 0 and the additive inverse of *a* as *-a*. The following results follow immediately and you will realize they are the same that we use in elementary algebra.

(4) $(x)0 = 0(x) = 0$

(5) $(-x)y = x(-y) = -xy$

(6) $(-x)(-y) = xy$

(7) $(-x)(y+w) = -xy-xw$

(8) $(y+w)(-x) = =-yx-wx$ where $x,y,w \in R$

It is easy to see that (**Z**, +, .) is a ring, with 0(Z) or 0 as the additive identity.

A ring R is commutative if the group (R, +) is abelian. It is also said to possess identity if the semigroup (R, .) has an identity.

It is clear that (**Z**, +, .) is a commutative ring with identity 1(Z).

All results 1 through 8 hold good and they are the ones we assume in elementary algebra. Of particular interest to us is the behaviour of zero reflected in (4): any number multiplied by zero gives us zero.

## Order in Z

In school we assume that given any two numbers a,b either $a<b$, $a=b$ or $b<a$

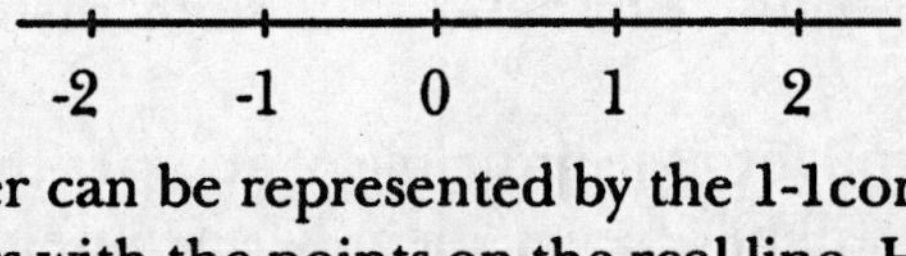


This order can be represented by the 1-1correspondence of the numbers with the points on the real line. However, this 1-1 correspondence is only an assumption, and cannot be proved rigorously. The integers when plotted on the line would appear as in the above figure.

We now wish to define "*less than (<)*" in **Z**.

Let x = C(a,b) where x is an integer and a,b $\in$**N**. We call x *positive* if $b < a$ in **N**. It can be proved that the definition is consistent i.e. holds good for all $(a,b) \in C(a,b)$.

The following result can be easily proved. If $x \in \mathbf{Z}$, one and only one is true.

(1) x is positive (2) $x = 0$ (3) $-x$ is positive. We reiterate that x is a class of ordered pairs of natural numbers.

Let T be the set $(x,y) \in \mathbf{Z} \times \mathbf{Z}$ such that y-x is positive. Using the above result it can be proved that T is an order relation in **Z**. We shall write this relation as $x < y$ (Z) or simply as $x<y$ when there is no confusion between "$<$" of natural numbers and "$<$" of integers. We also write $y>x$ if $x<y$. Clearly, the set of positive integers is

$\mathbf{Z}^+ = \{x|x>0 \text{ in } \mathbf{Z}\} = \{-x|x<0 \text{ in } \mathbf{Z}\}$

The following results can be proved in **Z**

(1) If $x>0$, $y>0$ then $x+y>0$

(2) $\mathbf{Z}^+ = \{C(S(n),1), n \in \mathbf{N}\}$

For example, $C(S(5),1) = C(6,1)$ which represents the positive integer 5.

(3) If $x>0$, $y>0$ then $xy > 0$

(4) If $x \neq 0$, $y \neq 0$ then $xy \neq 0$

## Embedding and Isomorphism

We pointed out earlier that mathematically, the natural numbers 0,1,2.. are not the same as the integers 0,1,2... In fact even the operations, addition and multiplication do not mean the same operations in **N** and **Z**. Nevertheless we mentioned that we can go about doing our arithmetic as if such distinctions did not exist.

A principle similar to the principle of abstraction will now be introduced. We will be able to "identify" the integer 1 with the natural number 1, integer 2 with natural number 2 and so on.

You will be able to appreciate the following theorem intuitively.

Let E be a mapping of **N** into $\mathbf{Z}^+$ defined by

$E(n) = C(S(n), 1) \in Z^+, n \in N$

Then E is a 1-1 onto mapping having the following properties.

(1) $E(a+b) = E(a) + E(b)$

(2) $E(ab) = E(a) . E(b)$

(3) $E(a)<E(b)$ if and only if $a<b$

Let us take $n = 8$, $a= 3$, $b = 4$ then the above assertions appear as

(a) $E(8) = C(9,1)$

(b) $E(3+4) = E(3) + E(4)$

(c) $E(3x4) = E(3) \times E(4)$

(d) $E(3) < E(4)$

In (a), 9-1 = 8, in (b) through (d) if you ignore E you will get the results which appear intuitively correct.

b' $3+4 = 3+4$

c' $3x4 = 3x4$

d' $3<4$

What's more, we can totally ignore the distinction between +, ., < of **N** and +, ., < of **Z**

*Isomorphism*

(1) Let o be a binary operation in a set A, and o' in B. A mapping E from A into (onto) A' is called (o,o') isomorphism of A into (onto) B if
$E(aob) = E(a)o'E(b)$

(2) If R is a binary relation in A and R' a binary relation in B then a 1-1 mapping of E into (onto) B is called a (R,R') isomorphism of A into (onto) B if for every a,b $\in$A. aRb, is true if and only if E(a) R' E(b)

You will find that the mapping defined from **N** into **Z** or onto $\mathbf{Z}^+$ is nothing but an isomorphism which *preserves* addition, multiplication and order. Intuitively this means that **N**, $\mathbf{Z}^+$ are structurally similar. Our naive belief of "mistaking" natural numbers for the integers seems to be partially vindicated.

If there is an isomorphism of S into S' with respect to operations or relations $(\alpha, \alpha')$, then S' is called an *extension* of S. We also say that S is *isomorphically embedded* in S' with respect to $(\alpha, \alpha')$.

Clearly we have shown that **N** is embedded isomorphically into **Z**. Thus we can "identify" the natural numbers with the corresponding positive integers.

In this chapter we have built integers on **N** and not on $\mathbf{N}^0$, but **Z** can also be constructed on $\mathbf{N}^0$. In that case the natural number 0 can be identified with the integer 0.

## Negative Integers

The integers obtained by removing from $\mathbf{Z}^+$ and 0 from **Z** are called the negative integers i.e. x is a negative integer if $-x \in \mathbf{Z}^+$. For every positive integer x we have a negative integer which is its additive inverse.

An integer x is called even if $x = 2y$ for some $y \in \mathbf{Z}$ and odd if $x = 2y+1$. It can also be proved that (1) an integer is either even or odd and (2) it cannot be both even and odd.

The natural numbers and integers may be compared as follows

| | | | | | | | |
|---|---|---|---|---|---|---|---|
| $\mathbf{N}^0$ | 0 | 1 | 2 | 3 | ... | (Frege and Peano) | |
| **N** | 1 | 2 | 3 | .... | | (Modern approach) | |
| **Z** | ....-2 | -1 | 0 | 1 | 2 | 3 | .... |

## Integral Domain

If (I,+,.) is a commutative ring with identity $1 \neq 0$, such that for $a,b \in I$, $a.b=0$ if and only if $a=0$ or $b=0$ then (I,+,.) is called an *integral domain.*

It can be proved that (**Z**,+,.) is an integral domain. The following properties hold good for **Z**. If $a,b,c \in \mathbf{Z}$, $c \neq 0$ then

(1) If $a.c = b.c$ then $a=b$

(2) If $c.a = cb$, then $a=b$

These are called the right and left cancellation laws, which we use in school. For example

$5x = 5b$

then $x = b$

*Order*

If (I,+,.) is an integral domain and "$<$" an order relation such that, for a, b $\in$ I

(1) when $a<b$ then $a+c<b+c$
(2) when $a<b$ then $a.c<b.c$

for all $c>0$ then (I,+,.) is called an *ordered integral domain.*
It can be proved that (**Z**, +, .,$<$) is an ordered integral domain.

*Positive Elements*

If (I,+,.) is an integral domain, then a subset $I^+$ is called a set of positive elements for I if for all a,b $\in$ I

(1) $a+b \in I^+$ if a, b $\in I^+$
(2) $a.b \in I^+$ if a,b $\in I^+$
(3) for a $\in$I exactly one of the following is true

$a \in I^+$, a=0, $-a \in I^+$

It can be proved that $\mathbf{Z}^+$ is a set of positive elements for **Z**
The following results can be intuitively appreciated in respect of the integral domain (**Z**,+,.)

(1) If $a \neq 0$, then $a.a \in \mathbf{Z}^+$

For example, (2) (2) =+ 4, (-2) (-2) = 4

(2) $1 \in \mathbf{Z}^+$
(3) If a, b $\in$ **Z** then a.b = 1 if and only if a=b=1 or a=b=-1

Note that (7) (1/7) = 1, but 1/7 is not an integer.

13

# The Hierarchy of Zeros

## Rational Numbers

The integers are a separate category of numbers though its subset can be "identified" with the natural numbers through isomorphic embedding. We now build the rational numbers which are one echelon higher than the integers.

The set **Z'** = **Z** - {0} is a semigroup under multiplication. It is not a group because an integer other than 1±1 has no multiplicative inverse. For example, in the commonsense arithmetic the inverse of 7 is 1/7 which is not an integer. Hence we have to construct a new type of numbers called the *rational numbers.*

We shall denote the set of ordered pairs (a,b) by *A,* where a, b ∈ **Z,** b ≠ 0 .

In A we define a relation E such that

(a,b) E (c,d) if and only if ad = cb. E is reflexive, symmetric and transitive. Hence it leads to disjoint equivalence classes such as C(a,b). The relation E will be shown by~. A rational number is an equivalence class defined above. The factor set A/E will be called the set of rational numbers and denoted by **Q**.

It is easy to see the motivation behind the definition of the equivalence relation. In elementary arithmetic a/b = c/d if and only if ad = cb (b,d ≠ 0)

Hence the definition that

(a,b)~(c,d) if and only if ad = cb

In ordinary arithmetic (a/b)+(c/d) = (ad+bc) / bd and (a/b) x (c/d) = ac/bd

This suggests the definition of addition and multiplication in rational numbers (which are classes).

Let (a,b)~(a',b') and (c,d)~(c'd') It can be proved that

(1) (ad+cb,bd)~(a'd'+c'b', b'd') and
(2) (ac, bd)~(a'c', b'd')

Hence if x = C(a,b) and y = C(c,d) then we can define addition and multiplication in **Q** as

x+y = C(ad+cb,bd)

xy = C(ac,bd)

Note that + and . on the left pertain to **Q** while those on the right pertain to **Z**, but we continue to use the same notations if there is no confusion. It can be proved that (**Q**, +) is a commutative group.

Its identity is the class C(0,1) and the additive inverse of x = (a,b) is -x = (-a, b). We shall denote the identity as 0(Q) or simply as 0. In school arithmetic this would be stated as: a/b has the inverse -a/b so that their sum is zero. We can also prove that (**Q**, .) is a commutative semigroup with identity C(1,1) which will be denoted by 1(Q) or simply 1.

We have already introduced the concept of a ring. It can be proved that (**Q**, +, .) is a commutative ring with identity.

An interesting property of the rational numbers is that every nonzero element has a multiplicative inverse. If x = C(a,b) its inverse x' is C(b,a) because xx' = 1. In school arithmetic this would appear as (a/b)x(b/a) = 1. We denote x' by 1/x.

This incidentally proves that ***Q*** - {0} is a group with respect to multiplication.

## Field

A system (A, +, .) is called a field if

(1) (A, +, .) is a commutative ring.

(2) (A', +, .) is a group where A' = A - {0}. It is easy to prove that (Q, +, .) is a field.

The following properties of this field **Q** can be intuitively appreciated

| | Properties | Examples |
|---|---|---|
| (1) | $1/(1/x) = x$ | $1/(1/5) = 5$ |
| (2) | $x(1/y) = x/y$ | $9(1/5) = 9/5$ |
| (3) | $(x/y)(y/z) = x/z$ | $(8/5)(5/8) = 8$ |
| (4) | $1/xy = (1/x)(1/y) = (1/x)/y$ | $1/35 = (1/7)(1/5) = (1/7)/5$ |
| (5) | $1/(x/y) = y/x$ | $1/(9/8) = 8/9$ |

## Order in Q

Let $x \in \mathbf{Q}$, $x = C(a,b)$. If $ab>0$ then it can be proved that if $(a,b) \sim (c,d)$ then $cd>0$. This enables us to define a set of positive rationals $\mathbf{Q}^+$.

$\mathbf{Q}^+ = \{x : ab>0, (a,b) \in x\}$

We can also prove the following theorem if $x \in \mathbf{Q}$, one of the following holds good.

$x \in \mathbf{Q}^+$, $x = 0$, $-x \in \mathbf{Q}^+$

This simply means that a rational is either positive, zero or its additive inverse is positive.

An important theorem results from this:

*Theorem*

The set $T = \{(x,y) : y-x \in \mathbf{Q}^+\}$ is an order relation in Q.

We write $x<y$ or $y>x$ if $(x,y) \in T$

We can prove that (**Q**, +, ., <) is an ordered integral domain.

If (A, +, ., <) is an integral domain and (A, +, .) is a field then (A, +, ., <) is called an *ordered field.* Thus (**Q**, +, ., <) is an ordered field.

## Embedding and Isomorphism

Earlier we showed that the natural numbers were embedded isomorphically into integers, so that they could be identified with positive integers. A similar process will work in case of **Z** with respect to **Q**.

Consider the mapping

E: **Z** $\rightarrow$ **Q**

defined by E(a) = C(a,1) where a $\in$ **Z** and C(a,1) $\in$ **Q**. Intuitively, this is identifying the integer *a* with the rational a/1 in elementary arithmetic.

The following results can be proved.

(1) E(a+b) = E(a) + E(b)

(2) E(ab) = E(a) E(b)

(3) $a<b$ if and only if $E(a) < E(b)$

Hence we find E is an isomorphism preserving addition, multiplication and order. We can thus say that **Q** embeds **Z** or is an extension of the integral domain **Z**.

Results 1 through 3 can be appreciated by removing "E" and using ordinary numbers. i.e. replacing C(a,1) by a/1. For example, 2+3 = 2/1 + 3/1

2.3 = (2/1).(3/1)

$2<3$ is equivalent to $2/1 <3/1$

What this means is that we can "identify" the integer 2 with the rational 2/1 and the integer 3 with the rational 3/1.

## Negative Rationals and Zero

If from **Q** we discard $\mathbf{Q}^+$ and 0, what remain are negative rational numbers. For every positive a $\in$**Q** we have the additive inverse -a which is the corresponding negative rational.

The isomorphic embedding of the natural numbers into the integers and the integers into the rationals can be represented as

| | | | | | | |
|---|---|---|---|---|---|---|
| $\mathbf{N}^0$ | | | 0, | 1, | 2, | ....... |
| **N** | | | | 1, | 2, | ..... |
| **Z** | ....-2, | -1, | 0, | +1, | +2, | ..... |
| **Q** | ...-2/1, | -1/1, | 0, | +1/1, | +2/1, | ...... |

0 in $\mathbf{N}^0$ is a natural number, 0 in **Z** is an integer, and 0 of **Q** is

a rational number. On account of embedding and isomorphism we can treat them *in practice* as the same ignoring their hierarchical status.

## Irrational Numbers

In elementary mathematics a rational number is one which can be expressed as a ratio of two integers $p/q, q \neq 0$. Those numbers which are not rational are called irrational numbers. The equation $x^2 = 2$ has no solution in terms of rational numbers because $\sqrt{2}$ is not rational.

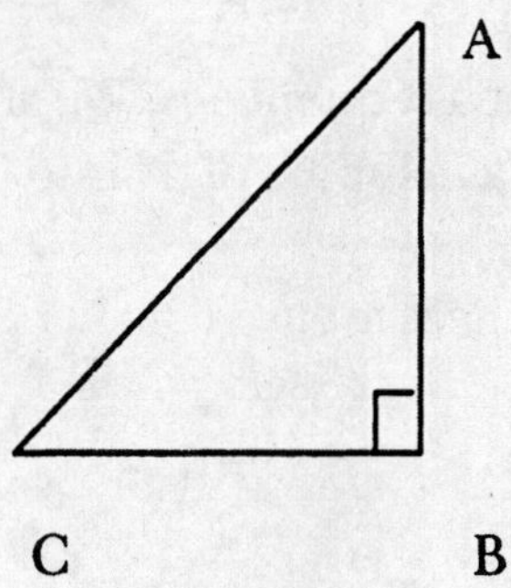


Fig. 13.1

In school we study the Pythagoras theorem according to which the square on the hypotenuse of a right angled triangle equals the sum of the squares on the other two sides. In fig. 13.1 where angle B is a right angle,

$AC^2 = AB^2+BC^2$

Suppose $AB = BC = 1$ then $AC^2 = 2$

What is the length of AC? The Pythagoreans thought such a length was "incommensurable" or *alogos* ("inexpressible") or *arrotos* ("having no ratio"). Note that what they meant was AC could not be expressed as a ratio $p/q$, $q \neq 0$ which is the characteristic of a rational number. The Babylonians (ca 2000 BCE) were aware of the Pythagorean equation, but possibly could not provide the proof of the theorem. They knew that the triplets such as (3,4,5) could form a right angled triangle $3^2 + 4^2 = 5^2$

Unlike the Greeks, they even calculated the length of $\sqrt{2}$. Their approximations were 1.4142129 and 1.414213562. It is not known whether they were aware that the irrationals existed as a different type of numbers. The Egyptians, too, dealt with numbers which we call irrational. Their value of $\pi$ which is the ratio of the circumference to its diameter was 3.1605 which has an error of about 1%. Nevertheless, they like the Babylonians, did not seem to be aware of the fact that they were dealing with a distinct type of numbers.

## Sequences and Real Numbers

Most of us know what a sequence is. We shall formally define a sequence $a_n = F(n)$ as a mapping of **N** into **Q** which is an ordered field.

Some of the sequences are:

E1

(a) $a_n = 1/n^2$
(b) $a_n = 8$
(c) $a_n = (-1)^n + 1/n$
(d) $2 - 1/n$

Intuitively we know the behaviour of these sequences. In case of (a), the terms are

1,1/4,1/9,.....

$a_n$ becomes smaller and smaller. We can make $a_n$ as small as we please and our intuition tells us that the sequence should "tend to zero" i.e. approach the "limit" 0. The sequence (b) is a constant sequence. In (c) the first term is either +1 or -1 while the second terms approaches zero. Hence $a_n$ has no definite limit its value can be made as close to +1 or -1 as we desire. The sequence (d) obviously tends to the limit 2, because 1/n approaches zero.

The following two definitions are important

A sequence is called *fundamental* if for each e>o in **Q** there is n(e) $\in$**N** such that

$|a_n - a_m| < e$ for all $m, n \geq n(e)$. "$n(e)$" shows that the number *n* depends on *e*.

A sequence $(a_n)$ converges to *a* if, for each $e>0$ in **Q** there is some $n(e) \in$ **N** such that

$|a_n - a| < e$ for all $n \geq n(e)$ in **N**

*a* is called the limit which can be proved to be unique. We write $L(a_n) = a$.

Intuitively the limits of $(a_n)$ in E1 a,b,d are 0,8,2 respectively, while (c) has no limit. Note that in case of a fundamental sequence no limit is specified.

The following theorem is important

T1

If $(a_n)$ is a covergent sequence then it is a fundamental sequence.

Its converse is not true i.e., there may be a sequence which is fundamental but which does not converge to a limit in **Q**.

We can appreciate the following theorem intuitively

T2

If $(a_n)$ is a fundamental sequence in **Q** then exactly one of the following is true:

(1) $L(a_n) = 0$

(2) $(a_n)$ is positive

(3) $(-a_n)$ is positive.

$(a_n)$ is called positive if for some positive $e \in$ **Q** and some $m \in$ **N**

$a_n \geq e$ in **Q** for all $n \geq m$ in **N**. We can prove the following results

(1) If $L(a_n) = a$, and $L(b_n) = b$ then

$L(a_n + b_n) = a+b$

$L(a_n b_n) = ab$

Consider the set F of all fundamental sequences in **Q**. We define a binary relation E such that $(x_n)E(y_n)$ if and only if $L(x_n - y_n) = 0$ where $(x_n), (y_n) \in F$

It can be proved that E is reflexive, symmetric and transitive.

Hence E is an equivalence relation. This leads to disjoint equivalent classes.

*Definition*

We define a *real number* as an equivalence class $C(x_n)$ where $(x_n)$ is a fundamental rational sequence. We denote the set of real numbers by **R**.

The definition appears strange to us, but recall that many numbers were defined earlier in terms of equivalence classes.

*Binary Operations in* ***R***

The following results can be proved.

(1) For $(x_n) \in F$, $L(x_n) = a \in \mathbf{Q}$, if and only if $(x_n)E(a)$ where (a) is a constant rational sequence.

(2) If $x_n, x'_n, y_n, y'_n$ are rational sequences such that $(x_n)E(x'_n)$ and $(y_n)E(y'_n)$ then

$(x_n+y_n)E(x'_n+y'_n)$

$(x_ny_n)E(x'_ny'_n)$

Let $x = C(x_n)$, $y = C(y_n)$

then the above results facilitate the definition of addition +(R) or (+) and multiplication .(R) or (.) in **R**.

$x+y = C(x_n+y_n)$

$xy = C(x_ny_n)$

The operations can be proved to be well defined.

It can be proved that (**R**, +, .) is a field. Note that if (a) is constant rational sequence, we can write C(a) = a(R) or simply a when *a* on the left hand side is a rational while that on the right side is a real number. This will be more lucid later.

The zero of the real numbers is C(0) = 0(R) which can be denoted simply by 0. If $x, y \in \mathbf{R}$, then $x+0 = 0 = 0+x$ and

$x.0 = 0 = 0.x$

Remeber that our "real zero" is a class of sequences having the limit 0 in **Q**. The additive inverse of $C(x_n)$ is $C(-x_n)$. The multiplicative identity is again a class of sequences C(1) whose limit is 1. The multiplicative inverse of non-zero real number

$C(x_n)$ is $1/C(x_n)$ such that $C(x_n)C(y_n) = C(1) = 1$

We have omitted the proofs of most of the results.

## Order in R

Let R+ be the equivalence classes of positive sequences. We can prove that if $x = C(x_n)$ then exactly one of the following is true

$x \in \mathbf{R}^+$, $x = 0$, $-x \in \mathbf{R}^+$

This trichotomy introduces an order relation

$T = \{(x,y): y-x \in \mathbf{R}^+\}$

We write $x<y$ or $y>x$

This makes $(\mathbf{R}, +, ., <)$ an ordered field.

## Isomorphic Embedding

The real numbers belong to a rung which is higher than that of the rational numbers. We use the common technique of isomorphic embedding of **Q** into **R** so that the rational numbers can be identified with a subset of **R**

$E: \mathbf{Q} \to \mathbf{R}$

$E(x) = C(x)$ where x is a rational number whose image is the class $C(x)$ of fundamental sequences whose limit is x.

As before, E can be proved to be an isomorphism preserving addition, multiplication and order.

i.e.

$E(x+y) = E(x)+E(y)$

$E(xy) = E(x)E(y)$

$E(x)<E(y)$ if and only if $x<y$

Thus we can identify the range of E with the rational numbers. If you delete "E" from the above statements, the left and right hand sides will appear identical.

Hence we can treat the "real zero" 0(R) as if it were the "rational zero" 0(Q) the real 2 as the rational 2/1 and so on.

We mentioned earlier that all fundamental sequences are not convergent. This means that there are "gaps" such as $\sqrt{2}, \pi$ etc.

The construction of **R** helps us bridge this gap. These gaps in **R** represent those real numbers (which are classes of fundamental sequences) which are not rational. These real numbers are called irrational numbers.

It can be proved that a rational sequence $(x_n)$ is fundamental in **Q** if and only if it is fundamental in **R**.

An ordered field is called *complete* if every fundamental sequence is convergent in it. The following important theorem can be proved:

The field of real numbers is complete.

## Integers and Fractions as Relations

We have used the mapping route to create a hierarchy of numbers and zeros. We shall briefly outline how the older thinkers like Peano, Frege and Russel derived the higher numbers from $\mathbf{N}^0$.

Let n be a cardinal number then n+1, n+2,..... n+m where m is an inductive number are also cardinal numbers. We define + as the relation of n+1 to n, +2 as the relation of n+2 to n. In general n+m is relation of n+m to n. It can be proved that the relation is one-one. The converse relation is defined in a similar way: -1 is the relation of n to n+1 etc. -m is the relation of n to n+m. We thus get positive and negative integers as "relation" The integer zero(0) may be treated as the relation of n to n itself.

From the integers we can create fractions and signed ratios. The fraction m/n is defined as a relation between two inductive numbers a and n if an = bm. It can be proved that the relation is one-one provided m or n is not zero. The relation o/n is the same whatever n is. We call this the zero of the rational numbers.

Let us note that in this approach, the fraction 0 "is a relation of relation of 0, the natural number". We will not pursue this subject further but point out that the higher numbers have to be defined using the methods, which appear strange to us.

These circuitous methods used by mathematicians raise a question: why is there a schism between theory and practice? Is it not possible to have a unified theory of all real numbers in which zero appears as zero of all categories, there being no necessity of derived numbers. No such theory seems to exist at present. However, there is a ray of hope. The approach of Frege may be contrasted with that of Peano and modern mathematicians. Frege's natural numbers include zero while the other methods have to derive their "first" zero. It may be possible one day to define real numbers in which rationals and irrationals appear as subsets, of the real numbers, the integers appear as a mere subset of the rationals, and the natural numbers as a subset of the integers. We can then assign the same meaning to addition and multiplication. We will also be able to say "this is *the* zero."

Before we conclude a summary of the hierarchy of zero is presented.

## Summary of Arithmetical Zeros

**$N^0$** (1) (Peano) "Serial Approach"
Zero denoted by 0. There are infinitely many zeros corresponding to infinitely many systems of the natural numbers. Zero is the number which is not the successor of any number. It is a *relative zero* or *variable zero.* Using the principle of abstraction, **$N^0$** is identified with the natural numbers we use in practice. In particular, this zero can be "identified" with the commonsense zero.
(2) Frege-Russell - "Logical approach". Zero denoted by 0. There is only one system of **$N^0$**. Hence there is only one zero which may be called *commonsense zero, absolute zero* or *quantitative zero.*

**N** Mapping (Modern) Approach
There is no zero. The first element is "One". There are infinitely many systems of natural numbers "identified" with the numbers we use in practice through the principle of abstraction.

**Z** (Modern Approach)
Denoted by 0 or 0(Z). This is a derived zero because the zero does not exist in **N**. It is a class of ordered pairs of natural numbers "equivalent" to (1,1) where 1 is a natural number.

**Q** (Modern) Zero is denoted by 0(Q) or 0. It is a derived zero: an equivalence class of ordered pairs of integers equivalent to (0,1) where 0,1 are integers.

**R** (Modern) - Zero is denoted by 0(R) or 0. It is a derived zero: an equivalence class of fundamental rational sequences equivalent to the sequences having the limit 0 where 0 is a rational number.

In practice, we can forget the different type of "zeros" on account of (1) the isomorphic embedding of lower categories into the higher categories of numbers (2) identification of natural numbers using the principle of abstraction. Thus all zeros may be treated as the commonsense zero we use in practice.

In the following, various numbers are compared along with their zeros

| | | | | | | | | |
|---|---|---|---|---|---|---|---|---|
| **N⁰** | Peano, | Frege | | 0 | 1 | 2 | 3 | ..... |
| **N** | Modern | | | | 1 | 2 | 3 | ..... |
| **Z** | ... | -2 | -1 | 0 | +1 | +2 | +3 | ..... |
| **Q** | .... | -2/1 | -1/1 | 0 | 1/1 | 2/1 | 3/1 | ..... |
| **R** | ..... | -2 | -1 | 0 | 1 | 2 | 3 | ..... |

14

# Other Mathematical Zeros

## Complex Numbers

We have shown how the real numbers are constructed. The significance of **R** is that these numbers have a one-one correspondence with the points on the real line.

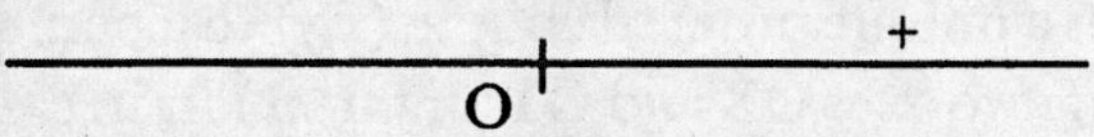


We can plot all rationals as well irrational numbers on the line. This is, of course, an axiom. In reality we do not really know how points can be defined, but our assumption has worked in practice and has solved the problems of irrational numbers, which were faced by such mathematicians as Pythagoras.

However, when we deal with algebraic equations we find some of the equations cannot be solved. For example, the equation
$x^2+1=0$

implies $x^2 = -1$

and we do not know a real number whose square is -1. This problem was solved by Carl Gauss using a geometrical method. Suppose we assume that $x = \sqrt{-1}$ does exist in some sense and call it "i". We treat it as a number different from a real number but assume that it obeys the algebra of real numbers. We can treat *i* as, say, x in algebra and write 2i, 3i,....-i, -2i,... etc. in the same way as we write 2x,3x...-x, -2x, and so forth. We define a complex number z as

$z = a+bi$, where a, b are real numbers

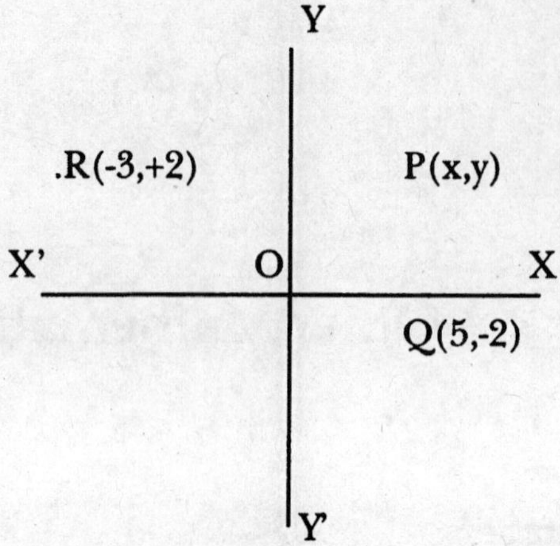


Fig. 14.1

Descartes introduced what is now known as *coordinate geometry*. An extension of the co-ordinate system on the real line, it designates a unique ordered couple (x,y) to a point P in a plane containing two axes OX and OY (Fig. 14.1) As in case of the real line we assume that there is a one-to-one correspondence between the points in a plane and ordered couples of real numbers. However, instead of designating P as (x,y) Gauss represented it as x+iy where $i = \sqrt{-1}$. Thus the points Q, R would appear as 5-2i and -3+2i.

Thus while "1" is the unit along the real x axis, "i" is the unit along y axis which is the imaginary axis. If we assume, that the normal operations in arithmetic hold good we will get the following results in the set of complex numbers

$z_1 = x_1+iy_1$
$z_2 = x_2i+iy_2$
$z_1+z_2 = x_1+iy_1+x_2+iy_2$ (a)
$= (x_1+x_2)+i(y_1+y_2)$
$z_1z_2 = (x_1+iy_1)(x_2+iy_2)$ (b)
$= x_1x_2+i^2y_1y_2+i(x_1y_2+x_2y_1)$
$= x_1x_2- y_1y_2 + i(x_1y_2+x_2y_1)$
Remember $i^2 = -1$

Both (a) and (b) are "complex numbers". In x+iy, x is called the real part while iy is the imaginary part.

It can be easily proved that these definitions are consistent. This means we can treat real numbers as a subset of complex numbers. Remember that a real number like 7 lies an X axis while an imaginary number, say, 8i lies on Y axis, while 7+8i lies at the point (7,8).

The zero of the complex numbers is 0+0i which is the origin O and is denoted by 0.

However, modern mathematicians do not build new numbers in this fashion, because the method introduces a new quantity "i" which is not in our original set of premises.

## Ordered Couples

Complex numbers are defined as the set of ordered pairs in **RxR**. We denote a complex number as z=(a,b) where a and b are real numbers. Note that there is no reference to geometry nor do we, by the sleight of hand, create $i = \sqrt{-1}$.

We define the addition and multiplication as below

Let u = (a,b) and v = (c,d) be complex numbers then

u+v = (a+c,b+d)

uv = (ac-bd, ad+bc)

This has a correspondence with the earlier definitions of the last section.

It can be proved that the definitions do not lead to any ambiguities. We can also prove that the set of complex numbers **C** with the operations (+) and (.) is a field. Note that the operations should be denoted by +(C) and .(C) but we can drop C so long as there is no confusion.

The additive identity is 0(C) = (0,0), and the multiplicative identity is 1(C) = (1,0) which for convenience can be denoted by 0 and 1.

It can be proved that i = (0,1) is such that $i^2 = (-1,0)$. However -i = (0,-1) also gives $(-i)^2 = (-1,0)$.

This imples $z^2 = -1$ has two roots, $+i$ and $-i$

The following results can be proved :

(1) If $z = (a,b)$ is not zero then a,b cannot both be zero and $a^2+b^2$ is a positive number.

(2) If $z = (a,b) \neq 0$, its multiplicative inverse is $[a/(a^2+b^2), -b/(a^2+b^2)]$

Unfortunately (**C**, +, .) is not an ordered field.

Two questions now arise :

1. Is a complex number a *number*?
2. What is the significance of complex zero?

The complex field lacks one important property, its elements have no order. Nevertheless we can isomorphically embed **R** into **C**. Mathematicians usually consider a field roughly equivalent to numbers in the abstract sense.[1]

It is difficult to classify the complex zero. We can identify it geometrically with the origin which makes it a relative zero. However, we might gain more insight if we consider the isomorphic embedding.

Consider the mapping

$f : \mathbf{R} \rightarrow \mathbf{C}$

$f(a) = (a,0)$

It can be proved that it is an isomorphic embedding of (**R**, +, .) into (**C**, +, .). The real number *a* can be identified with the complex number (a,0). In this sense we can say that (0,0) can be *identified* with the real number 0. In this abstract sense we may say that (0,0) is a quantitative zero.

A difference between the complex numbers and other derived numbers needs to be pointed out : the integers, rationals and the real numbers were defined as equivalence classes while complex numbers are ordered pairs not *sets*.

There is another reason why the complex zero should be treated as a quantitative zero. Recall the properties of the real zero mentioned in Chapter 1. The complex zero behaves in the same way. If z is a complex number then

1. $0+z = z = z+0$
2. $0.z = 0 = z.0$
3. $0/z = 0, z \neq 0$

## Matrices

A matrix of the order mxn has m rows and n columns and has either real or complex numbers as elements.

$$\mathbf{A} = \begin{bmatrix} 2 & 1 & 0 \\ 1 & 0 & 2 \end{bmatrix}$$

For example, A is a 2x3 matrix, its element $a_{23} = 2$ (second row, third column)

We define the addition of two matrices both of the same order mxn as the matrix of the order mxn whose elements are the sum of the corresponding elements of the matrices. For example if

$$\mathbf{B} = \begin{bmatrix} 2 & 0 & 3 \\ 0 & 1 & 0 \end{bmatrix}$$

which is also 2x3

$$\mathbf{A} + \mathbf{B} = \begin{bmatrix} 4 & 1 & 3 \\ 1 & 1 & 2 \end{bmatrix}$$

With this operation we can prove that a set of real matrices of the order mxn is a commutative group. Its identity is the zero matrix. For example in the above case

$$\mathbf{0} = \begin{bmatrix} 0 & 0 & 0 \\ 0 & 0 & 0 \end{bmatrix}$$

and the additive inverse of, say, A is -A =

$$\begin{bmatrix} -2 & -1 & 0 \\ -1 & 0 & -2 \end{bmatrix}$$

Are matrices numbers? They are an array of numbers which are used in statistics. What type of zero is the zero matrix? First, each order of the matrix has its own zero. Hence different zeros are not comparable. But any zero matrix is not a relative in the sense in which the origin in space is. For convenience we may call it a quantitative zero since each element is a number and is zero.

Multiplication is defined only when (mxn) matrix pre-multiplies (nxp) matrix to give (mxp) matrix. When multiplication is compatible, we get

$0A = 0$ and $A.0 = 0$

Hence the zero matrix seems to behave in accordance with our concept of nothing.

However, we do not have a field of matrices and matrices are usually not treated as numbers. There are what are known as "skew fields" of matrices but we need not consider them.

## Mathematical Zeros

We may now summarize our findings in Part II regarding the śūnya or zero in mathematics.

In the arithmetic which we study in school, by zero we mean only one number which has the implication of nothing : when added to another number the latter does not change, when multiplied by another number, we get back zero, and when divided by any non-zero number our answer is zero.

However, in abstract mathematics mathematicians have a hierachy of zeros: the zero of the natural numbers, the zero of the integers, the zero of the rationals and the zero of the real numbers. What's more, the only commonsense zero is the natural number zero defined in the Frege's method. All other first-level zeros are relative. In fact there are infinitely many relative zeros. Of these, we select the right zero (quantitative zero or *nothing*) using the principle of abstraction. All the higher-level zeros are "derived zeros" which are a class of numbers belonging to the rung immediately below.

While there is a hierarchy of zeros, the principle of embedding and isomorphism allows us to treat all zeros as identical *in practice*.

The complex zero differs from other higher-level zeros in that it is not a class but an ordered couple (0,0) of the "real zeros."

As we move beyond the real zero the question arises as to whether the other zeros in mathematics: complex zero, zero matrices etc. are really numbers. They share many properties of the zero we use in school but they do not fit into the commonsense concept of zero qua *number*.

# Part III

## Philosophy and Religion

# Infinite Void of Consciousness

## Vedānta

In Chapter 5 we mentioned that there are six orthodox Indian schools of philosophy apart from Buddhism. From the viewpoint of those who believe in mysticism or spiritualism Vedānta is the most important school, for two reasons. First, it offers a solution to contradictions which we face in life; happiness-misery, love-hate, hot-cold, instinct-culture and so forth. When people face such contradictions, they either turn to the philosophy of nothingness and nihilism or mysticism. Mysticism includes religion inasmuch as it is based on faith and intuition rather than rationality. But mysticism is not a very appealing word because it is also associated with black magic, sorcery and such other dark areas which we shun. The second reason why Vedānta is important is that though mystical in nature it has a tremendous appeal to intellectuals: there is almost no mumbo-jumbo and dark area. It is a model of equality not only between man and woman but also between men and animals, and even between the inanimate and animate objects. Vedānta and especially monism may not be practiced or fully understood by the masses, but the masses certainly respect those champions who propagated the monistic philosophy; Śaṅkarācārya, Vivekānanda and many others.

*Vedānta* means "the end of Vedas". It contains the teachings of Upaniṣads. However, according to many scholars such as

Sadananda, as a philosophical school Vedānta includes the Upaniṣads, Brahma Sūtras of Vyāsa, also called Bādarāyaṇa, and the *Bhagavad Gītā*. These three sources are collectively called Prasthānatrayī.

## Vedānta and Advaita

While there are different schools of Vedānta they all have a common core. They consider such questions as "What is the Ultimate Reality?" "How is the apparent world and its phenomena connected with the reality?" "What happens after death?" All these schools believe in the existence of God. They regard the Ultimate Reality as one, Supreme Consciousness and transcendental. They call it Ātman or Brahman. They believe that God's existence cannot be proved logically. In this they are close to the Western agnostics, but they differ from the agnostics in that they believe that Brahman can be felt or realized.

The most important and intellectually elegant school is monism (*advaita*). Vyāsa is usually regarded as its founder. Other important exponents are Śukadeva, Gauḍapāda and Śaṅkara. The last is perhaps the most famous monk who lived between sixth and ninth CE. He wrote a number of commentaries.

## Ātman or Self

The conception of Self in Śaṅkara's philosophy is borrowed from the Upaniṣads. The Self is all-pervading, self-existent, eternal, immortal and self-illumined Consciousness. It is beyond the phenomenal world which we perceive and in which we find time, space, matter etc.

The Self is within the body and also outside the body. We are born, we grow and experience the phenomena, and die. Ātman or Self is merely a witness. It sees the changes but is changeless and pure consciousness. I as an individual feel that I exist, my body exists, my mind exists and so on, but this is only an illusion. In fact neither I nor you nor anyone nor even any inanimate things exist. What exists is Self or Ātman. Some of the verses from scriptures are worth quoting.

"Ātman, tinier than the tiniest and greater than the greatest, rests in the hearts of creatures. The desireless one being free from grief realizes that glory of Ātman through the purity of senses and mind". (*Kaṭha 2-20*)

"The wise one does not grieve, having known the bodiless, all-pervading supreme Ātman who resides in all impermanent bodies" (*Kaṭha 2-22*)

"The Ātman, hidden in all beings reveals (itself) not (to all) but is seen only by the wise through their subtle and pointed intellect" (*Kaṭha 3-13*)

"Realize Ātman to be distinct from the body, sense-organs, mind, buddhi and non-differentiated matter. It is the Witness of their functions, comparable to a king" (*Śaṅkara in Ātma Bodha 17*)

"Know That to be indestructible by which all this is pervaded. None can effect the destruction of the Immutable" (*BG 2-17*)

## Brahman

According to monism the Ultimate Reality is Brahman which is all-pervading, eternal, self-existent, self-illumined and pure Consciousness. According to Śaṅkara Brahman alone exists. The phenomenal world is cosmic illusion called māyā. A few quotations will elucidate the point

"Realize that Brahman which is neither subtle nor gross; nor short nor long; without birth and change; without form, qualities or colour" (*Ātmabodha,* 59)

"The Supreme Brahman pervades the entire universe outwardly and inwardly and shines of Itself like the fire that permeates a red-hot iron ball, both inside and outside and shines of itself." (*Ātmabodha,* 62)

"Brahman is other than the universe. There exists nothing that is not Brahman. If any object other than Brahman appears to exist, it is unreal like mirage" (*Ātmabodha,* 63)

"All that is perceived or heard is Brahman and nothing else. Attaining the knowledge of Reality, one sees the universe as the non-dual Brahman, Existence-Knowledge-Bliss" (*Ātmabodha,* 64)

Ātman and Brahman are identical. The individual soul or *jīva* does not realize this fact because of its ignorance. Monism is not just the intellectual philosophy, it teaches you how to realize that you are not different from Ātman which is Brahman, the Ultimate Reality.

**Māyā**

If there is only one infinite consciousness called Brahman, how is it that we see the world of plurality?

According to Śaṅkara who adheres to the advaita school of monism, the universe is *māyā* or cosmic illusion. It merely means that to us *One* appears as *many.* The word *avidyā* or *ajñāna* is used to indicate the individual's ignorance which makes him perceive Brahman as plurality. The word Prakṛti is also used by Vedantins to denote māyā.

However, from another viewpoint, māyā is the power of Brahman.

A few characteristics of māyā may be mentioned. Māyā is unconscious (unlike Brahman the infinite consciousness), but is not real since it is dependent on Brahman, Māyā conceals Brahman. The language of contradictions and oxymorons is often used to describe māyā. It is neither identical with Brahman nor distinct from Brahman. It conceals both positive and negative principles. *Āvaraṇaśakti* is its power to conceal, while *vikṣepa-śakti* indicates its power to project plurality. It is neither real nor unreal. It is not real because it is an illusion, it is not unreal because from Brahmanic point of view, it cannot be divorced from the One. Māyā, like Brahman is beginningless. Nevertheless, in one sense it can be removed qua avidyā. The doctrine of monism or advaita is not a mere theoretical model, it also teaches how to remove avidyā and realize Brahman through knowledge.

Advaitism or nondualism can best be captured in the various aphorisms or *mahāvākyas*. A few of them are mentioned below.

That thou art (*SV, Chāndogya* 6-10-3)

This Ātman is Brahman (*AV, Māṇḍukya* 2, *Bṛhadāraṇyaka* 2-5-19)

Consciousness is Brahman (*RV, Aitareya* 5-3)

I am Brahman (*YV, Bṛhadāraṇyaka* 1-4-20)

## Upādhi

While the monists believe in one Ultimate Reality they use a few technical words to explain the phenomenal world and creation. For example, Īśvara or God is that aspect of Brahman which is associated with māyā to create the universe. Īśvara is also called Saguṇa Brahman. The word Nirguṇa Brahman is used to indicate the formless Ultimate Reality.

While Ātman (Self) is Brahman, the individual self feels that it is a separate entity. This is due to what is called *upādhi,* a limitation imposed by māyā. The following metaphor is often quoted: the space occupied by a closed vessel appears as limited, but in reality it is only the sky or void.

Brahman associated with māyā is sometimes called the material cause of the universe while Brahman qua Consciousness is the efficient cause of the universe. But these are merely two ways of stating that there is one and only one Brahman and the rest is an illusion.

Śaṅkara posits two realities. According to him all external and internal phenomena belong to the "apparent reality" and Brahman alone is the absolute Reality.

## Prāṇa

There are different views on prāṇa or life-force. The Yoga system describes several modification of prāṇa while Vedānta describes ten forms of prāṇa. Some Vedāntins believe that the material existence is the result of the vibrations of prāṇa which is the same as māyā. It would appear, therefore, that everything gross or minute, huge material bodies as well as sound and electromagnetic fields are mere patterns of the prāṇic vibrations. This aspect is found relevant by some modern physicists, as we shall see later.

## Realization

While many philosophers speak of the "liberation from bondage" or the liberation from the cycle of birth and death, extreme monism cannot recognize the concept of liberation, since we are always free: it is only an illusion which makes us feel that we are different from Brahman. The monist would show you the path of *self-realization* and not liberation. It is through true knowledge that you attain realization. This path is often called *jñānayoga* (*jñāna* for "knowledge"). Scholars often cite various stages of the path towards attaining this goal. This knowledge is also called Ātmavidyā or Brahmavidyā. It consists of progressive stages which give you the inner conviction that

1. Brahman alone is real and the universe is unreal.
2. There is only one Brahman without second.
3. This Self is Brahman i.e., I am Brahman.
4. The entire universe is Brahman.

## Brahman and Consciousness

If there is only one Reality the infinite Brahman which is consciousness, how would the Western scholar interpret this philosophy? It might be argued that behind the phenomena is the single *noumenon,* or the thing-in-itself, which is the Reality that is an infinite conscious void. However, our concept of void itself belongs to the phenomenal world and it may be a mistake to literally interpret void as the sky or ether, also called Ākāśa. Nevertheless, Ākāśa is believed to be the most important symbol of Brahman and is often identified with Brahman.

It should be emphasized that the Supreme Consciousness is all-pervading. This implies that in one sense Brahman is present even in inanimate objects or individual consciousness.

# 16

# Superconsciousness beyond Void

## Void and Space

In the last chapter we mentioned that Vedānta regards the world as illusory and posits that there is only one Reality, infinite consciousness. Vedānta also describes the evolution of the universe at the phenomenal level and assumes five subtle elements; space or ether (Ākāśa), air (vāyu), fire (agni), water (ap) and earth (pṛthvī). Each element is believed to have evolved out of the element listed immediately before, and Ākāśa evolved from Brahman associated with māyā. In reality, however, Brahman is associated with each element. Ākāśa has a special place in scriptures. It is considered one of the most important symbols of Brahman and often equated with Brahman. Ākāśa is associated with sound. So important is space that we can think of "conscious infinite void" as the closest description of Brahman a mortal can make.

The *Chāndogya Upaniṣad* (1-9-1) asserts that Ākāśa is the essence of the world. Swahananda comments that Ākāśa mentioned here is not bhutākāśa (phenomenal sky) but Brahman.[1] The *Brahma Sūtras* (1-1-22) endorse this view and contend that "The Supreme Reality is named Ākāśa in this scripture"

The same Upaniṣad in (3-12-9) maintains that Brahman is Ākāśa outside the body as well as inside the body. It is also within the heart. It is nothing but the all-pervading Brahman. In (3-13-4) the Upaniṣad identifies both Ākāśa and udāna (the air that proceeds from the sole of the foot) with Brahman . It exhorts you to meditate on them to acquire nobiiity and strength.

In (4-40-4) the *Chāndogya* says that prāṇa is Brahman, Ka(joy) is Brahman and Kha(ether) is Brahman. Incidentally Brahman is also described as Existence-Consciousness Bliss. This bliss mentioned as Ka above is not ordinary joy but the supreme Bliss. In the next verse (4-40-5) the Upaniṣad again asserts Ka(Bliss) is Kha(space) and Kha(space) is Ka (Bliss) and both in reality, are Brahman; beyond the phenomenal world.

Dattatreya's *Avadhūta Gītā* is a text which contains what may be called the extreme views on monism. It is written from the viewpoint of one who has realized Brahman and hence some of its stanzas appear strange, if not arrogant.

In (1-6), the author says that there is no doubt that "I am that God who is the Self of all, pure, indivisible, like the sky, naturally stainless".

In (1-58) he asserts he has no need of knowledge, reasoning, space (phenomenal) or samādhi (superconscious state attained in rājayoga at the last stage). I am naturally the perfect consciousness, the Real (i.e., Brahman) like the sky, spontaneous and steady.

Chapter III of the *Avadhūta Gītā* is most interesting. In most of the verses Dattatreya asserts "I am the nectar of knowledge, homogeneous Existence like the sky" i.e., "I am Brahman"

"You have no name and form even to the extent of allusion, nor any substance differentiated or undifferentiated. Why do you grieve, O you shameless mind? I am the nectar of knowledge, homogeneous Existence, like the sky" (3-33)

or again,

"I have told you all that is essential." There is neither you, nor anything for me or for a great one nor is there any teacher or disciple. The supreme Reality is natural and exists in its own way. I am the nectar of knowledge, homogeneous Existence, like the sky" (3-42)

"Pure, vast and homogeneous like the sky, the Self is the same in all and devoid of all. It is the homogeneous Being divested of essence, non-essense and change. Why do you who are the identity in all grieve?" (5-27)

The above discussion should confirm our intuition that Brahman is the infinite void or the sky of consciousness. However, let us see what Dattātreya has to say about the void elsewhere.

"There exists neither total void nor voidlessness...." (1-76)

"... There is no space or absence of space...... (5-5)

"There is nothing which pervades or is pervaded. There is no abode nor is there lack of abode. How can I speak of void and nonvoid?..." (4-9)

Hence when we say that Brahman is the conscious void, the void (like the sky) must be treated as a metaphor. We cannot transcend the phenomenal world and see what the real void is.

## Consciousness

While Brahman is the primordial principle of consciousness, the question now arises as to what type of consciousness it is. There are grades of consciousness: it may be safely believed that a fish, a dog or an ape has consciousness; but in the ascending scale, humankind may be said to possess the highest type of consciousness. But if we are considering the omnipresent consciousness which is responsible for creating and organizing the universe, it must be much higher than human consciousness. Vedantists call it pure consciousness. Aurobindo describes it as the Supermind. The monists are aware that realization implies the ascent of man from the human consciousness to superconsciousness. Nevertheless, this very superconsciousness manifests itself in different forms in nature. As Aurobindo points out, "Man's consciousness can be nothing else than a form of Nature's consciousness. It is there in other involved forms below mind, it emerges in mind, it shall ascend into yet superior forms beyond mind. For the force that builds the worlds is a conscious force, the existence which manifests itself in them is conscious Being and a perfect emergence of its potentialities in form is the sole object which we can rationally conceive for its manifestation of this world of forms"[2]

Aurobindo assumes that the "mind" must be identical with the Supermind though in the phenomenal world it appears inferior and takes different forms.

The pure Consciousness or the Divine Supermind is believed to have a triple status, Truth (sat), Consciousness (cit), and Bliss (ānanda), which is called Saccidānanda that "must be a spaceless and timeless absolute of conscious existence that is bliss; but the world is, on the contrary, an extension in time and space and a movement, a working out, a development of relations of possibilities by causality — or what so appears to us — in time and space"[3]

Ākāśa and consciousness have considerable resemblance. Both are infinite but appear to be limited by the upādhis. An enclosed space is not different from the infinite Ākāśa and the consciousness of a jīva is the same as the infinite consciousness.

The hierarchy of consciousness is not only found in different species of creatures, it is believed to be reflected in human beings as different states. The *Māṇḍukya Upaniṣad* describes four such states, the fourth or Turīya is identified with Brahman, and is, of course, the goal of those who want to realize Truth.

According to the *Māṇḍukya*, all is Brahman or the Self which consists of four quarters. The first quarter is Vaiśvānara whose sphere is the waking state. In this state consciousness enjoys the outer world through various senses. Taijasa is the second quarter whose sphere is the dream state. The consciousness is internal and it enjoys subtle objects. The state of deep sleep is the third quarter called Prajña. Prajña is a mass of consciousness with bliss. At this level everything becomes undifferentiated. Prajña is the Lord of all and omniscient. It is the inner "director" and the source of all. This is also the place of origin and dissolution of all beings. At this stage the sleeper does not desire anything nor does he see any dreams.

The fourth state is Turīya. Turīya is not conscious of the internal world, nor conscious of the external world nor is it an undifferentiated mass of consciousness. It is neither conscious nor unconscious. It is unseen, beyond the grasp, uninferable, unthinkable, indescribable. Its valid proof is the single belief in the Self in which the phenomenal world disappears and which is unchanging, auspicious and non-dual. That is the Self which has to be known by the one who aspires to realize Truth.[4]

You may observe that Turīya or Brahman is described in contradictory terms because it is indescribable. This has led some students to ask whether Turīya is a mere void. The teacher explains that it is not mere void. "An illusion cannot exist without a substratum; for the illusion of silver, snake, human being, mirage etc. cannot be imagined to exist apart from the corresponding substrata of the mother of pearl, rope, stump of a tree, desert etc".[5]

Incidentally, Om or Aum the revered symbol is identified with Brahman. The first three states described above are equated with the three mātrās (moras) of Aum: A (waking), U(dream), M(dreamless sleep). The fourth state Turīya is identified with *amatraḥ* (that which lies beyond three mātrās of Aum), which means Turīya or Brahman is the complete Om.[6]

## Negations and Contradictions

Like any other mystical experience, Brahman is indescribable. One of the ways to refer to it is therefore using negatives and contradictions. One of the most popular methods is to describe it as *neti neti* ("not this, not this")[7].

The Hindu philosophers usually do not believe in the one-time creation of the world but posit a cyclic process in which the universe evolves and dissolves. In the Vedas this process is described as the breathing out (evolution) and breathing in (dissolution) of Puruṣa or Cosmic Person. However, those monists who believe in absolute nondualism must accept this description metaphorically if the indescribable eternal Brahman is to be believed.

The principle of "Opposites" is found even in the earliest literature, the Rigveda(10-129) This hymn is referred to as the Creation Hymn (Nāsadīya).[8]

There was neither non-existence nor existence then, there was neither the realm of space nor the sky which is beyond. What stirred? Where? For whose protection? Was there bottomless water? (1)

There was no death and no immortality. There was neither day nor night. That One breathed without air with its own vibrations. There was nothing other than that. (2)

Darkness concealed darkness in the beginning. All was water. The life force was covered with emptiness. That One emerged through the power of heat (3)

Desire came upon that One in the beginning which was the first seed of the mind. Poets (kavi)seeking in their heart with wisdom found the bond of existence and non existence.(4)

The cord was placed across. Was there *below*? Was there *above*? There were those who sowed seeds and there were powers. There was impulse below and giving out above. (5)

Who knows really? Who can proclaim the scene? From where was it produced? From where is this creation? The gods appeared later, with the universe. Who knows from where it has arisen? (6)

From where has this creation arisen? Perhaps it created itself, perhaps it did not. The one who looks down upon it from the highest heaven only knows. Or perhaps he does not know. (7)

This hymn can be interpreted in several ways. The contradictions are mind-boggling and reflect the doubt existing in the mind of the poet. If it is interpreted from the viewpoint of the monist we may say that One refers to Brahman and the poet speculates on the origin of Braman itself i.e., "the origin of the existence of existence itself" (8)

An interesting verse appears in the *Taittirīyopaniṣad* (2-7) "In the beginning there was indeed Nonbeing. From that, Being sprang up that of itself assumed a self. Hence it is called the self-made". It is difficult to interpret the verse. According to Sarvananda, it does not connote "an agnostic conception of a primal non-existence".[9] In support of his contention he cites the *Chāndogya* (6,2,1-2) according to which "absence of attributes cannot be equated with non-existence or absurd or self-contradictory like a human horn or a square circle".[10] According to the *Rigveda* (10-129) Brahman is above Being and Nonbeing. "Śūnya or Void is one among the thousand appellations of Viṣṇu. The German mystic Bohme said, "The Nothing bringeth itself to a will".[11] The only conclusion we can draw is that Brahman is indescribable.

It is worthwhile to quote Dattātreya in the *Avadhūta Gītā* "Here is the One without void and absence of void, without purity and impurity, without whole and the part..." (5-87)

While Brahman is described as infinite consciousness, which implies physical inertness, it is also not different from the universal activities. These are only two aspects of Brahman. According to Aurobindo, "It is an eternal passivity which makes possible the perfect freedom and omnipotence of an eternal divine activity in innumerable cosmic systems. For the becomings of that activity derive their energies and their illimitable potency of variation and harmony from the impartial support of the immutable Being, its consent to this infinite fecundity of its own dynamic Nature".[12]

Aurobindo refers to our earlier allusion to Creation out of Nonbeing and says that *Nonbeing* is only a word. When we speak of Being appearing out of Nonbeing we are speaking of a temporal succession. But in reality this is impossible because Being and Nonbeing lie beyond time. According to him

Nonbeing refers to a contrary affirmation of Brahman's freedom from all cosmic existence. "The Nonbeing permits the Being, even as the Silence permits the Activity"[13].

The monists like Aurobindo argue that just as Nonbeing is not nullity, phenomenon is not phantasm: in a way it is a form of, Truth.

Interestingly the hathayoga refers to Brahman as *Śūnyāsūnya* which means the *One* who is beyond śūnya (zero) as well as nonzero.

17

# Buddhism and Śūnyavāda

## Buddhism

Śūnyavāda is one of the four schools of Buddhism. Buddha means the "Enlightened One" or the "Awakened One". This was the epithet first given to Siddhārtha Gautama of Sākyas, who was born around 563 BCE in what is now Nepal.

Siddhārtha was the son of a king. An astrologer had predicted that either he would be a universal king (cakravarti) or if he renounced the world, he would become a famous redeemer. The king took utmost care to keep him surrounded by luxuries. He tried to ensure that Siddhārtha would never come near ugliness, sickness and death.

However, the prince on four occasions saw sights which had a lasting effect on him: a decrepit doddering old man, a diseased man lying on the street helpless, a corpse, and finally a monk with a shaven head. When the prince saw how a man could suffer he lost the zest for worldly pleasures. He was tormented by the thoughts of disease and suffering for six years. One night he left his wife and his son and went towards the forest in search of truth.

For the next six years he experimented with many spiritual methods; rāja yoga, extreme asceticism and so forth. Dissatisfied, he began to believe that the extremes had to be avoided and the middle way was the best course. Once he sat down under a pipal tree at Gaya in meditation. After going through a turmoil of temptations and fear, Siddhārtha emerged with Great Awakening. The tree under which he sat began to be called Bo tree ("Bo" for *bodhi* or enlightenment.)

For the next half a century the Buddha wandered from place to place preaching his message.

## Buddha's Teachings

Buddha's enlightenment made him depend on ethical and moral teaching rather than on intellectual speculation. He taught how to minimize suffering and misery. According to Buddha there are ten metaphysical questions which are totally useless for the actual mode of living. They are:

(1) Is the world eternal? (2) Is it noneternal? (3) Is it finite? (4) Is it infinite? (5) Are the soul and the body the same entity? (6) Are they different entities? (7) Does an enlightened person continue to live after death? (8) Does such a person cease to live after death? (9) Does such a person live or not live after death? (10) Does a realized person neither live nor not live after death?

These are metaphysical questions that cannot be answered. This is why Buddhism is considered close to agnosticism.

Buddha always remained silent and refused to answer these questions. He was more interested in making people aware of the sorrows of life. Unfortunately after Buddha's death his silence was "interpreted" in different ways which led to many schools of Buddhism.

Buddha taught the Four Noble Truths. These are (1) Suffering exists. (2) There is a cause of suffering (3) Suffering can cease (4) There is a means to stop suffering.

(1) *Suffering exists.* Suffering (*dukkha*) exists as disease old age, death etc, but life itself should be viewed as suffering which is born of attachment and desire.
(2) *There is a cause of suffering.* According to Buddha every cause has an effect. There is an endless chain of cause and effect. This doctrine is called *pratītyasamutpāda.* There are twelve

links in this chain, called dvādaśanidāna. These links are:

1. Ignorance (avidyā) (A)
2. Previous impressions (saṃskāras) (S)
3. Initial consciousness (vijñāna) (Vi)
4. The body-mind complex or unity (nāmarūpa) (N)
5. The five cognitive senses and the mind (ṣaḍāyatana) (Sa)
6. Contact of senses with objects or touch (sparśa) (Sp)
7. Past experience of senses (vedanā) (Ve)
8. Thirst to enjoy oneself (tṛṣṇā) (T)
9. Mental clinging or attachment (upādāna) (U)
10. Will to become (bhāva) (B)
11. Birth (jāti) (J)
12. Death (jarāmaraṇa) (M)

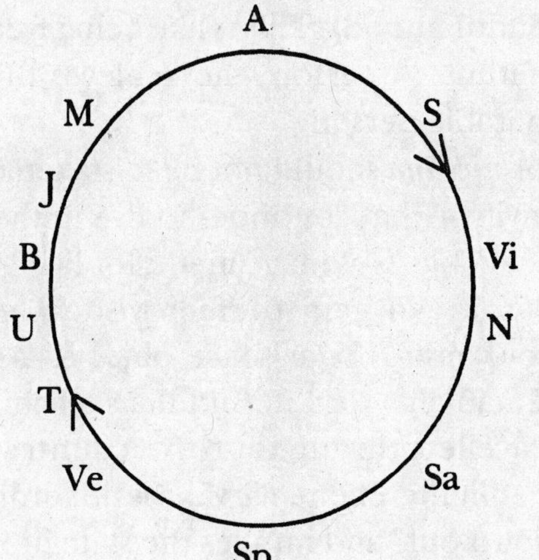


Fig. 17.1

The arrows show the flow in the cause-effect chain

It is because there is a will to *become*, a person is born (B to J) The will to become comes from our clinging to sense objects (U to B) and so on. The most interesting link is the initial consciousness in the cells which gives rise to the body-mind organism. Buddhism believes in rebirth. Note the link, past experience (Vi) — initial consciousness (N).

The twelve-link cycle (Fig. 17.1) continues till one knows how to break it. This method leads to the cessation of suffering.

## End of suffering

This is the third Noble truth. If one learns to break the cycle one is not subject to "conditioned life" and there is no suffering. This can be achieved by following Buddha's four Noble Truths. Desire, attachment and avidyā are the impediments which need to be eliminated. Buddha's thinking seems to have common elements with karma yoga and jñāna yoga.

Control of desire and contemplation of Truth can lead a person to a state of perfection and wisdom. This is the state of *Buddhatva* (Buddhahood). This is like being free or liberated in one's own lifetime. A person who achieves this goal is called *arhat* or a venerable person.

The state of *nirvāṇa* should not be mistaken for somnolence or lack of activity. Arhat continues to live in the world: he may use the external objects as instruments for living, but there is no attachment. You can gain perfect wisdom when you have withdrawn your mind from sense objects. We also find the elements of Patañjali's yoga in Buddha's teachings.

Buddha travelled throughout the country preaching for 45 years after enlightenment. Nirvāṇa is not ordinary extinction - it means "blown out" and implies the state in which the cause of suffering is extinguished. As we mentioned earlier, Buddha avoided metaphysical questions. He did not elaborate on what the state of nirvāṇa was. This means that "liberation" can only be felt and is not describable.

The fourth Noble truth is that there is a means to stop suffering. Buddha was not a metaphysician who wastes his time in arguments and speculation. He unfolded a complete system of *sādhanā* (practice) which consists of eight steps. They are:

right views (*samyagdṛṣṭi*), right intent (*samyaksaṃkalpa*), right speech (*samyagvāk*), right conduct (*samyakkarmānta*), right livelihood (*samyagājiva*), right effort (*samyagvyāyāma*), right mindfulness (*samyaksmṛti*), right meditation (*samyaksamādhi*)

## The Path to Nirvāṇa

*Right views* — A right view means correct knowledge of the Four Noble Truths. This is not just the theoretical knowledge, but capacity to feel the nature of one's ignorance; imperfection and impermanence of the world and being aware of one's relationship with the world.

*Right Intent* — Right intent or resolve implies a firm determination to transform oneself: the student should give up attachment to external objects, enmity, and his conduct should not be harmful to others.

*Right speech* — The right intent would be worthless unless it is followed by the right speech which implies avoidance of idle chatter, gossip, defamation, lying, perjury, sarcasm or any speech that can cause physical or mental injury to others.

*Right Conduct* — This includes five vows (*pañcaśīla*) and behaviour conforming them. The five vows are non violence, truthfulness, nonstealing, non sensuality, nonpossessiveness (sometimes interpreted as nonintoxication). You will appreciate that these fairly agree with five of the Ten Commandments. Pañcaśīla provides the ethical code for the followers of Buddha.

*Right Effort* — This implies that negative thoughts must be replaced by constructive thoughts which lead to the correct method prescribed by Buddha.

*Right Mindfulness* — This implies that we should remember the ephemeral nature of objects and the pleasure they give us. The power of mind is expressed in the Buddhist text *Dhammapada* "All we are is the result of what we have thought".[1]

*Right Meditation* — The first seven steps prepare you to make your mind one-pointed. According to Buddha there are four stages of meditation:

1. The practitioner makes his mind peaceful and investigates truth through concentration.
2. The student at this stage has expelled all doubts and accepted the Four Noble Truths fully. This is the stage of duality where the practitioner is the enjoyer and peace is the object of his enjoyment.
3. In this stage the student transcends peace and joy and is aware only of his existence.
4. The last stage is the culmination of meditation where even the bodily existence is not felt: this is the state of total indifference. It is Nirvāṇa. What is it like? Can we call it nothingness? As we saw earlier, Buddha refused to answer such questions. We shall see later how this stage is interpreted by later Buddhists.

Buddhists believe that there are four levels of wisdom. At the lowest level is *śrotāpanna,* one who has entered the eight fold path of liberation. The next level belongs to *sakṛdāgāmin,* one who will come back to this world only once. On the third echelon is *anāgāmin* who will not return to this world. The last level belongs to an *arhat,* one who is liberated in this very life. This stage is comparable with *jīvanamukti* of Hindus.

## Theories in Buddhism

Before we study the *Śūnyavāda* we must get acquainted with Buddha's philosophical and moral views. While Buddha avoided being dragged into metaphysical questions and answers, we can perceive four doctrines in his teaching.

*The Doctrine of Dependent Origination* (*prātityasamutpāda*)

According to this theory nothing exists without cause and everything has some effect. Accidental origination found in some modern scientific theories is alien to Buddhism.

It is this theory of dependent origination which led Buddha to find the way to break the cause-effect chain and search for the state which is transcendent and unconditional which should be the goal of life. Buddha regarded this doctrine necessary to understand his teaching. He called it dharma or "eternal law".

Closely related to this theory is the *theory of universal change.* Everything we perceive or feel is ephemeral and undergoes change from moment to moment. If we cannot detect these changes it is because of the limitations of our senses as well as the fact that the change may be too small from one stage to another. According to Buddha, "That which seems to be durable will perish; that which is high will be laid low"[2]. This doctrine of impermanence subsequently led to the *doctrine of momentariness* (*kṣaṇikavāda*). This phenomenon of continuous change is illustrated by the stream of water or a flame. Similar sentiments were expressed by the Greek philosopher Heraclitus who said that the objects of our experience are in perpetual flux.

Unlike some Vedic darśanas, Buddha does not accept the existence of a soul — He views a human being as a complex of five ever-changing states called pancaskandhas. These components (*skandha*) are (1) form (*rūpa*) — the material body (2) feeling (*vedanā*) of pain, pleasure, indifference etc. (3) perception (*sañjanā*) (4) post impressions (*saṃskāra*) which may be memories and predispositions which are latent (5) consciousness (*vijñāna*). When this combination dissolves or is destroyed, the existence of the human being disappears.

Buddha does not discuss God. He is more concerned with our feelings in life and how dukkha can be eliminated.

## Problems of Nothingness

Two questions relating to void, and nothingness emerge from Buddha's teachings.

(1) The first relates to the cause-effect cycle depicted in fig. 17.1 . The stage of death is again linked with birth. How do we explain these links? Who is the experiencer of these links? After death there is no conscionsness nor is there any soul. Hence we cannot speak of the "identity" which

feels, say, tṛṣṇa and who has the "will to become". The mark of individuation in animate beings is consciousness. If everything is extinct what is that which participates in the cycle? Is it *nothing* or something indescribable? If *A* dies, can we say that *A* is born again?

(2) The conception of *Nirvāṇa* raises a similar question. If etymologically Nirvāṇa implies extinction, what remains? Nāgasena was one of Buddha's disciples. It would be interesting to know his views through a dialogue. When he was asked what Nirvāṇa is, he posed a counter-question.

"Is there a thing called wind?"

"Yes respected sir"

"Please sir, show the wind by its color or configuration or as thick or long or short"

"Respected sir, this is not possible. The wind cannot be grasped in the hand or touched. Nevertheless it exists"

"Sir, if it is not possible for you to show the wind, we can say there is no wind"

"Respected Nāgasena, I know that there is wind. I am convinced of its existence but I cannot show it"

"In the same way, sir, Nirvāṇa exists but cannot be shown"[3]

With respect to Nirvāṇa we are on a firmer ground *vis-a-vis,* the problem relating to the interval between death and the next birth. We can say that Nirvāṇa is a state that cannot be described.

## Śūnyavāda

It was mentioned earlier that Buddha maintained silence on most metaphysical puzzles. He called such problems indescribable (*avyaktani*). Nevertheless his teachings as well as silence was interpreted in different ways by his followers.

As happens to any tenet, as time elapsed there were further interpretations and reinterpretations, with the result that at present there are about thirty schools of Buddhism, of which four are considered most important. They are: (1) Śūnyavāda, also called Mādhyamika, (2) Vijñānavāda or Yogācāra; (3) Sautrāntika, and (4) Vaibhāṣika.

We shall consider Śūnyavāḍa in detail and treat other schools only briefly.

The schism between the Śūnyavāda and other schools stems from a philosophical problem. What is reality? Is it mental or nonmental?

The Śūnyavāda, which was founded by Nāgārjuna. (ca 150-250 CE), maintains that reality is neither mental nor nonmental. Everything we perceive outside or inside is unreal. It is like the objects in a dream. The whole universe is unreal.

Śūnyatā (emptiness) is the word used by the followers of this school. The objects, feelings, and thoughts exist in one sense. I can see a table, I can touch it, I use it for writing or other purposes, but it is the table of the phenomenal world.

What we call "thing" has the following features:

(1) a thing has an inherent nature (2) all things are subject to the law of dependent origination (3) all things appear to exist in the phenomenal world. However, in the ultimate sense they are empty.

However, the śūnya of the Mādhyamika is not *nihil* or *nothing* as we normally understand by "zero". It means that the Ultimate Reality is indescribable. The Śūnyavāda, therefore, is not nihilism which we considered in Chapter 6. If the Śūnyavādins contend that things are neither real nor unreal, their contention is based on the following argument: Everything we know is causally connected, hence it cannot be real. But it is not unreal because it exists in some sense, and anything that is unreal cannot come into existence. We cannot also say that (1) a thing is both real and unreal (2) a thing is neither real nor unreal because these statements are self-contradictory. The Western logician would say that they violate the "law of contradiction" and the "law of the excluded middle".

In fact, there are two types of truth, empirical or phenomenal (*saṃvṛti satya* or *vyavahārika satya*) and transcendental or absolute (*paramārtha satya*). Corresponding to these two realities there are two śūnyas. The first nothingness or Śūnyatā relates to the phenomenal world to which the law of dependent origination applies. The nature of a thing (dhamma) is dependent on another thing. We have also mentioned that according Buddha's teaching there is momentariness and changeability. Śūnya in relation to the phenomenal world connotes all these characteristics of impermanence and cause-effect chain. Śūnyatā also implies that it is the intrinsic property of a thing which makes it dependent on a cause.

It is through this relative non-being we have to search for the ultimate Truth. This Truth is nirvāṇa. However, since this state is indescribable because it is beyond the phenomenal world of cause-effect chain and is not conditioned, this Absolute Truth (paramārtha satya) is also śūnyatā which cannot be described in terms of the phenomenal world. This transcendental śūnyatā has a different import for those who have attained true wisdom or nirvāṇa. This very śūnyatā or nothingness for them provides a potential for everything.

## Other Schools

The other important school is Vijñānavāda whose founders were Asaṅga, Vasubandhu, Diṅnaga and Dharmakīrti. This school contends that the external objects are unreal while the mind is real in the sense, it is subject to the rule of dependent origination. Since our perception cannot be differentiated from the external objects, the existence of the external world cannot be proved. This school is also called Yogācāra because it borrows from yogic methods.

The third school is *Sautrāntika* or "representationalism" according to which both mental and external worlds are real.

The fourth school is Vaibhāṣika or direct realism. According to this school external things are directly known by perception. In this it differs from the Sautrāntika school according to which the external world is inferred from the mental impression.

After Buddha, Buddhism split into two main streams, Mahāyāna ("great vehicle") which believed in the liberal interpretation of Buddha's teaching and silence. Thus it has elaborate metaphysics. The other stream is *Hīnayāna* ("small vehicle") which tried to adhere to Buddha's original teachings. Hence there is minimum metaphysics. This is also called Theravāda. Śūnyavāda and Vijñānavāda belong to the Mahāyāna which spread to northeast: Tibet, China, Mongolia, etc. The other two schools belong to the Hīnayāna which through South India spread to Sri Lanka, Burma, Indonesia and Thailand.

18

# Fullness in Emptiness

## Nothing and Death

People commit suicide because they suffer mentally or physically. They believe that their death would lead to extinction of suffering, assuming of course, that there is nothing after death. Even those who believe in afterlife may take this extreme course because the suffering is unbearable. This is understandable. There may also be people who, as we explained in Introduction, find life empty and hollow after a tragedy or even on account of boredom which characterizes the wealthy but lonely people in the West. If such pathological ennui reaches a certain point, a person may end his life.

But there are also people who are well-contented, who have enjoyed the various stages of life, discharged their duties according to the social and religious norms, but who feel that there is nothing more to be done on this earth. Possibly such people feel that they were born for a certain purpose, and when the goal is met there is no sense in living.

We hear the stories of many holy men who accept "voluntary death", wrongly called samādhi, at the appropriate time. Some of them may be apocryphal. A report which appeared recently in newspapers makes one wonder how a contented man can end his life. This is the story of a person from the Indian State of Kerala. For some years he had been petitioning the court to grant him permission to end his life. The person maintained that he had fulfilled all his duties, lived his life fully and was well-contented. His mission in this life was complete since he has nothing more to do. It is possible that he was motivated by the desire not to be a burden on his children if he underwent prolonged sickness before death.

There have been many such petitions to the judiciary. The petitions were justified on the ground that an attempt to commit suicide is an offence under the Indian penal law. I always thought that such petitioners were hypocrites seeking publicity. However, when I read in the paper that this man really committed suicide after waiting in vain for some years for the court's consent, I had to change my perception about human nature. This is a singular case of jumping from "a peaceful nothingness" into the valley of apparent extinction.

It is interesting to get acquainted with the thoughts of two eminent metaphysicians of the twentieth century, T. Krishnamurti and Osho. Both had unconventional views and both were popular among the intellectuals in India and abroad.

## J. Krishnamurti

Jiddu Krishnamurti (1895-1986) was born in Madras. Annie Besant educated him in England. He was proclaimed the Messiah in 1925 by the Order of Star in the East founded by Besant. However, Krishnamurti proved to be a rebel and dissolved the Order. One who has read him often feels that Krishnamurti's yearning for freedom had roots in the institutional halo which was imposed on him. In India many minors are appointed the head of a mutt (monastery) or as the heir apparent. When the boys grow up they may find that the spiritual glory does not suit their temperament, but very few of such misfits have had the courage to rebel and abdicate the spiritual throne.

The book *The Ending of Time* is a dialogue between Krishnamurti and physicist David Bohm; and gives us an insight into what Krishnamurti has to say about conflict, time, nothingness and void.

## Time and Becoming

Krishnamurti believes that humanity in the process of development took a wrong turn somewhere. He attributes this to humankind's desire to *become* something. This is ascribed to conflict which in turn is the result of the feeling "I am different from you". It is the ego which is at the root. "If there is no ego there is no problem, there is no conflict there is no time - time in the sense of becoming or not becoming; being or nonbeing".[1] Time and psychological knowledge are inseparable and are our enemies. It is necessary to destroy the patterns of knowledge our brain has learned for millions of years. When there is no "me", no time, not even meditation, there is *nothing* which is the source of everything. In *nothing* lies the energy which can lead us to creation.

It is necessary that our mind is totally cleansed of time or the acquired knowledge. This leads to the extinction of the individual mind. There is nothingness which is the universal Mind. This Mind is everything and is energy. Emptying of the particular mind leads to the universal Mind. One should go one step further and conceive of the death of the universal Mind to reach the *ground* which has neither beginning nor end.

In one sense accepting the psychological patterns we have acquired for millions of years is irrational, and is the root of becoming and conflict. Paradoxically, it is *insight* which rids us of our "me" and "mine". According to Krishnamurti Vedānta means the end of knowledge. This end is necessary if we want to be free. The traditional ways, prayer, church, books etc. to acquire freedom and truth are useless. The way to freedom lies in the new mind, and that can be acquired only when we empty our present mind with contents called knowledge.

It was pointed out that insight plays a crucial role. Insight encompasses total human activity. Krishnamurti agrees with Bohm that insight is the all-pervading energy which illuminates the brain and dispels darkness. The question now arises as to why everyone does not acquire insight. The problem has to do with love which seems to be almost identical with insight. Somewhere on the way of evolution humans lost this basic characteristic of loving and turned in the wrong directions. It is the division between the ego and the rest which is the center of darkness. The root cause is knowledge and time and becoming. Krishnamurti asserts that apart from the psychological movement (becoming) there is another Movement independent of time which is undivided. This is the ground where there is no "my insight" and "your insight". There is no death in this. Movement. Mind emerges from this Movement as a ground and dies back in the Movement. At one place Krishnamurti asserts that true meditation can begin only when the mind is empty.

Does life have meaning? If by life we mean what goes on for millions of years, life has no meaning, but we can find meaning when the brain is totally free. But this is difficult because when it is threatened, the mind takes shelter in time i.e., in conventional behaviour. Emptying of mind is the beginning of contemplation. When the mind extricates itself from time, it can be the universe — a state of meditation in which there is no past.

## Emptiness and Freedom

But what is emptying of mind? Krishnamurti asserts that he is not talking of the pseudo-emptiness created by one who runs away from pleasure, pain and suffering. He means total emptiness. Such emptiness is the movement of energy. It is not material reaction which appears in time. This movement of energy is timeless. This is the movement which has no cause, no beginning, and no end. Paradoxically in this moving energy there is stillness. It is this movement, which is beyond time, that is the source of creation. What it creates is always new.

Krishnamurti speaks of two orders, the order in the individual mind, full of contradictions and reactions, and the universal order which has the base in the movement which is still. The universal order does affect the order in the mind. The latter gives security but not freedom. For complete freedom we should have enough courage to relate to the universal order. Those who renounce the world, the saints and the monks, cannot have complete freedom. He posits that the universe and the mind which have been totally emptied are identical. The universe is like the body of the absolute Mind. Those who say that God is always there or Brahman is always present are making dangerous statements, since "always" implies time. In freedom when the individual mind is the universal mind, emptiness is a prerequisite and time is not present.

The march from the particular to the general and from the general to the universal is what happens when there is complete freedom which gives total security. Just as for the scientist, phosphorous is phosphorous which is neither mine nor yours, in the same way love, grief and so forth do not belong to a particular individual, they are general. When we reach the stage of generality our further journey is deeper taking us to the universal. We might then find what we call the purity of love, compassion and intelligence. This needs our total participation, the mind, heart and the whole being.

Krishnamurti appears difficult, but the common characteristics of mysticism are there for us to see. "Movement in stillness" is an excellent example. Another feature of mysticism viz. *nothing* as the source of creation, (in this case creation that is ever new) reminds us of the point or bindu which encloses the void, but is a potential source of creation.

## Osho

Osho, formerly Bhagwan Shree Rajaneesh was immensely popular in India and the West. Many meditation centers sprang up in several parts of the world in the 1970s. His method is known as "loving meditation". He is regarded as an unconventional godman loved as well as despised. His meditation involved a personal devotional relationship between his devotees and him.

Osho admired Buddha's teachings. The latter said, "There is no self. You are an emptiness, utter silence, a nonbeing".[2] However, according to him Buddha's approach was negative with the result that people took his message literally. If we are nothing, then why worry about life? What is there to achieve if we are just a void? He felt that one of the reasons why Buddhism died in India was the other philosophies being positive were more attractive. While Buddha rightly diagnosed the disease viz. egoism, he went to the other extreme and suggested emptiness as the solution. Ordinary people found it difficult to grasp the essence of his message. For them dropping the ego for liberation appeared strange. If there was no ego, where is the question of liberation?

Osho accepts Buddha's message but tells his devotees that "You don't have a self because you are part of the universe; you are not nothing" [3]. If you don't have a self, it is because you are a part of the great Self. The idea is to convey the fact that we are not separate from rivers, mountains, sky, other people and the entire nature. The emptiness is only a metaphor. If we have room with furniture we may remove a piece of furniture one by one. In the process, the emptiness which was divided into parts by the furniture, has become full.

Osho asserts that emptiness *is*, but it has its own fullness. Suppose we do not know what is love, we need neither hate it nor accept it nor reject it. If we relax we will find that our state of "letting go" melts into the universe. Nothingness becomes fullness.

It is only when we see the other side of the emptiness viz. wholeness, that we acquire true knowledge. Mere emptiness may relieve you of your worries but it cannot offer anything concrete as gain. Enlightenment can come when you transcend these opposites or contradictions of void and wholeness. What you need for this is mere silence.

Osho cautions that the apparent non-existence may hide the precious existence. The roots of the tree without which the tree cannot exist lie hidden under the ground. Osho seems to have been influenced by the Upaniṣads and the *Bhagavad Gītā.* The body is not the real self. The true existence, Self, lies inside and is immortal. He recalls an apt historical anecdote. When Alexander set out for India, his friends asked him to bring a true sanyāsin (monk). After conquering a part of the Punjab, he went in search of a true sanyāsin. He was directed to a famed yogi. Alexander the Great expressed his wish to take the sanyāsin to Greece. The sanyāsin refused. Alexander was furious and reminded him that he was a conqueror and could do anything he desired. To the emperor's astonishment the poor sanyāsin had the audacity to call him ignorant and a fool. You may kill me, that will only destroy my body. My true Self is indestructible. If you behead me as well, you will only see my head rolling. According to this anecdote, Alexander was stunned and had no moral courage to kill the person who claimed that by destroying his body, Alexander would not annihilate his true Self.

Osho believed in moderation and appropriate self-control. According to him total renunciation, fasting and self-torture is hypocrisy. " I am in favour of the self-discipline that happens like the falling of a dry leaf. Certain things drop out from life, become meaningless, and life is transformed".[4]

He makes a distinction between the *opposite* and *absence.* For example, darkness is not the opposite but absence of light. We cannot throw a bit of darkness on light to dim it or extinguish it. His message is that darkness cannot be fought, but a lamp has to be lighted to dispel it.

19

# Taoism and Zen

## Taoism

If we consider Taoism of China and Zen of Japan we find a continuum of a philosophy which begins with contradictions and merges into "unity in emptiness".

Taoism (pronounced as "Dowism") was born in China. Its author was called Lao Tzu which means "the Old Boy". His real name is not known. Lao Tzu did not preach, but he wrote a volume *Tao Te Ching* or "The Way and Its Power" which has profoundly influenced the Chinese society.

The word "Tao" has three broad interpretations. First, like the Indian Brahman Tao cannot be perceived and its existence is transcendental. If we try to describe Tao, our expressions will not reveal Tao. It is above all, beneath all and behind all. It is the Womb from which everything has emanated. According to *Tao Te Ching*, it is ineffable, eternal and the greatest of the great. Taoists have a terse maxim: those who know, don't say, those who say, don't know.[1] This interpretation of Tao is called the way of the Ultimate Reality.

The second interpretation calls Tao the "way of the universe" which is manifested as the organization of the universe including the laws of the universe. This is similar to the conception of Ṛta:

"We must praise Eternal Order (Ṛtam samsantah) and think in a straight way" (RV 10-67-12)

As the way of the universe, Tao, like Brahman, is immanent. In the third sense, Tao refers to the way of human life as an organic part of the universe.

*Te* means "power" and *Tao Te Ching* has been translated as *The Way and Its Power.* Scholars divide Taoism into three subdivisions. Religious Taoism, Philosophical Taoism and the last is nameless which is heterogeneous. All schools try to manipulate *te* in human beings either by efficiently using it or by trying to increase it. We shall, however, consider those aspects of Taoism which interest us most.

The first concept that interests us is *wu wei.* Though its literal translation is "inaction", in Taoism it means *effective action* in social relationship. Another concept, *Ch'i* which means "breath", is important for those Taoists who have incorporated practices similar to raja yoga of ancient India, which consists of eight steps leading to samadhi or the superconscious state. The Taoist yogi, too, strives for liberation and when the realization comes the yogi has extraordinary awareness which is complete serenity and bliss. The Taoist yoga has a strong component of mysticism.

The principle of *wu wei* is extremely important for the philosophical Tao. Here we find contradictions interwoven around this concept. Though wu wei is supreme action it implies inaction, gentleness, and simplicity. Creativity is sought through the relaxation of mind. We must stop trying to struggle more and more and "let go" the mind to find its own peaceful state. In Chapter 27, the *Tao te Ching* contends that we may move in such a way that a foot-print is not shown, speak in such a way that the tongue does not slip and reckon so well that no counter is needed.

Those who believe in this principle of "effective action in inaction" contend that they are searching for effective voids in life and nature - empty spaces through which the action is swift but silent. *Tao te Ching,* the contradiction is expressed as: "Nothing is as soft and yielding as water, but its power to dissolve what is hard and rigid is not exceeded by any other substance. The soft can conquer the hard; the gentle can more than counterbalance the rigid"

But the author laments that though we know this truth, it is difficult to follow it in practice.

**Relativism**

A characteristic of Taoism is the principle of relativism of values. A closely allied to relativity was the concept of *yin/yang* which Taoists borrowed from their ancestors. The concept is symbolically represented as shown in the figure below.

The concept embodies the pairs of opposites: male/female, bright/dark, firm/yielding, good/bad etc. Yang is the male principle with creative power associated with heaven and movement. Yin is the passive female element endowed with intuition associated with stillness. The symbol is called *T'ai-chi T'u* or "Diagram of the Supreme Ultimate". The dark portion is *yin* while the bright is *yang*. The diagram has a rotational symmetry displaying a cyclic and continuous movement. According to Kuei Ku Tzu. (fourth century BCE) " The *yang* returns cyclically to its beginning, the *yin* attains its maximum and gives place to the yang".[2] The significance of the two dots is that when one force reaches its zenith, it has already acquired the component of the opposite.

Those who meditate on this symbol claim to have access to the mysteries of the universe, which no intellectual debates can unfold. Taoism through *yang-yin* principle tries to syncretize the apparent dichotomies. While Taoism recognizes relativity , its answer seems to be not nothingness but reconciliation.

Two stories are worth narrating. The first relates to a farmer whose horse has run away. When his acquaintances sympathize with him, the farmer says, "who knows what's good or bad?". His equanimity pays and the horse returns the next day bringing with it a hoard of wild horses. His friends now felicitate him for the windfall. The farmer replies calmly, "who knows what is good or bad?". He is vindicated, for the next day his son in an attempt to mount one of the wild horses falls and breaks his leg. Again the sympathy from the friends, and in reply, the stoic question, "who knows what is good or bad?". The farmer is right. The next day soldiers come for the compulsory recruitment of young men. The farmer's son is exempted because of his injury.

The other anecdote relates to the death of Chuang Tzu's wife. When a friend comes to offer condolences, he is surprised to find Chuang Tzu singing and drumming and apparently enjoying himself. When the friend expresses his shock that instead of shedding tears, Chuang Tzu is in a jovial mood, the Taoist replies that those who are born are born to die - it indicates a natural change. My wife is sleeping in a place between the earth and heaven. To wail and shed tears would be tantamount to deny the law of the nature.

## Zen

Buddhism was exported from India to China, where it blended with Taoism and was called *Ch'an*. From China, Ch'an went to Japan where it is called Zen.

Taoism depicts the coexistence of the opposites and incorporates the principle of equanimity and resignation. It recalls the Indian philosophy embodied in Chapter 2 of the *Bhagavad Gītā* in which Kṛṣṇa asks Arjuna to rise above the pairs of opposites. Zen implicitly recognizes the pairs of opposites but its reaction appears inconsistent, bizarre and befuddling.

The Zennist who behaves unpredictably can point out Buddha's Flower Sermon as the archetype of the Zen puzzle.

Standing on the mountain and surrounded by his disciples, Buddha did not *sermonize,* he merely held aloft a golden lotus. How would the disciples interpret this gesture? Only one disciple Mahakasyapa seems to have understood the Master's message. This was revealed by his knowing smile. Buddha appointed him his successor. If this mode of communication sounds incredible to us the Zennists' behaviour reflecting their philosophy leave us stunned. As Hudson Smith points out, "Entering Zen is like stepping through Alice's looking glass. One finds oneself in a topsy-turvy wonderland where everything seems quite mad - charmingly mad for the most part, but mad all the same. It is a world of bewildering dialogues, obscure conundrums, stunning paradoxes, flagrant contradictions, and abrupt non sequiturs, all carried off in the most urbane cheerful and innocent style imaginable."[3]

Zen believes in the immediate experience and not in the intellectual debate. It is not interested in credos, doctrines and abstractions.

According to Chuang Tzu, if someone asks about the Tao and another answers him, we may conclude that neither knows it. Nevertheless, the Zen master "teaches" his disciple through "direct pointing" which illumines the pupil as a unique experience.

Some examples of quaint behaviour of the Zennists are briefly given below.

If a disciple asks the master "what is the meaning of Zen?" he may just make a gesture such as lifting the index finger. Or he may kick a ball. But the disciple may not be that lucky, he himself might receive a kick from the master.

A neophyte refers to Buddha with reverence. The master's reaction is to ask him to rinse his mouth and not to utter the "dirty word" again. Po-cheng, a Zen master was asked if the Buddha nature can be sought. The master's answer was "It's like searching for an ox when you are riding it".

One who claims to know what Buddhism means, writes a poem to the effect: the body is the Bodhi tree, the mind is like a bright mirror. Be careful, keep it clean and don't allow dust to gather upon it. However, another contradicts him with a quartain which means Bodhi or True Wisdom is not a tree. The mind is not a shining mirror. Since there is *nothing* from the first, it is useless to talk of wiping off the dust. And this is accepted as the true Zen thought.[4]

## Satori

In Zen *satori* implies the immediate experience of enlightenment or knowing the Buddha nature of the universe. In connection with satori three words, zazen, koan and sanzen are of importance.

Zazen means "seated meditation". The aspirant may sit in the lotus position for hours or days, his eyes half-closed. This method seems to have been borrowed from India. When the aspirant awakens with the Buddha-mind, he applies his experience to his daily activities.

*Koan* means a problem or a riddle. Some examples are:

1. How did your face look before your ancestors were born?
2. A cow passes by a window. Its head, horns and the legs all pass by. How come that the tail did not pass by?

The *Koan* training is calculated to expose the student to new experience through the world of contradictions, opposites and oxymorons. The result is a new understanding that cannot be gained through logic.

*Sanzen* in Rinzai sect implies "consultation related to meditation" In the Soto sect it is called *dokusan.* Twice a day a student meets his master in private. He mentions a *Koan* he is working on and explains his own solution. The master may accept the explanation, which is a rarity; he may reject it so that the student gets a further opportunity for seeking the right experience. The teacher's role is that of a guide during the long training of the student, but the teacher is merciless and the student has ultimately to find the correct experiences which are the solutions of his *koans.*

The training in *zazen, koan* and *sanzen* may lead a student to the mystical enlightenment, *satori.* It may come as a sudden flash after years of what appears to be useless efforts.

While Zen appears to be unconventional, its practitioners contend that for those who have attained satori, life is good, the world appears beautiful. The Zennist does not become a recluse, he comes back to the ordinary world with his new experience. It allows him to see the world as it is. According to Smith "Zen wears the air of divine ordinariness"[5]

To the Zennist the way leads to unity, but to the outsiders and to the trainees, the path to satori is bizarre. The shocking utterances made by the master are bound to make common people feel that, this weird way reflects the effects of confusion caused by contradictions. Overawed by contradictions, man not only turns to mysticism but uses methods which appear even blasphemous. For example, a Zen master may ask his trainee to indulge in such apparently horrible acts as tearing off scriptures to pieces, or to treat the venerated words as Buddha or nirvāṇa as dirty. Only in the *lefthand tantra* one finds a parallel, where the practitioners use liquor, fish, mudras (gestures), meat and sex in their worship. The goal is to bridge the gap between the divine and profane. .

The Zennists claim that when the masters ask the students to indulge in the unconventional behaviour, it is only part of the training from which the trainees learn something they would not learn otherwise. The ostensible blasphemy does not in reality indicate any disrespect to Buddha's teachings.

When a disciple attains *satori* he is believed to be at the starting point of his path and not at the end of it. Further *satories* can take the Zennists to the higher levels of freedom.

## Unity and Emptiness

The practitioners of Zen would certainly deny that their philosophy leads to nothingness of the skeptic. But in their philosophy one finds a blend of unity and emptiness that is reminiscent of the pronouncements of the extreme monists of ancient India.

"It is true that Zen values unity, but it is a unity that is simultaneously empty (because it erases the lines that divide) and full (because it replaces those lines with ones that connect)"[6].

A reconciliation of the extreme opposites viz. life and death in the following words of Ruth Fuller Saki reminds one of the Indian *advaita* or monism.

"When this realization is completely achieved, never again can one feel that one's individual death brings an end to life. One has lived from an endless past and will live into an endless future. At this very moment one partakes of Eternal life - blissful, luminous, pure".[7]

20

# Śūnya and Void in Tantra

## Śiva - Śakti

"Tantra" literally means "looms" or "weaving". It is believed that we are born with a pattern which is in equilibrium with nature. However, our defective life-style disturbs the pattern. Tantric worship is aimed at reweaving the fabric of life.

The *sādhanā* (practice) incorporates breathing exercises, meditation, mantras, *yantras* (geometrical figures), *mudrās* (gestures) and *maṇḍalas* ("circles") and *haṭhayoga* involving various physical postures.

Tantra treats human body as a microcosm containing the diverse counterparts of the macrocosm or the universe. The sādhanā is calculated to harness the forces of the universe by polarizing their internal counterparts.

Most tantric schools believe in the primordial Pure Consciousness which the nondualists call Brahman. In tantra this Reality is designated as Śiva or Parama Śiva. His power (Śakti) is merged with him. This is the feminine aspect of Śiva who is treated as static and consciousness, Śakti is called Great Mother or Mahā Kuṇḍalinī. This dynamic Goddess (Devī) is the creator of the universe. In reality Śiva-Śakti is one and inseparable but on account of the power called Māyā-Śakti the female negates perfect consciousness (*Cit*). The result is the illusory universe.

## Bindu

*Bindu* means "point" or "dot" but can also means a drop. It has several meanings. But conceptually it has no dimensions. In linguistics it means anusvāra (.) which indicates nasalization. Paradoxically this bindu encloses a void. The bindu as a whole is the state of active Śakti in which "I" and "This" merge. In this state the bindu is Śiva-bindu which indicates Śiva the experiencer. However, when consciousness differentiates, between "I" and "this" (object), Śiva experiences the universe as extension.

There is a cycle in which the universe evolves and then dissolves. In dissolution the universe reverts to a mathematical point. The Śiva-bindu Śakti which creates the universe is considered as a mathematical line "without magnitude". It is coiled around the bindu and is in the compressed form. In other words, when Śakti is dormant the line is also a point. She is called Kuṇḍalinī Śakti or Mahā Kuṇḍalinī. When active, it becomes a straight line converting itself into a triangular pyramidal figure in three dimensions called Śṛṅgāṭaka. This movement ultimately leads to the creation of the universe.

Most tantric schools accept thirtysix categories or *tattvas*. The highest tattva according to the text *Śāradā Tilaka* is Śiva-tattva. Śiva in his transcendental aspect is changeless but in his immanent form as Śakti, he appears to change and is called Sakala Śiva. Śiva-tattva refers to this Sakala Śiva. From Śiva-tattva emanates Śakti-tattva. From the latter originates *nāda* (sadakhya tattva). Nāda means the unmanifest *śabda* (sound). From nāda evolves bindu (Īśvara tattva) which we have already mentioned.

This bindu is usually called Parabindu (supreme bindu). Parabindu is described as the state of the letter "ma" of the Sanskrit alphabet before manifestation. It consists of Śiva-Śakti-tattva surrounded by Māyā or Parama Kuṇḍalinī.

As we mentioned earlier this Parabindu has paradoxical properties: a bindu of no dimensions, but yet enclosing space or void called *śunya.* This bindu symbolizes the Brahman state of Śiva (Brahmāṇḍa) which is the void as well as the guṇas (sattva, rajas, tamas — three properties of matter created by Śakti). This is also the symbol of the indissoluble Śiva-Śakti duo. Parabindu is also called ghanāvasthā or "massive consciousness" of Śakti which is nothing but Cit associated with undifferentiated Śakti. This is also called Parama (supreme) Śiva. This bindu is also the abode of all gods (devatās).

Parabindu divides itself into three entities; the first is called Bindu the second is nāda and the third is bīja (mantras like oṃ, eṃ, iṃ etc. ) All the three products of Parabindu are themselves bindus - dimensionless. The first Bindu has the nature of Śiva, bīja (bindu) is Śakti and nāda-bindu is Śiva-Śakti. The union (yoga) of these three bindus is the threefold Bindu (tri-bindu) which is Para or supreme, subtle (sūkṣma) and gross (sthūla).

The dynamics of the various bindus is extremely complicated and varies from school to school. From our point of you, suffice it to say that these bindus represent dimensionless śūnyas (zeros). They are the union of Śiva and Śakti or the void surrounded by a circle. The primordial bindu viz. Parabindu or Tribindu can be described only in terms of an oxymoron - dimensionless, supreme, subtle yet gross.

## Microcosm

Tantra has an esoteric anatomy according to which the central channel of energy called suṣumnā runs from the base of the spine to the crown of the head. Along the axis of the suṣumnā are six main cakras or lotuses which are the junctions of energy currents. They are *mulādhāra* in the region of anus, *svādhiṣṭhāna* at the reproductive organs, *maṇipūra* at the naval, *anāhata* at the heart, *viśuddha* at the throat and *ājñā* between the eyes. At the crown is the inverted thousand-petalled lotus called *sahasrāra.*

In the mulādhara lies the kuṇḍalinī (śakti) which is coiled like a serpent. Under normal circumstances it is dormant. The worshipper using several methods awakens the kuṇḍalinī which, breaking through various cakras reaches the sahsrāra. This is the stage when the tantric merges with the Supreme God Śiva. It may be recalled that the body (microcosm) and the universe (macrocosm) are believed to be similar. Just as Mahā Kuṇḍalinī coils around Parama Śiva in the universe, in the mulādhāra, its counterpart kuṇḍalinī coils round "svayambhu-liṅga" (*svayambhu* for "self-generated" *liṅga* for "phallus" the symobl of Śiva)

## Great Void

According to the text *Śat Cakra Nirūpaṇa,* in the sahasrāra is the full moon without blemish resplendent like the clear sky. Inside it is the Triangle called A-ka-thadi. Inside the triangle is śūnya. Śūnya has been translated as the Great Void, but can also mean bindu ("point") and in this case it should be treated as Parabindu.

This Great Void is served by all gods in secret. This shining Parabindu is also called Īśvara (manifest Brahman). Metaphorically the center of Īśvara is the abode of Brahman. In the northen Śaiva and Śākta sects there is also the concept of *śūnyātiśūnya* ("the highest void") an experience related to Sadāśiva.

It has also been suggested that the Great Void is the "body" (śarīram) of the Parabindu.

According to Toḍala Tantra "The Supreme Light is formless (*Nirākara*) and Bindu is imperishable. Bindu means the void (śūnya)"[1]

According to verse 42 of *Ṣat-Cakra-Nirūpaṇa* this void (śūnya) is well-concealed and difficult to attain. It is extremely minute "the ten millionth of the size of the end of a hair". This subtle śūnya is said to be the root of liberation (mokṣa). The śūnya also manifests *nirvāṇa kalā* or the void (*antaḥ-śūnya*) along with *amā kalā.* It is believed that the moon has seventeen kalās (digits) but only the nectar-dropping amā and nirvāṇa kalā are revealed to those who can reach the śūnya through meditation. This void is the source of Bliss which is not "pleasure" but means liberation.

In this minute void is the god Parama Śiva who is both Ātman and Brahman. He is also the union of rasa (the Bliss of liberation) and virasa (the bliss stemming from Śiva and Śakti or power.) The latter is the female component of Śiva-Śakti. He is also the sun that destroys nescience and delusion.

We shall not describe the kuṇḍalinī dynamics in details. The Kuṇḍalinī Devī is aroused by the sādhaka. The serpent rises, moves towards the sahasrāra and reaches the Great Void where it unites with Parama Śiva. The tāntrik who sees this void and experiences the entire process is liberated.

The Parabindu is described with details which differ from texts to texts. The Śaivas (a sect) call it the abode of Śiva. These who follow Viṣṇu call it Parama Puruṣa. Some call it Hari Hara. Some also call it Devī and *munis* (sages) call it Prakṛti-Puruṣa (i.e., Śakti-Śiva)

Before we end we may mention that the word bindu is applied to various spaces and substances. For instance, it means semen or a drop which is not dimensionless. In general the concept of bindu incorporates the existence of dimensionless void surrounded by the coiled line compressing the void. Though dimensionless and void, the bindu is the seed of creation. It is the potential from which the whole universe emerges.

## Bindu in Upaniṣads

The conception of "bindu", however, antedates tantra. It is found in several Upaniṣads. The bindu refers to the anusvāra which implies nasalization but can mean either the third mora (mātrā) or 31/2th mora of Om. Om, which is believed to be pronounced as A-U-M, has 31/2 moras the last 1/2 mātrā represents silence or reverberation. In the symbol ॐ (Om) the bindu appears over the crescent and is called *candra-bindu.*

The *Nādabindu Upaniṣad* (*nāda* for "unmanifest sound") is believed to impart the secret meaning of the nasal-point. According to it the true yoga involves meditation on Om. This is the yoga of realizing Brahman.

In *Brahmabindu Upaniṣad,* again, the bindu (reverberation) refers to the higher (unmanifest) Brahman, while Om represents the symbol of Brahman.

The *Amṛta-bindu Upaniṣad* (*amṛta* for "elixir") condemns all bookish learning and emphasizes the importance of Om. The sound-om is a means to reach Brahman. The soundless *m* (*asvara makara*) or the silent 1/2 matra is the part that is to be meditated upon, because it is nothing but immortal Brahman.

The Dhyānabindu (*dhyāna* for "meditation") is the doctrine of bindu which relates to dhyāna. It maintains that the silence of meditation corresponds to the subtlety of Brahman: it is a thousandth of a hundredth part of hair's tip, nay, it is still a fraction of this when we come to the 1/2 matra of Om. Although this Brahman is a minute dot, it is all-pervading.

In the *Tejobindu Upaniṣad* this bindu is depicted as the point of tremendous power. It also mentions the contradictory nature of Brahman.

The "bindu" thus seems to convey the dimensionless point which embodies omnipotent and omnipresent Brahman. The point enclosing the void is also the potential for infinite creation. In essence, the doctrine of bindu is: *there is infinite in zero.*

21

# Being and Nonbeing

## Realism and Idealism

A word closely related to nothing is nonbeing. To understand the concept of being and nonbeing, we will have to consider what the ancient and modern philosophers have to say about them.

The question which troubles even laypersons is: What is the nature of the world? Is it the same as it appears to us? There are two broad philosophies, realism and idealism which discuss this aspect. There are scores of subschools in each of these categories.

Those who call themselves realists accept the minimum requirement that things or objects exist independently of the human mind or experience. In Chapter 4 we discussed atomism. Democritus, Leucippus and Epicurus may be called some of the earliest adherents of realism, though there were a few differences of opinion among them.

In modern times, Thomas Hobbs (1588-1679) made two important contributions to the theory of knowledge or epistemology. First, the knowledge of the external world begins with sensation. Second, the knowledge of external objects is indirect rather than direct. What this implies is that our perceptual world is caused by the real world but we do not know whether it is an exact replica.

Galileo (1564-1642) being a scientist had a slightly different approach to the external world. He assumed that certain properties of an object were primary, and others secondary. If you see a body, its size, motion, and the number of objects in its neighborhood may be taken as authentic perception. But he thought that "tastes, odors, colours etc.. on the side of the object in which they seem to exist are nothing else but mere names, but hold their residence solely in the body; so that if the animal were removed, every such quality would be abolished and annihilated".[1] In other words certain qualities were secondary dependent on the observer's perception.

Rene Desecrates (1596-1650) towing the line of Galileo went further and postulated that there were two irreducible substances instead of one; mind and matter. The mind was responsible for thought or consciousness. The essential quality of matter is extension in space. His dualistic philosophy may be briefly described as follows:

1. The senses cannot reveal the essential nature of the external objects. They cannot even guarantee the existence of such objects.
2. However, he was certain of the mind - in fact, *his* mind. He maintained that "I think; therefore I am" (*cogito ergo sum*). However, his "cogito" has been under severe criticism as we shall see later. Also, it is difficult to infer that others have minds, from his premise "cogito". The existence of others' minds can only be surmised by commonsense and analogy: the fact that other people behave in similar way as we do.

George Berkeley (1685-1753) was an opponent of realism. His philosophy is captured in the famous dictum *esse est precipi*: "to be is to be perceived". Thus if you are looking at a moving automobile, its shape, colour, structure, motion everything that you can perceive totally is the thing before you. We have no need to refer to an object divorced from our experience.

According to Berkeley, "I have an idea of something" is equivalent to "I directly perceive something". His idealistic philosophy is called *presentative* theory of reality to distinguish it from *representative* theory of Locke (1632-1704). Locke asserted that knowledge comes from the object, the conscious mind and the ideas which the mind harbours. According to him there is "agreement or disagreement" between ideas and external reality. Since the object which he assumed to be the original cause of knowledge, is not perceived directly there is no way to test whether there is "agreement or disagreement". This is a serious lacuna in Locke's theory.

Berkeley can be called an extreme idealist. He contended, "The things immediately perceived are ideas which exist only in the mind". This has been interpreted as his belief that reality is dependent on the mind. In this respect two observations need to be made. First, one can have hallucinations and illusions. We can scientifically disprove the illusory existence of these "existents". This is a serious defect in the Berkelian theory. The only solution to this in conformity with idealism would be to give a separate existential status to "objects" one sees in illusion or dream. Second, at the subatomic level, matter is believed to behave in a strange manner. The behaviour of this micro-world seems to be dependent on the observer. The quantum theory which has thrown light on such phenomena will be discussed later.

Thomas Reid (1710-1796) criticized. Berkeley's view that the senses gave us the knowledge of only sensations. Reid contented that Berkeley uses the word "idea" in a broader way than was necessary. His fault was the inclusion of perception in the concept of ideas. Reid says that if we are pricked by a pin, we do feel the sensation but we know that the sensation is not the pin. We perceive that object which pricked us has dimensions, weight, colour and so forth. What Reid was objecting was Berkelian idealism rather than his presentative theory. Reid's contention that the characteristics of an object exist independent of our mind is called *commonsense realism.*

Actually, Berkeley is a modern idealist. Idealism existed in ancient Greece. To understand its development we will have to consider the philosophies of the early Greek thinkers.

Heraclitus (535-475 BCE) contented that objects are constantly in flux. We have to employ our intelligence along with senses if we want to know the real nature of an object. "Eyes and ears are bad witnesses for men unless they have souls that understand the language".

Parmenides (515-440 BCE), Heraclitus' contemporary went a step ahead and argued that if the object was always changing it is impossible to know its real nature. The real nature may be called the *being* of an object. The flux implies that the object reveals to us not as being but "becoming" which is ever-changing. This suggests that we have to not only think of being (what the object is) but also of nonbeing. (what the object is not). Parmenides' conclusion was that since we cannot think of what is not, *nonbeing* is nothing. "You cannot know what is not". What we see is only the appearances behind which the real being hides. He thought that this real being could be known only through reason.

Consider the following two statements: (1) what *is* is (2) what is *not* is not.

According to Parmenides the first is true, and the second, according to Parmenides is meaningless. In the second case, if we want to make a statement about nothing or nonbeing first we have to think of something which is negated. This is a contradiction. In his own words, which influenced generations of Greek intellectuals:

Come now I tell-thee and do thou hear my word and heed it — what are the only ways of enquiring that lead to knowledge. The one way assuming that being *is* and that it is impossible for it not to be, is the trustworthy path, for truth attends it. The other that not-being is and that it necessarily is, I call a wholly incredible course, since thou canst not recognize non-being (for this is impossible) nor couldst thou speak of it, for *thought* and *being* are the same thing. [2]

"What *is* is" can be interpreted as what *is* is eternal, indestructible, constant and so forth. Suppose someone asserts "What *is* is noneternal".

This means that what *is* has the capacity to become what is *not.* This implies "what is, is not" which is a self-contradiction.

## Kant and Hegel

Kant (1724-1804) belongs to the school of philosophers called objective idealists. For him the mind was a source of object's "form" — the structure but not the content. The object we perceive is the *phenomenon*, but behind this lies the unexperienced and unfathomable entity which he called *Dang an sich* or the thing-in-itself.

Hegel (1770-1831) based his philosophy on Kant's. According to him all attempts to establish the existence as a thing without the participation of the mind is futile. He maintained that whatever exists *is* and must be an object of human consciousness. Even such a statement as "the unknowable may exist without our knowledge" is self-contradictory. For Hegel whatever we experience, both actual and possible, *is* the world. He rejected Kantian thing-in-itself and thus made *being* synonymous with the mind, in a way.

Democritus who was mentioned in Chapter 4 was a realist who maintained that the object was logically independent of the mind. Berkeley (1685-1753) on the other hand belongs to the other extreme end of the spectrum. He rejected the idea of matter. In his subjective idealism only the mind and its ideas — only particular ideas exist. In short Bishop Berkeley contended that material objects only exist through being perceived. In Hegel appears the synthesis of the two opposite views. "Democritean obective object is recognized as an object for thought and Berkelian knowable object is recognized to be a thought about the object".[3]

Hegel's method of reconciling the opposites is known as the Hegelian dialectic Hegel considered being as the primal category. If we inspect different objects, they can be distinguished by colour, shape, size etc., but the common property they have is being. Using the dialectical technique with the help of "reason" the basic notion of being leads to other secondary categories: cause, effect, plurality, unity, substance, quality, existence and non existence which follow from our experience.

Hegel contented that the concept of *being* necessarily involved the notion of *nothing*. When we assert that an object has being we simply mean it *is*. We do not refer to the secondary characteristics. However, when we think of *nothing*, the earlier being is always considered. When our thoughts oscillate between being and nothing, they give rise to what may be called *becoming*. Becoming is the process by which being becomes nothing and nothing becomes being. In the Hegelian dialectic "becoming" plays the role of removing the tension created by the opposites: being and nothing. In the dialectical process being-nothing-becoming indicates reconciliation of two ideas: an equivalent thesis (positive idea), and antithesis (negative idea). Synthesis, the last stage represents the mode of reconciliation. Whenever there is synthesis our knowledge has ascended to a higher level. This process of thesis-antithesis-synthesis continues. At each stage whatever is unnecessary is thrown out and what is essential is retained. This represents an upward movement of knowledge.

Hegelian dialectic is important because "contradictions" are endemic to life. Hegelian thought leads to one solution. There are also other solutions such as turning to mysticism or embracing the philosophy of nothingness.

## Neorealism

In early twentieth century Russell, Moore and others promoted what is called neorealism. A manifesto on American New Realism set forth by six neorealists appeared in 1910. Its implications on being and nonbeing are profound. The important articles contained in the manifesto are mentioned below:[4]

1. The entities (objects, facts etc.) which are studied in logic, mathematics and physical sciences are not mental in any usual meaning of the word mental.
   This article reflects Alexius Meinong's (1853-1920) general theory of objects according to which not only physical objects but also ideas and fictitious entities should be treated as real. Thus a "golden mountain" or "Lord Kṛṣṇa" are existents.
2. The being and nature of the entities do not depend upon their being known. For example, neither Frankinstein's monster nor Mr. Hyde are nonbeings.
3. The degree of unity, consistency or connection subsisting between the entities is matter that should be decided empirically.
4. As far as the present knowledge goes, the evidence is in favour of pluralism and not monism.
   This is in contrast to Advaitism according to which existents A,B,C are mere appearances of the ultimate reality viz. Brahman.
5. There is no logical evidence to show that organic theory of knowledge or "internal" view of relations hold good.
   3,4,5 together rebut the doctrine of "objective realism", the tenet which teaches that an assemblage should be treated as a whole. For neorealists "internal relations" is a myth. If a whole consists of parts A and B, the Gestalt or complex, (A,B) is a nonbeing if A and B are treated as existents.
6. Things known may continue to exist unaltered when they are not known. Their existence is not correlated or dependent on the fact that anyone experiences, perceives or conceives them. The things may pass in and out of the cognitive relation *without prejudice to their reality*.

This is a clause that encompasses the common notion of realism.

7. Cognition belongs to the same world as that of its objects. It has its place in the order of nature.
8. The objective content of consciousness is any entity in so far as it is responded to by another entity in a specified manner exhibited by the reflex nervous system. Thus physical nature, for instance is, under certain circumstances, directly present in consciousness.
9. The specific response which determines an entity to be content of consciousness does not directly modify such entities otherwise than to endow them with objective status. In other words, consciousness selects from a field of entities which it does not create.

Statements 7-9 reflect the relational theory of consciousness. They do not accept the views of other philosophers that consciousness is either an entity itself or a characteristic of the mind. The neorealist believe that the objects may or may not enter into a cognitive relationship, but they are not altered merely by the process of cognition.

The realists hold that the things known are not products of the knowing relation nor essentially dependent for their existence or behaviour upon that relation. They contend that this doctrine has three claims upon our acceptance: first, it is the natural, instinctive belief of all men, and for this, if for no other reason, puts the burden of proof upon those who would discredit it; secondly, all refutations of it presuppose or even actually employ some of its exclusive implications; and thirdly, it is logically demanded by all the observations and hypotheses of the natural sciences, including psychology.

22

# Existentialism

## Limitations of Rationality

Existentialism reflects a rebellion against social norms and philosophical orthodoxy. While rationalism appeared quite attractive especially in those times when there was rapid scientific progress, people were aware of the limitations of rationalism. Rationalism cannot fully explain ethics and morality leave alone the concepts of God, death and after life.

Humans, unlike inanimate objects and even other living creatures, play a double role in nature. As subjects they think, act and create. As objects they find that they are used as instruments by society seriously curtailing their freedom. The artists, writers and those who are engaged in creative work find this subject-object dichotomy strange and stifling. The existentialist is concerned with this human predicament. He treats a being as unique and his emphasis is more on feeling and freedom than on thinking. *Being* cannot be expressed in terms of a system.

This is precisely why existentialism cannot be called a school of philosophy. It would be unthinkable for the existentialists to issue a manifesto comparable to the programme of neorealists mentioned in the last Chapter.

Hegel was an inveterate rationalist. Paradoxically in his writings existentialists have found the grist for their mill. In his *Philosophy of Mind* he describes the process of "alienation" or "estrangement" in which the experiencer not only faces the distinction between the "datum" and "thought" but also externalizes them. When we see a chair, the chair and its idea appear to be divorced from consciousness. It is as if we happen to be related to them by chance or accident. For Hegel, reason could reconcile the dichotomy and the experience could be made more intelligible.

For the existentialist reason cannot synthesize this schism — the particular experience should be treated as unique and not belonging to a category.

## Freedom and Authentic Living

Soren Kierkgaard (1813-1855) was a staunch Christian. He, however, launched an attack on the demands of society and state on individuals who were treated as passive parts of these institutions. He was also against speculative philosophy.

Kierkgaard rejected Hegel's attempt to reconcile the opposites through reason. For him our personal experience, our existence in the world and our encounter in which we *feel* rather than *think* is what is important. For him personal experience and impersonal experience are two opposite poles. Every person faces the option of either being or not being himself. According to him our society severely restricted our choice of freedom. He advocated what is called *authentic living* in which the person exercises her innate freedom — the freedom to feel and select.

Friedrich Nietzsche (1844-1900) was equally sensitive to the plight of individuals in the wake of the orthodox society, state and religion. However, his reaction was anger unlike Kiergaard who showed despair. This led Nietsche to his doctrine that we must exercise the inherent Will to Power to control the environment.

Henri Bergson (1859-1941) was a French philosopher who belonged to the anti-intellectual and pro-intuition movement. According to him our excessive dependence on rational analysis made us lose our identity as unique beings.

Edumund Husserl (1859-1938) has left deep impress on existentialism. According to him the units of experience are signs or phenomenal objects that have signification independent of the experiencing self and the objects experienced. We recall the Descartes' famous words: *cogito ergo sum.* Husserl and the later existentialists maintain that the consciousness which thinks is not the same as the basic consciousness. The fundamental undifferntiated mass of consciousness, Husserl thinks, is passive, a witness. This is the transcendental ego which is different from the ego that participates in the world. While Husserl emphasized on our being a witness to understand our being-in-the world, Martin Heidegger (1889-1976) concentrated on the participating ego. According to him it is only when we are deeply engaged in the world fully that *Dasein* is understood. By Dasein he means the proper mode of existence. Dasein is revealed to us only when we live authentically exercising our freedom but accepting responsibility as actors.

According to Heidegger if we do not live authentically, it is to avoid dread, the origin of which lies in our very being.

The human condition in which we perpetually face the contingent and have to exercise our choice with responsibility appears painful. It appears that our achievements are delusions and happiness a mere evasion. Heidegger's thinking leads to only one value: *realizing the nothingness of human existence.* His solution is that we should live authentically, accept the existential dread and not evade it though the palliatives of social norms.

The subjectivity of existentialists has created a dilemma for them. Since they do not subscribe to a tenet, how shall they communicate something that cannot be conceptualized? Many existentialists have resorted to the writing that is not analysis. They write through stories, novels, diaries and so forth and like painters try to express their feeling. However, since their language is often ambiguous it can be interpreted — like abstract painting in many ways. It may even lead one to think that existentialism is "almost anything" and hence, in essence, "nothing".

## Other Existentialists

Karl Barth was a theologian who tried to reconcile Christianity with existentialism. He was considerably influenced by Kierkgaard and asserted the supremacy of faith over reason. He agreed with Kierkgaard that it is the inner crisis which can give man a glimpse of God. He was a staunch adherent of the Bible and maintained that God's words were revealed only at the time He thought appropriate.

Jean Paul Sartre is called an atheist existentialist and is one of the most influential figures in literature and philosophy of the 20th century. His contribution to existentialism will be considered in the next Chapter.

Karl Jaspers was another existentialist who thought human beings were treated by society as tools and not as individuals who are free. Like Kierkgaard, he believed, that situations which produce crises in man's life were often the source of our contact with unlimited reality.

Gabriel Marcel was an existentialist who rejected dualism contained in the pairs, thought-existent, self-God, subject-object. His thesis was that such dichotomies were artificial, attributable to epistemology rather than ontology. He pinpointed the circularity in our perception that knowledge is contingent on "a participation in being for which no epistemology can account because it continually presupposes it". He concurs with Bergson in assuming that we cannot know the "reality" of an existent. The only way we can experience reality is through our communion with it. This, of course, is in tune with what all existentialists contend: supremacy of experience over reasoning.

23

# Consciousness and Nothingness

## Sartre

Since existentialism is highly subjective, there are no "schools" of existential philosophy. Nevertheless, the philosophy has a common core viz. human existence.

Jean Paul Sartre (1905-1980) is usually called an "atheist existentialist" while Paul Tillich (1886-1966) is regarded as a religious or Christian existentialist. Such classifications are only a matter of convenience.

Born in Paris, Sartre graduated from Ecole Normale Superieur. He taught at Lycee du Havre and also studied under Husserl and Heidegger at Institut Francais. Sartre wrote plays such as *Les Mouches* ("The flies") and novels like *Nausea. L'etre et le Neant* ("Being and nothingness") is perhaps his most important work on philosophy. He was also the founder and editor of the periodical *Les Temps Modernes.* He also wrote screenplays and essays. He was awarded the Nobel prize for literature in 1964. Though abstruse at many places, he is certainly one of the most important existentialists of the 20th century.

Sartre rejected Desecrates' argument that "I think therefore I am". The consciousness which asserts "I am" is not the consciousness that thinks. This led Sartre to posit a *pre-reflective cogito* which is the primary consciousness. He calls this *non-thetic* or *non-positional* self-consciousness. For this, to be and to know are the same. The other self-consciousness is thetic or positional in which consciousness reflects deliberately upon itself, its own acts and states. This means that it treats itself as an object.

For Sartre the pre-reflective consciousness is non-personal. If you perceive a table, your first reaction should be "there is consciousness of the table" and not "I am conscious of the table. For him, Ego ("I" as well as "me") comes into existence only when the original consciousness becomes the object of reflection. This makes Ego transcendent in the same way as the world is. However, the difference is that the world does not depend on consciousness, while Ego is constituted by it. Ego has two aspects "I" the unity of actions and "Me" the unity of states and qualities.

## Nihilation

Sartre lays down the concept of *nihilation* in his *The Psychology of Imagination.* In imagination, an object is posited as absent or non-existent.[1] This means that our ability to imagine comes from consciousness which should have the power to nihilate an object or make it into nonbeing. Though consciousness is *in-the-world,* it is separate from objects which, he says, are *in-the-midst of the world.* There is thus a separation between the things in the world and consciousness. Since the cogito in the primary form is non-positional, if it is conscious of an object, it is merely consciousness of not being an object. This shows that consciousness has the power of withdrawing: it nihilates the object and covers it with a region of nonbeing.

In imagination there is double nihilation. When we imagine, we posit a world in which the object is *not* present so that we can create a pseudo-world in which it *is* present. The second nihilation arises from the fact that we consider the object in the pseudo-world as not belonging to the real world. Sartre connects nothingness with freedom in a strange way: the power to imagine implies freedom. "The unreal is produced outside of the world by consciousness *which stays in the world,* and it is because man is transcendentally free that man can imagine" [2]

## Being as Superfluousness

Sartre's concept of Being includes *Being-in-itself* and *Being-for-itself.* The definition of Being is simply "Being is". Being-in-itself is the non-conscious being. It is the Being of the phenomenon. It is plenitude and its fullness engulfs our knowledge. In his novel *Nausea,* the hero Roquentin realizes that Being, general or particular (himself), is *de trop,* that is existence is contingent and gratuitous. There is no reason why Being should *be.* It is there and beyond it Nothing. Sartre expresses similar views in his *Being and Nothingness.* "Being in-itself is never either possible or impossible. It *is.* This is what consciousness expresses in anthropomorphic terms by saying that being is superfluous (*de trop*) — that is that consciousness cannot derive being from anything; either from other being or from a possibility or from a necessary law. *Uncreated,* without reason for being, without any connection with another being, being-in-itself is *de trop* for eternity" [3]

While Being-in-itself is unconscious, Being-for-itself is conscious Being. Though part of Being, it is the nihilation of Being-in-itself. According to Sartre man or the For-itself can pose questions and can also be in question in his own being. He traces this to the existence of Nothingness. He postulates that Nonbeing is a condition of any transcendence toward Being. While Being-in-itself merely *is,* man is the being "who is what he is not and who is not what he is". Man continuously makes himself.

Sartre's contention is that consciousness is *Nothingness.* But as nothingness it also reveals Being. The world cannot exist without consciousness: rivers, seas, trees, mountains different species of animals, all exist as such because of consciousness: without it there would be simply beings. Consciousness itself is Nothing, but it is because of it that things as plurality and differentiation exists.

The For-itself is nihilation of Being as the nihilation of individual being. It is not the absolute Nothing, it is just an individual nonbeing. Sartre contends that Being-in-itself is logically prior to Being-for-itself. The split between the original Being into two dimensions ("in-itself" and "for-itself") has no external cause. "Nothingness lies, coiled in the heart of being like worm"[4]

The For-itself not only originates in the In-itself, it can continue its existence only because of being. Sartre distinguishes two types of negations. The "revealing intuition" displayed by consciousness is "internal negation". It continuously negates the In-itself by realizing inwardly that it is *not* the In-itself. The "external negation" enables consciousness to distinguish between two objects, say a table and a chair. Thus the For-itself "nihilates the In-itself both as a whole and in terms of In-itselfs or objects"[5]

Sartre maintains that "man is the being by whom nothingness comes into the world". The For-itself has a paradoxical existence: it is nothing, but in relation to being, by being the nothingness of a particular being, it has a kind of marginal being which it acquires by nihilation. The For-itself thus can never reach fullness of the region of being we call In-itself. Nevertheless qua nihilation it *is*.

## Consciousness and Freedom

Sartre regards consciousness as free since it is not "full" unlike In-itself. If it were full being it would have no need of choosing and thus would not be "free".

We may describe the For-itself as an internal nihilation of Being, a revelation of Being. It is a choice as well as a desire of Being. According to Sartre this is possible *because* it is not Being. As far as the dynamic aspect and activity is concerned, it is For-itself which is the actor despite it being dependent on Being and though itself it is not a Being. But Sartre postulates that the For-itself yearns to *be*. It is in pursuit of Being for ever but its desire is never fulfilled, it tries to escape its nothingness but all its efforts are futile. When Sartre views consciousness as Desire he finds that its essential structure is negative but the results are positive. Consciousness as Sartre sees it is always consciousness *of* something. Thus the consciousness is of the object *as* desirable. Desire is neither in the world nor in consciousness. It is a manner in which it relates to the world and its objects. This desire appears in two ways. Every specific desire of the For-itself determines an aspect of the person. The sum total of such desires makes the individual unique. However, all these desires are ultimately based on a foundation of its intimate relation with the In-itself. *The basic desire therefore is to be In-itself which the For-itself can never achieve.* Sartre depicts this as a confrontation between the For-itself and In-itself.

The desire in the Eastern philosophies is often depicted as an evil that has to be destroyed in order to reach the higher level of existence. For Sartre, For-itself *is* desire and we cannot think of destroying it. This is so because the For-itself, though a nihilating aspect of Being, derives its meaning from its very project of desiring Being which it can never possess. For the Eastern religion like Buddhism desire leads to Guilt. For Sartre, guilt is harbouring the illusion of possessing an absolute Self. Clearly, Sartre regards the failure of For-itself to merge with Being as guilt. We cannot dissociate failure and despondency from guilt.

Sartre adheres to the principle that for man qua For-itself has the ideal of possessing Being. In order to achieve fullness, it may transform itself into God which is the epitome of fullness that lacks nothing. Thus, Nothingness which is For-itself in pursuit of Being, may see God as its goal. But this is only for the majority who are religious-minded. There are agnostics and atheists for whom there may be transformation of desire into other ideals.

Sartre, however, faces a dilemma. If the In-itself like God is fullness, how can it be affected by the so-called Nothing or a "hole" inside it? He does not seem to have an answer in terms of cause. In every philosophy there have to be basic premises, else the cause-effect chain will lead to an infinite regress. Sartre appears to take the internal rupture of the Self into "For" and "In" as basic and we need not explain why "For" which is Nothing should affect "In" which is Being. While the common perception is that reason is absent in existentialism, it has a place in Sartre's thinking. For him, the basic or first relationship of consciousness with Being is non-rational or rather pre-rational. However, Sartre recognizes knowledge and reason as the bridge between the For-itself and In-itself. It is through reason that For-itself perceives the external world and gains knowledge. However, being free, the For-itself may choose to live with infinite possibilities: it may reject reason totally, it may decide to become purely rational or it may accept reason in different proportion.

## Pursuit of Being

Unlike Freud, Sartre regards consciousness as translucent. This leads him to reject the unconscious as well as the Freudian Id, Superego, Ego, and the universal Oedipus complex. He considers them as secondary structures.

What is the nature of the For-itself? Since it is ever in pursuit of being the metaphor of an arrow in motion is often likened with it. We cannot say that at any given time the arrow will be at a certain position, say, at A and if it is at A whether it is stationary or moving at that instant. Due to its nature of perpetually projecting itself to future possibilities the For-itself is more a process than a substance.

Sartre's views on the (human) body are interesting. In a sense the body is man's *facticity* or "Being there in the world". Facticity actually is the For-itself's necessary connection with the In-itself and hence with the world as well as the past. Facticity is that which helps one say that the For-itself *is* or *exists.* Facticity of freedom is also depicted as the fact that "freedom is not able not to be free". As Being-there-in-the-world, our facticity determines the physical limitations to the operational range of the For-itself. The body as the synthesis of physical elements is contrasted for ever with For-itself which is Nothingness. Nevertheless, the facticity does not belong directly to the In-itself except when it becomes a corpse. One might even argue that the For-itself *is* the body. True, For-itself *per se* is Nothing and the senses belong to the body but the For-itself feels or perceives the external world through the senses. As Sartre points out, "It would be impossible for me to realize a world in which I was not and which would be for me a pure object of a surveying contemplation. But on the contrary it is necessary that I lose myself in the world in order for the world to exist and for me to be able to transcend it. Thus to say that I have entered the world or come to the world or that there is a world, or that I have a body is one and the same thing" [6]

Sartre uses the Greek word *ekstasis* to indicate "standing out from". The For-itself is separated from its Self in three successive ekstases.

(1) The For-itself nihilates the In-itself in temporal dimensions; past, present and future, though in a sense it still belongs to the In-itself.
(2) There is what may be called *reflection* in which the For-itself tries to view itself from outside.
(3) The For-itself realizes that it has a Self for others (*Being-for-others*), the Self which itself cannot grasp.

## The Other

Sartre believes that we cannot prove the Other's existence since the Other is a For-itself outside our experience. The existence of the Other is not an ontological necessity. I can conceive a world in which I alone exist. However, Sartre accepts the Other's existence as a "contingent necessity". The conception of the body establishes a link between the Other and me. My body is not only the body-for-me, it is also the body for the Other and the body seen by the Other. Hence when I see the body of the Other, its movements assure me that it is the Other's For-Self which is the center, which is the subject. It is through the Look of the Other I realize that my body and I are the object and the Other is the subject. But the Self the Other sees, qua object, I cannot grasp. When I look at him, the Other is the object and when the Other looks at me, I am the object. This see-saw of the subject-object and the mutual "Looks" is the foundation of Sartrian love, hate, sadism, masochism as well as indifference. In fact it is the basis of the human relationship.

Sartre appears abstruse and outlandish. Since existentialists are highly subjective, their work, like that of a painter can be interpreted in several ways. Could we gather the bits of his thinking and try to build a philosophy that appears intelligible to the common man, and is logically consistent? Logic is not an anathema to Sartre. In fact without the minimum principle of reasoning no communication is possible.

I think, we can have a minimal model based on Sartrian concepts. I may summarize what, I feel, is the essence of his thought

(1) For Sartre consciousness is Nothing. What Sartre implies is that consciousness is not substantial like mountains, chairs, rivers, seas and the human body; it is not a material being.

(2) Being *is*. It is what it *is*. It is clear that unlike the neorealists Sartre does not include the entities which merely have logical existence, say, numbers, the golden mountain or the unicorn.

(3) In case of some beings consciousness may emerge. There is an internal rupture of the Being leading to Being-in-itself which is the unconscious mass, and the Being-for-itself. The latter "nihilates" the In-itself and is consciousness. Nevertheless, it depends on the In-itself for its emergence. The initial rupture is an unexplained premise. The For-itself is consciousness which wants to *be*

and pursues this project throughout life without success. This dichotomy between the In-itself and For-itself is only apparent. In fact, the Sartrian philosophy has the germs of the modern thinking that there is a unity between the body and the mind. Nevertheless the mind is the product of the body. Sartre's Nothing only conveys the idea that the mind cannot exist materially though it is a part and parcel of the Being. The For-itself is the bridge between the individual and the external world.

(4) Sartre recognizes two layers of consciousness (consciousness is always *of* something) (1) Unreflective consciousness which is implicit and does not give rise to any knowledge (2) the reflective consciousness, in which the consciousness tries to become its own object.

(5) Sartre regards the For-itself as that which is "condemned to be free". In fact, the freedom the For-itself enjoys is absolute only in the sense that it can indulge in imagination i.e., because it is Nothing. But when associated with its body it is certainly subject to the constraints of the physical world.

(6) The existence of the "Other", the external world or the external consciousness cannot be proved. Through feelings we have to accept them as "concrete indubitable presence".

24

# Nonbeing and Anxiety

## Threat from Nonbeing

Existentialists widely differ from one another in their views on being and nonbeing. Paul Tillich (1886-1966) is usually associated with "Christian" existentialism. He provides an explanation of different types of anxieties resulting from human existence.

Like Sartre he believes that nonbeing is dependent on being which it negates. Being has ontological precedence over nonbeing. Moreover nonbeing though in itself is devoid of qualities, it "borrows" them from being. This means we can speak of a specific being-nonbeing which are qualitatively connected. Tillich rejects the idea of a primordial nonbeing which could have existed before Being. Such a premise would imply that the "aboriginal being would be neither nonbeing nor something, that becomes nothing in contrast to something".[1]

Tillich treats nonbeing as a source that threatens being. While Sartre too mentions the threatening For-itself, in his theory the In-itself plays almost no role in confrontation since it is unconscious.

Nonbeing threatens being from three directions. First, the ontic (From *on* "being") self-affirmation of being, which is basic, is undermined. This results in the anxiety of fate and death. All of us are instinctively aware of our ultimate annihilation. This anxiety of death is inseparable from existence. But in the shadow of this anxiety lies a relative anxiety which stems from uncertainty and contingency. This is the anxiety of Fate. Though apparently we are subject to the cause-effect chain, our power to control the chain is limited. There is no reason why we were born or why we are what we are. Contingency affects us every moment and none of us is free from the attendant anxiety.

The second anxiety arises because nonbeing attacks from another direction: it threatens spiritual self-affirmation on being. Spiritual self-affirmation implies our ability to create or to *be* from moment to moment by living spontaneously. The anxiety appears in two ways. In relative terms we feel emptiness from moment to moment. In absolute terms it indicates meaninglessness. According to Tillich this threat of nonbeing to the spiritual life is implied in man's finitude and actualized by man's estrangement.

Our ability to doubt arises from the fact that though we participate in the world, we can yet remain aloof and cogitate. This is the normal Cartesian doubt. In doubt there is a component of not having. If this component becomes gigantic and swallowing, the doubt does not remain methodical questioning but has become existential despair. The man may try to wriggle out of this situation by avoiding to ask questions or doubt. In this process he "escapes from his freedom" in order to escape the anxiety of meaninglessness. Tillich points out that in this attitude meaning is saved but the self is sacrificed.

There is another possibility; the person may become a fanatic. Instead of becoming passive and complaisant he may become violent and persecute dissenters.

Ontic anxiety and the anxiety of self-affirmation though different cannot be divorced. My being encompasses my relation to meaning. The threat to spiritual being is also a threat to the whole being. This is evidenced by the fact that a person may wish to end his being leading to ontic extinction when he cannot withstand the despair of emptiness and meaninglessness. Tillich regards death instinct as a spiritual and not an ontic phenomenon. However, he is also aware of the vicious circle in which being is threatened by nonbeing on ontic as well as spiritual side.

Being is also threatened by nonbeing from the third side in which the moral self-affirmation is undermined. When we judge our own selves in regard to our actions, we, as judge, may condemn the culprit within us. This leads to an anxiety which is anxiety of guilt in relative terms and the anxiety of self-rejection absolutely.

Tillich maintains that since nonbeing is mixed with being, there is ambiguity, whatever the moral code to which we are subject. This ambiguity and the negativity involved leads to guilt which may ultimately lead to the feeling of self-rejection. Man may react to this situation in one of the following ways. He may show defiance against the negative (his own) judgement or he may opt for the "moral" way and derive self-satisfaction which may have a component of self-sacrifice. These options are usually called anomism and legalism. Whatever the option, anxiety continues to threaten since we do not know whether we have exercised self-affirmation rightly or wrongly. The anxiety may come into the open leading to guilt and self-rejection.

## Despair

Though Tillich mentions three types anxieties he contends that one does not find an anxiety in the pure form. Usually nonbeing threatens from all directions and the very existence of a person is threatened. When the situation reaches a point when non-being feels victorious, the limiting stage has arrived and that is *despair.*

The very finitude of being condemns it to remain in the hopeless state. It is a tragedy that while being has been subjugated by nothing, the former still retains its feeling, the feeling to suffer. Tillich calls this "despair within despair".

One might think that suicide may put an end to this unbearable suffering. But suicide does not mean an escape from total anxiety. Mere anxiety of existence and meaninglessness perhaps could be made extinct. But we cannot escape guilt and condemnation. A person under the weight of guilt feels that suicide cannot end misery. Tillich feels that guilt is qualitatively infinite and "cannot be removed by a finite act of ontic self-negation".[2]

Tillich was a devout Christian and his thinking that there is "no exit" from despair accompanied by guilt possibly reflects his religions belief. He also mentions "the immortal soul" in relation to despair. A person who feels intense guilt and sin perhaps subscribes to the idea that death is not the end and he is answerable for his sin even after death.

It would be interesting to analyze the statistics relating to suicides. Suicides take place in all societies. A person may commit suicide because he is suffering physically and mentally. We may say that such a person escaped ontic anxiety. There is no dearth of suicides committed by the people who feel "empty". This is especially so in affluent societies where there is excess of the sources of pleasure, loneliness and drug addiction. But people *do* end their lives because they feel terribly ashamed to face society because of the perceived sins they have committed. The Western society, especially, though technically Christian, has different attitudes to life than the Christians of, say, three hundred years ago.

Tillich discusses anxieties which are existential and not "neurotic". In practice, however, when the pain of the very existence reaches the point of despair, neither a psychiatrist nor a clinical psychologist would call the underlying anxiety "non-neurotic".

Nevertheless, one feels that it is possible to provide a theoretical explanation to Tillich's contention that guilt does not easily lead to self-destruction. If a person is capable of feeling guilt, whatever the moral code she adheres to or whatever religion she belongs to, she feels the need to be strongly punished. When the guilt is not punished from external sources, she inevitably resorts to self-flagellation which may appear in neurotic and psychotic disorders such as depression, obsessive compulsive disorder or even physical acts of violence against oneself. It may be recalled that Henry III who held himself responsible for the murder of his friend, Thomas Becket, archbishop of Canterbury, had to indulge in flogging himself. Suicide implies annihilation of being and the very end of self-punishment. The person suffering from guilt may chose to remain alive under self-torture.

25

# Conflict and Contradictions

## Contradictions and Doubt

In Chapter 6 (Nihilism) and Chapter 21 (Being and Nonbeing) we discussed negation, relativism, pluralism and contradictions. There is no doubt that the world we live in is full of contradictions. At the emotional level we face such pairs of opposites as happiness and misery, love and hate, success and failure and so forth. Coupled with relativism a given source can induce opposite emotions in different people depending on their constitution and station in life. At the intellectual level, a phenomenon can be interpreted in diametrically opposite ways.

Contradictions are not confined to human psychology, though admittedly they appear to be growing more complicated as society advances. But even in the inanimate world one finds the pairs of opposites which we mentioned earlier: hot and cold, dry and wet, dark and sunny, long and short and so forth. These contradictions become magnified because every person has her own way of looking at things.

The method of Cartesian doubt is a commendable principle in science and philosophy: it asks us to be patient, doubt, and not believe in our senses totally. However if doubting passes beyond a certain point it becomes a hindrance in epistemology. No knowledge of any practical utility is possible. Extreme skepticism, as Russell points out, can only take us to solipsism or the belief that only I and my consciousness exist.

However, we cannot wish away the contradictions inherent in the world we live in. It is not usually realized that the emotional and intellectual consequences of these contradictions are far-reaching. First, those who are optimistic may use the Hegelian technique to synthesize the opposites and reach a higher level. But this is possible only in philosophy and science. A zealous person may not be able to achieve synthesis in practical problems because the tools with which he wishes to bring about reformation may be beyond his control, and the world at large may not allow him to implement his method of synthesis. Second, those optimists who do not get the necessary help from society may be impatient and resort to revolutionary path which may lead to destruction and chaos not followed by reconstruction.

Third, the intellectual who sees contradictions *ad infinitum* may become a skeptic or cynic. The philosophy of nothingness in whatever form it appears is caused more often than not by contradictions. Fourth, we may become skeptics or cynics through the emotional routes when we are subjected to the blows of contradictions (success and failure) and we realize that we cannot control our own destiny. Whatever the individual route to skepticism and cynicism, the phenomenon is reflected in society as social schizophrenia. We may go to church or temple though we may not believe in the tenets of the religion they represent. I may deliver a sermon on social justice, equity, and socialism as a government minister though I may have scant regard for these principles or I may be so confused that I do not know how these words in my own speech should be interpreted.

Fifth, if the contradictions and opposites have an emotional impact which a person cannot withstand, she may become a neurotic or a psychotic.

Finally, one may turn to mysticism to reconcile contradictions. Religion and mysticism offer a solution to our anxiety generated by contradictions. What is especially important is that some of the mystical paths are intellectually appealing.

The most important contradiction we face in the intellectual sphere is morality. What should be the standard of ethics and morality? We find that different societies practice different codes of conduct. This shows that there is no universal code of morality innate to human existence. How do we reconcile these contradictions with the doctrine of personal freedom which the liberal intellectuals among us pretend to profess?

Let us consider the case of sex and marriage. In most western societies and non-western democracies like India, a man and a woman can have sex legally provided both are unmarried adults. But premarital sex is not as rampant as the permissive laws might appear to indicate. Millions of people live with the painful dilemma of "to do or not to do". In some countries sex with a married person is allowed with the consent of the spouse. In India the law is not symmetric. One cannot have, sex with a married woman without her husband's consent, while a married man requires no consent from his wife to have relations with an unmarried woman. Even if we ignore such nuances, wife-swapping and husband-swapping or legal promiscuity is not a rule because the moral dilemma acts as a counterweight. The very institution of marriage has been questioned by many people, but even those who stoutly oppose this institution on intellectual grounds rarely practice living together without marriage - except in a few countries.

The legal and social constraints imposed on marriage and sex have been debated *ad nauseam* but the contradictions and dilemmas have not disappeared. Some of these constraints are well known. Marriage with a close relative is prohibited, but the definition of the close relative is not universal. The husband is usually expected to be older than the wife, but a young girl marrying a man in his eighties is bound to raise eyebrows. There are also sources of conflict in other areas of sex: homosexuality, bestiality and so forth.

Let us take the case of a crime such as cheating, theft, lying or killing. While people usually condemn these acts, exceptions are generally tolerated on account of "extenuating circumstances". Society usually permits lying in many cases. Killing is usually justified in war or criminal justice, but it usually raises moral dilemmas.

The way in which we solve these conflicts depends upon our own upbringing. But life nevertheless remains a perpetual source of contradictions, relativism and attendant anxiety.

I recall a novel mode of living suggested by the author of a book I read a decade ago. The author has a great belief in personal freedom and free enterprise. He is aware of the legal and moral fetters that restrict our freedom, but his novel solution is to accept the fact that every human being seeks pleasure. We should shape our life in such a way that this pleasure is maximized. In other words we should base our behaviour in terms of cost-benefit analysis, neither on any legal duties nor on any moral code. You may steal, lie, cheat, provided the net result of your activities is positive pleasure. For example, if you find an opportunity to swindle a bank to the tune of say a million dollars, calculate how much you have to pay as bribe to the bank employees, police and other officials who are likely to be involved in the chain that leads from the crime to justice. In other words you take a calculated risk. If your calculations show that your (1) net gain is $ 800,000 with no punishment (2) $500,000 gain with a nominal imprisonment of six months, you may choose the option that suits you. What is necessary is that you have a neutral attitude to morality or law and a keen mind to weigh all the pros and cons.

I have not seen a better application of what is called *operations research* in human life. However, it is doubtful whether the author himself practices what he teaches. But this is another dilemma: should we practice or not practice what we teach?

## Instinct and Culture

In human society, contradictions and dilemmas can be traced to instinct and culture.

All types of instincts including hunger and sex lead to competition either because resources are limited or because many people may wish to satisfy the instinct from the same source that satisfies the instinct. Men may quarrel over the same woman and women over the same man. There may be disputes over the same property. Several aspirants may fight for the position that can give power.

The instinct *vs* culture again is a potent source of conflict. It may manifest in crime when we cannot control our instinct and transgress the cultural norms. It may also result in the "inner conflict". A person may be tormented by a mental conflict when he is unable to decide whether a particular act he has committed is a sin or not.

What is usually not realized is that there are innumerable sources of conflict within a given culture. Not only do people fight over what should be the correct law relating to rights and liabilities, they may quarrel over what is the worth of a cultural product like painting or sculpture.

In the realm of intellectual activities, one peculiar source of contradiction may be cited. Suppose a well known philosopher writes a book. This work can be interpreted in several ways by the readers. It may be praised as the greatest text ever written by some, or may be written off as trash by others. Many commentaries may be written on this book. The next generation will not only read the original book; but also the commentaries, and express their own interpretations. As time passes the succeeding generations will interpret and reinterpret the original work and after many generations there will be hundreds of interpretations, schools and subschools, some of which may contain diametrically opposite interpretations.

It was believed by some scholars that "hermeneutics" is the science of interpretation. However, anyone who has followed up the fate of a text over generations of readers will realize that any such attempt to create a science out of interpretation is a futile exercise. If a person considered important, a mystic, a prophet or a king uttered a simple sentence like "You rogue, I am my grandfather's grandson", five hundred years later you will find thousands of interpretations doing rounds and hundreds of commentaries written during the intervening period, all trying to interpret and reinterpret the original utterance. You are likely to be in the middle of the vortex of contradictions and only the philosophy of nothingness can save you from your plight.[1]

## Sophists

In the Western philosophy one can see the germs of skepticism in the teachings of sophists. The adjective "sophistical" is used today pejoratively. But during the days of Protagoras (ca 500 BCE), "sophist" meant "professor". A sophist taught those who could afford to pay the private teacher. Those students who wanted to be successful lawyers eagerly hired the services of the sophists.

A passage from the dialogue called *The Sophist* which is concerned with the definition of *sophist* will elucidate the art of sophistical arguments. "The art of contradiction making descended from an insincere kind of conceited mimicry, of the semblance making breed derived from image-making, distinguished as a portion, not divine but human of production, that presents a shadow play of words such is the blood and lineage which can, with perfect truth, be assigned to authentic Sophist"[2].

The most important sophist was Protagoras who was born at Abdera. In his book *On the Gods*, the beginning appears as "with regard to gods, I cannot feel sure either that they are or they are not, nor what they are like in figure; for there are many things that hinder sure knowledge, the obscurity of subject and the shortness of human life"[3]. His words clearly reflect the intellectual doubt about gaining knowledge. It is no wonder that such a philosopher in his *Theatetus* should maintain that "Man is the measure of all things", His dictum is interpreted to mean that knowledge is coloured by subjectivism, each person having his own interpretation of a phenomenon, and that there is no objective truth. It also implies relativism which we have already discussed in Chapter 5.

## From Sophism to Nothingness

The religious minded were shocked by the sophists' mode of argument which had scant regard for virtue. The sophists' method, solely based on logic which often resulted into opposite conclusions, given the inherent contradictions in the world as well as language, led to curious consequence. The sophists such as Gorgias often became rabid skeptics. According to Gorgias, nothing exists. If anything exists, it is unknowable and even if a person succeeds in "knowing" he could not communicate it to another. Gorgia's thinking succinctly shows that the fundamental contradictions in nature lead to skepticism and hence to the philosophy of nothingness.

That the sophists often used the playing upon words cannot be denied. Consider the following dialogue between Clesippus (C) and Dyonysodorus (D) in the *Euthydemus.* [4]

D- Do you say you have a dog?

C- Yes

D - And does he have puppies?

C- Yes, very much like himself.

D- And the dog is their father?

C- Yes, I surely saw him and the puppies' mother come together.

D- And he is not yours?

C- Certainly he is.

D- Then he is a father and he is yours. Hence he is your father and the puppies are your brothers.

An interesting puzzle appears in an anecdote, though not authentic, related to Protagoras. He trained a young man in legal arguments. He stipulated that the budding lawyer would pay his teacher the fees only if he won the first case and not otherwise. The story tells us that Protagoras brought the first suit against his pupil for the recovery of his fees.

We can understand why philosophers like Gorgias were confused by contradictions and felt that nothing can be said positively about anything.

However, sophism seems to have appealed to some pragmatists. F.C.S. Schiller called himself a follower of Protagoras. Russell guesses that this could be due to Plato's interpretation of Protagoras that one opinion can be better than another, though it cannot be truer. As we know very well, utility rather than truth is more important to the pragmatist.

26

# Cynicism and Scepticism

## Cynicism

Cynicism may be said to have been founded by Diogenes approximately at the time when Alexander lived. However, some credit should be given to his master Antisthenes, a disciple of Socrates, for some contribution in laying the foundation of this school.

Antisthenes was an aristocrat who lived in comfort in a conventional style. However, after the death of Socrates he seems to have developed a distate for the norms which he had followed earlier. Philosophical contradictions are believed to have changed him when he was old. He began to associate himself with ordinary working people. He lost belief in refined philosophy and began to preach the virtues of "going back to nature". He condemned any form of government, private property, marriage, and religion. Though he did not live in poverty he hated "artificial pleasure" not attributable to nature. His words "I had rather become mad than delighted" are quite famous.[1]

Diogenes was the son of a much hated money-changer and wanted to learn wisdom from Antisthenes. However, the famed philosopher appears to have disliked Diogenes initially and turned him away. The younger lad was stubbornly patient. He wanted to deface the conventions and customs as his father had "defaced coinage". His perseverance paid and Antisthenes accepted him as a disciple.

Diogenes treated every convention with contempt. He decided to live like a dog. He was called a cynic which means "canine". He is believed to have lived either in a tub or a pitcher. He lived unconventionally rejecting the customary forms of etiquettes, religion, dress and food. He maintained that he was a friend and brother of the humanity and even animals.

The word *cynical* has connotations today which did not accord with his philosophy. He believed in virtue. He condemned worldly pleasures and wanted liberation from desire. In this respect he can be compared with the Indian *karmayogi* who performs his duty, renounces desire and does not expect any fruits for his action.

In the third century, cynicism became quite popular, especially in Alexandria. However, it also changed to some extent. Cynicism of this age preached indifference and not aversion to good things in life. People were encouraged to be emotionally insulated, as it were, and one can see the germs of Stoicism which was to follow.

Cynics of this era published edifying pamphlets which taught people how one can live without worldly possessions, how simple food can lead to happiness. There is no reason why one should grieve over the death of relatives and friends. There is no need for excessive love for one's country. Whether the last advice emanated from pragmatism or the feeling of international brotherhood is not clear.

## Scepticism

We have already mentioned that contradictions and dilemmas lay behind the philosophy of sophists. Sophism may be said to be the harbinger of scepticism. Elements of scepticism are found even in Parmenides and Plato who questioned the cognitive value of perception. However, Pyrrho, who was in Alexander's army, is credited with the authorship of scepticism as a doctrine.

Pyrrho took contradictions to the realm of ethics and logic. He contended that there is no logical reason why one action should be preferred over others. It meant that you lived with the schism between theory and practice. As pointed out earlier, you may perform ritual though you may not believe in their effects. The philosophy also acted as a medicine for anxiety since the opposites can be reconciled. The adherents of skepticism asked you to live in the present without worrying about future which could not be predicted.

Russell aptly points out that skepticism as a philosophy is not merely doubt, but what may be called a dogmatic doubt. The man of science says, "I think it is so-and-so, but I am not sure". The man of intellectual curiosity says "I don't know how it is, but I hope to find out". The philosophical skeptic says, "nobody knows and nobody can ever know"[2].

Timon was Pyrrho's disciple. He has made a singular contribution to skepticism with his ostensibly irrefutable arguments. Greeks at that time recognized only deductive logic. But deduction was based on some general principles which were self-evident. Timon denied that any general principles can be admitted as axioms merely because they appeared to be self-evident. One had to prove everything. As Russell points out, this meant ".. all arguments will be either circular or an endless chain hanging from nothing. In either case nothing can be proved".[3]

A modern skeptic like Hume who can be compared with his Greek counterpart Timon did believe in phenomenon. But he doubted the inference from it. For example, he would contend that honey appears sweet, but he cannot vouch for it. The modern skeptic treats the phenomenon as an event and as such it is neither valid nor invalid. The modern skeptic would speak of the probability of what appears to be honey being sweet. He would also say that if two events A and B occur together whenever he notices them, their future association is highly probable.

Socrates as portrayed by Plato also has a skeptical side. Many of his dialogues do not reach any conclusion. Russell observes that "some the latter half of the *Parmenides,* for instance, might seem to have no purpose except to show that either side of any question can be maintained with equal plausibility."[4]

We may end the discussion on scepticism with an interesting anecdote relating to Carneades who was sent by Athens in 150 BCE to Rome on a diplomatic mission. In his first lecture at Rome, Carneades expatiated on the philosophy of Aristotle and Plato on justice. People in large number attended the lecture because the Greek culture was a fashion. In his second lecture he refuted everything he said in the first lecture with considerable success.

## Stoicism

Another school of philosophy which resulted form contradictions and nothingness is stoicism. This appeared after the death of Alexander and was imported to Athens by a Phoenecian merchant called Zeno (ca. 310 BCE). Will Durant finds a definite Oriental stamp of apathy in this philosophy. According to him both stoicism and Epicureanism are Greek reactions to "apathetic acceptance of defeat"[5]. The first philosophy projected melancholic resignation while the second had the facade of "be merry".[5]

Zeno's philosophy of *apatheia* relied on determinism which according to some philosophers was akin to Oriental fatalism. Just as Schopenhauer under the influence of the Eastern philosophy argued that it is useless for the individual to fight the universal will, Stoics accepted the contradictions of life as a "given", and advocated philosophic indifference to life.

Stoicism in a slightly different form is found in Indian philosophy and there is no doubt that Schopenhauer was influenced by Indian thoughts. The word *sthitaprajña* in Sanskrit is roughly equivalent to "*stoic*". In the *Bhagavad Gītā* (Chapter II, Sāṃkhya Yoga) Kṛṣṇa advises Arjuna to rise above the pairs of opposites and become a sthitaprajña (one who is stable in wisdom). Some of the verses from this Chapter are quite interesting.

"The contacts of senses with their objects generate, Arjuna, feelings of hot and cold, of pain and pleasure. They come and go and are independent. Bear them patiently. (2-14)

"That man is fitted for immortality whom these do not torment, who is balanced in pain and pleasure and steadfast" (2-15)

"Treating alike pain and pleasure gain and loss, victory and defeat, engage yourself in battle. Thus you will not incur any sin" (2-38)

"He whose mind is not disturbed by adversity, who does not crave happiness, who is free from fondness fear and anger, is the Muni of constant wisdom". (2-56)

It must, however, be realized that Kṛṣṇa asks Arjuna to be indifferent to the pairs of opposites because according to him a person has to perform his duty without expecting any rewards. The Indian doctrine of indifference is based on duty as well as on ultimate liberation, and is not based on pessimism.

## Epicureanism

A reaction to contradictions appears in another philosophy called Epicureanism, though this philosophy is usually mistaken for hedonism. Epicurus himself was a stoic, but his reaction to contradictions was different: he feels that total apathy is impossible, he exults the pleasure of intellect and not of senses. His philosophy is based on *ataraxia* or tranquility or equanimity. He warns against the ecstacies of sensual pleasure which may disturb the soul. Strife and death are inevitable. Hence there is no alternative to *ataraxia*— "to look on all things with a mind at peace". Peace connotes a method of creating void between a person and the world. In a sense Epicureanism though on the face of it appears as a pleasure-seeking philosophy, extols equanimity and insulation from strife.

To conclude, conflicts, contradictions and dilemmas which are inherent in human life as well as in inanimate phenomena, have led to different schools of philosophy. All these philosophies, however, contain a component of nothingness, void or insulation from strife.

# Space and Time

## Characteristics of Space

The most important property of space is that it can be occupied by material bodies. Since the objects can be of various sizes, the first concept that occurs to us is length. Length is a quantity whose magnitude can be measured in different units. However, numerical measurement is only a sophistication which is not needed in comparing lengths. The given lengths can be arranged in order ("less than" or "greater than") . What actually we need is an ordered series to compare lengths.

Another property of space is direction. We can think of a length AB as from A to B or from B to A. This helps us build coordinate systems; a real line having only one axis, a plane having two axes, and a system of three axes in three dimensions.

A characteristic of space is that there can be motion of a body in space.

The questions which interest us are "What type of zero is associated with space?" "Does a point which implies zero distance exist?" "What is meant by zero motion?"

## Vector Space

As is their wont, modern mathematicians define space in abstract terms, i.e. they assume the basic properties of the space we live in and try to construct a general space.

Let (K,+,.) be a field, then a set V is called a *vector space or linear space* over K if

(a) An operation say, "+" is defined in V such that (V,+) is an abelian group. Its elements are called *vectors*. The elements of K are called *scalars*.

(b) An external composition called scalar *multiplication* (.) which is a mapping of KxV into V is defined.

(c) These operations have the following properties

(i) $a(x+y) = ax + ay$

(ii) $(a+b)x = ax + bx$

(iii) $(ab)x = a(bx)$

(iv) $1x = x$

where $a,b \in K$, $x,y \in V$ and 1 is the multiplicative identity of K. We can prove the following results

(1) $0\,a = 0$ where $a \in K$ and 0 is the additive identity of V, called *zero vector*.

(2) $0\,x = 0$; 0 on the left is the zero of K while that on the right is the zero vector $\in V$.

(3) $a(-x) = -(ax)$

(4) $a(x-y) = ax-ay$

Let us pause and ponder over what these two zeros mean. We will confine ourselves to the fields of real numbers **R** or complex numbers **C**. The 0(K) is the quantitative zero subject to our comments on the complex zero. However, we do not know the exact nature of 0(V) unless V is specified. Nevertheless in view of the property (1) we tend to think that it is similar to a quantitative zero.

E1

(a) Consider a space over **R** or **C** which consists of a single vector 0, such that a.0 = 0 for all scalars *a*. V is called *zero space* and denoted by {0}

(b) Consider the set $\mathbf{R}^n$ of ordered n-tuples in which equality, addition and scalar multiplication is defined as follows:

$x = (x_1, x_2, \dots x_n)$, $y = (y_1, y_2, \dots y_n)$

(i) $x = y$ if and only if $x_1 = y_1$, $x_2 = y_2, \dots\dots x_n = y_n$

(ii) $x+y = (x_1+y_1, x_2+y_2, .......x_n+y_n)$
(iii) $a(x_1,x_2,...x_n) = (ax_1,ax_2....ax_n)$
where $a \in \mathbf{R}$

It can be proved that this is a "real" vector space of n dimensions. The zero vector is (0,0,....0)

## Metric Space

The linear or vector space mentioned above does not contain the concept of *distance.* A metric space introduces this idea through what is called *metric.*

Let X be a non-empty set. We define a *metric* on X as a non-negative real number d (which is a mapping from $X^2$ into **R**) which has the following properties.

(a) $d(x,y) \geq 0$, and $d(x,y) = 0$ if and only if $x = y$.
(b) $d(x,y) = d(y,x)$ (symmetry)
(c) $d(x,y) \leq d(x,z)+d(z,y)$ (triangle inequality)

where $x,y,z \in X$. Then (X,d) is called a *metric space.*

You will realize that d has the properties similar to what we call *distance* in our space.

The zero metric d = 0 is the distance between a point and itself. What's more,

(a) ensures that in no other case this distance is zero. This is certainly the commonsense zero.

E2

(a) Let X be a nonempty set in which the metric is defined as
$d(x,y) = 0$ if $x = y$
$= 1$ if $x \neq y$
this can be proved to be a metric space, its zero metric being the real 0.

(b) Consider the real line R. P(x), Q(y)... are points on the line, and
|x| is the distance of point P from the origin O(0). Then if
$d(x,y) = |x-y|$

this is called the *usual metric.* (X,d) is a metric space which is quite familiar to us.

(c) In the complex plane, Let P,Q be points having coordinates
$z_1 = x_1+iy_1 = (x_1,y_1)$, $z_2 = x_2+iy_2 = (x_2,y_2)$ (Fig. 27.1)

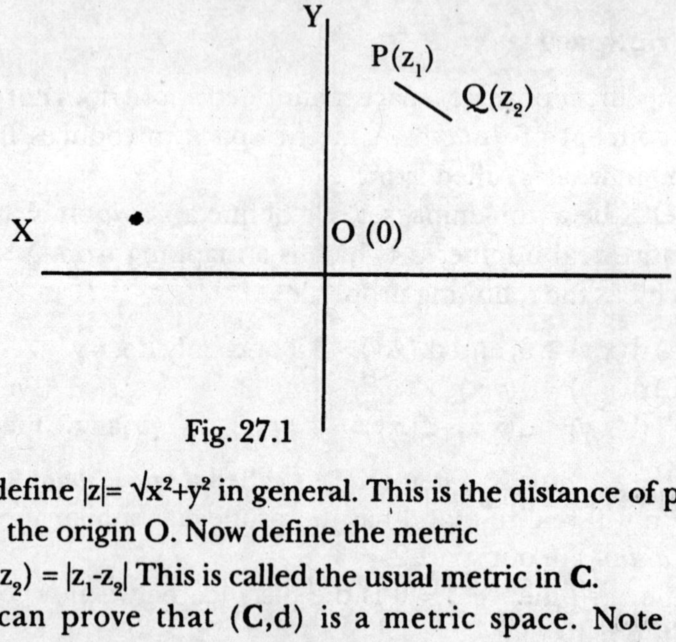


Fig. 27.1

We define $|z|= \sqrt{x^2+y^2}$ in general. This is the distance of point Z from the origin O. Now define the metric

$d(z_1,z_2) = |z_1-z_2|$ This is called the usual metric in **C**.

We can prove that (**C**,d) is a metric space. Note that $|z_1-z_2| = PQ$, the distance between two points.

Note that d = 0 is again a quantitative zero.

However, the origin which has the real coordinate 0 in (b) and complex coordinate 0 in (c) can be shifted and these zeros are merely relative.

## Normed Linear Space

A linear space need not be a metric space and a metric space need not be a vector space. The space in which we live has both these characteristics. Hence mathematicians construct an abstract space in which the properties of both spaces are incorporated.

Let N be a linear space in which to each vector we assign a

real number $\|x\|$ called the *norm* of x such that

1. $\|x\| \geq 0$ and $\|x\| = 0$ if and only if $x = 0$
2. $\|x+y\| \leq \|x\| + \|y\|$
3. $\|ax\| = |a|\|x\|$ where a is a scalar.

We call N *normed linear space.*

The following results are stated without proof

(a) The normed linear space N is also a metric space with the metric

$d = \|x-y\|$

(b) $|\ \|x\| - \|y\|\ |\ \|x-y\|$

## Euclidean Space

In E1 (b) we mentioned that $\mathbf{R}^n$ leads to a vector space. We now introduce a norm

$\|x\| = \sqrt{(x_1)^2 + (x_2)^2 + \ldots\ldots (x_n)^2}$

in which the metric is $\|x-y\|$. This is called the Euclidean Space in n dimensions.

Of particular interest is the three dimensional Euclidean Space with which we are familiar and in which, $\|x\|$ is the distance of a point from the origin. If (x,y,z) are the coordinates of point P

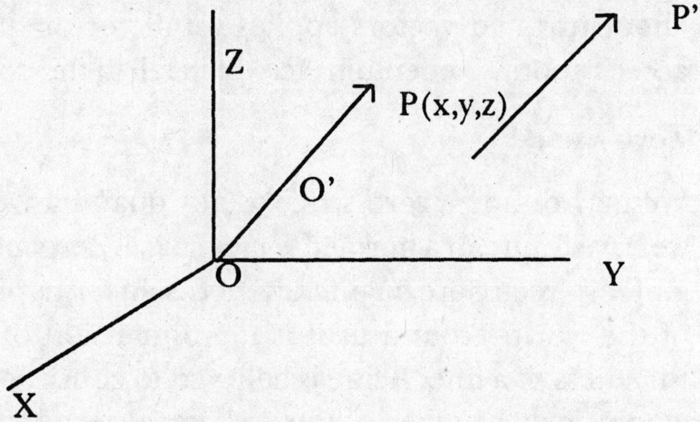


Fig. 27.2

$OP = \sqrt{x^2+y^2+z^2}$

OP is a vector whose components are (x,y,z) and direction as shown in figure. Note that we can shift the origin to O'. If O'P' is parallel and equal to OP, vectors OP and O'P' are equal.

We have the following zeros to consider.

1. The origin O(0,0,0). This is a relative zero, since it can be shifted.
2. Vector OO i.e. when O and P coincide. In this case the vector is (0,0,0) which is a quantitative zero; its magnitude $=\sqrt{0^2+0^2+0^2}=0$
3. Distance OP or O'P' when P coincides with O (i.e., P' coincides with O') the distance is obviously zero.

It is interesting to see that (x,y,o) where x, y are real numbers is the z-plane which is a normed vector space in its own right . This is a *subspace* of $R^3$. Again (x,0,0) is a line which is x-axis. This in itself is normed vector space. This is a subspace of $R^2$ as well as $R^3$. Note that the zeros in this space can be written as (0,0) and 0 and interpreted in the same way as (0,0,0).. What's more, any plane or any line are two dimensional and one dimensional subspaces of $R^3$ with similar interpretations of the zeros.

It is necessary to remember that though a vector in fig. 27.2 appears as geometrical segment with direction what we have said about normed vectors applies to all vector quantities; force, acceleration, momentum etc. which fall in the domain of physics.

## Zero Space

We may define a zero space as any quantitative zeros in space we have found in a normed vector space. Zero metric or distance and zero vector are quantitative zeros. In terms of our perception of the world around us it is the dimension of a point or the thickness of a line. A line is believed to consist of points. Hence a point may be taken as the archetypal zero space.

Lotze has made strong arguments against the concept of point.[1] If a point exists, what is its *being*? Indeed it looks strange that anything that has no dimensions should have existence.

However, some philosophers such as Russell argue that there is a difference between being and existence. A person, stone, river etc. have existence. A centaur or vampire does not exist but it can have a "being". An imaginary object does not exist but can have being in as much as it can be a logical subject. In mathematics and science we often use abstractions or concepts which have being. They are parameters which can conveniently describe the universal phenomena. A point and a line are such beings. The conception of a spatial as well as a material point has served geometers and physicists well. We should accept these entities in this sense. This is also consistent with the neorealist's thinking.

Is space continuous or there is a void in the space itself? This question again can be answered in a similar way. Geometry and physics accept continuity. For example, we assume that between two points on a line there is another point. In fact we assume a second order continuity in the real numbers in which irrationals appear with the corresponding points on the real line. The physicist can legitimately assert that there are no "gaps" in space (energy and material particles are excluded) because we can transmit electromagnetic waves over long distances and receive audio-visual data on television.

Apart from the quantitative zero, we also have the "zero of the scale" or the relative zero which refers to the origin of a set of axes.

## Time

Unlike (our) space, time flows in one direction. What's more, we cannot move back into what is our past. Like space we have a relative zero in time: any instant can be taken as the zero from which events are measured. We also have a zero time interval which is the time interval between an instant and itself. An instant again has a being in the same sense as a point has a being. Most of our remarks made in respect of points are applicable to instants. Both, instants and points have served us well in science as parameters.

## Zeno's Paradox

Philosopher Zeno created many puzzles. One of them relates to motion. "If everything is at rest or in motion in a space equal to itself, and if what moves is always in the instant, the arrow in its flight is immovable"[2].

To demystify this paradox we must consider the concept of motion. In motion there is a triangular relation: a material point occupies a spatial point at a given instant of time. We can speak only of the *motion* of a material point which, say, occupies spatial points $s_1$, $s_2$... at time $t_1$,$t_2$... . The whole idea of motion is that there should be a *finite* distance covered by a material body in a *finite* duration of time. The paradox viz. at any instant an arrow is at rest arises in not recognizing this fact.

To determine whether a material point M is at rest or in motion at any given instant we have to apply the following criteria suggested by Russell.[3]

An instant such that a *time interval* containing the given instant otherwise than as an end-point can be assigned, at any instant within which interval M is in the same place is a moment when M is at rest. An instant when this cannot be done is an instant when M is in motion. M occupies *some* place at neighbouring instants on either side. At an instant when there are such intervals, but all have this instant as end-points, M is in the state of transition from rest to motion or *vice versa*.

The crux of the notion of motion lies in the finite distance covered in finite time.

# Part IV

## Science

# 28

# Epistemology

## Logic and Empiricism

Epistemology, which discusses how knowledge is acquired, is usually treated as a branch of philosophy and one might wonder why it finds a place in the part relating to science. There are two reasons. First, deductive logic forms an inseparable source of the theory of knowledge. Though historically treated as a subdivision of philosophy, it is more akin to mathematics and, like mathematics, is regarded as an exact science. Second, epistemology of "nothing" has vital importance in distinguishing mysticism or religion from science. We shall, therefore, treat epistemology more as an instrument to detect "nothing" rather than a branch of philosophy.

We acquire knowledge through our senses which include the mind. In this connection, there has been an unnecessary controversy between two schools of epistemology - rationalism and empiricism. The rationalists maintain that logic (we shall use the word "logic" to indicate deductive logic unless otherwise stated) is the main determinant of human knowledge while the empiricists hold that experience is the most important factor in acquiring knowledge. This has led to what is called *analytic-synthetic* dichotomy. The following examples will elucidate the controversy.

E1

(a) The moon is either a star or not a star.
(b) The moon cannot be both a star and a non-star.

(c) John is a man. All men are mammals. Hence John is a mammal.
(d) If a,b,c are real numbers and $a<b$ and $b<c$ then $a<c$.
(e) Hydrogen is lighter than oxygen.
(f) A human being cannot live for more than 300 years.
(g) The sun sets in the West every evening.

All these statements appear to be true. However, the statements (a) through (d) seem obviously true. They belong to either logic or pure mathematics (logic and pure mathematics are almost synonymous). The statements (e) through (g) contain an element of uncertainty and are dependent on our observation. For example, there may be a celestial accident and the earth may stop orbiting the sun, in which case (g) may be false. Or, it may be possible in future for a man to live for more than 300 years. The statements in the first category are sometimes called *analytical* and those in the second group *synthetic.* The analytical statements are cent per cent true or false, while such assertion cannot be made about synthetic statements: we can only speak of the "degree of probability". Thus the truth of (g) is highly probable.

Incidentally in case of logical statements we use many "laws" whose names we may not know. For example, (a) demonstrates the *law of the excluded middle* which is formally "A is either B or not B". There is no third possibility. (*Tertium non datur*). (b) exemplifies the *law of contradiction* which says that "A cannot be both B and not B". (c) is similar to *syllogism.*

Some philosophers like Ayn Rand severely attack the analytic-synthetic dichotomy. According to them, knowledge is acquired by the application of logic to experience. The dichotomy is artificial since the mind which uses logic is a part of nature which is explored. Nevertheless many epistemologists treat logic as a special source of knowledge because its truth or falsehood is "100% sure"

## Induction and Memory

Induction is a method by which we make a general inference on the basis of a limited number of observations. There are many rules which the scientist has to follow to make the inductive inference highly probable. You can appreciate the degree of probability of the inferences in the following cases.

E2

(a) Humans are mortal.

(b) A student reads the biography of Hitler and concludes that all German speaking people are cruel.

(c) X who is a Miss world asserts on a TV show that a particular product is highly nutritious. The sales of the product double in just one month.

(d) There is a huge container in which wheat is stored. You take a small sample only from the top layer. The sample is found to be slightly moist. You conclude that the entire quantity may contain moisture.

(e) Gregor Mendel's laws in genetics were rejected by many communists because he was a monk.

We may say the truth of (a) is, highly probable. In (b) the student's inference is faulty because he uses insufficient statistics. Ex. (c) contains a wrong inference because X is not an authority on nutrition. Ex. (d) is an instance of weak induction because the sample was taken only from one place and was not *representative* of the bulk. Ex. (e) illustrates what is called the "argument against man". Mendel's being a monk has nothing to do with the truth of his laws which have to be scientifically verified.

We cannot discuss in detail what makes induction highly probable; but it is necessary to point out that the principle of induction itself cannot be proved. It has to be accepted as an axiom under certain circumstances.

Memory is another source of knowledge, but is fallible.

However, modern instruments which record and store audiovisual data have reduced the chances of error in remembering a scientific result.

Testimony is another source of knowledge and is used also in law courts. However, testimony, too, depends upon the memory of the person who testifies. Its credibility is also linked with the integrity of the person making an assertion.

Analogy is another source of knowledge immensely useful in science. Suppose x and y have properties a,b,c. It is found that x has property d then analogy suggests that y has property d. Analogy may be treated as a type of induction.

## Propositional Function

In Chapter 3 we mentioned that there was a difficulty in defining the null set extensionally. Let us see if this obstacle can be overcome.

A *proposition* is a statement which is either true or false.

E3

(a) The Ganges is a river in India.
(b) Churchill was a President of the United States.
(c) Washington D.C. is a man.
(d) x is a man.

(a) is a proposition which is true, (b) and (c) are false propositions, and (d) is not a proposition since we do not know what x is.

Consider the following statements

(a) Plato is a man.
(b) Gandhi is a man.
(c) Lincoln is a man.
(d) Zero is a man.

We start with (a) and replace Plato by Gandhi, Lincoln and Zero successively retaining the other parts of the sentences. The new sentences may be true or false. The generalized form of these can be written as *x* is a man.

Since "x" is not fixed, the above is not a proposition but a *propositional function* which can be denoted by fx, f(x), $\phi$x, $\phi$(x) etc. x is a *variable* or *argument.* Of course, it is assumed that f(x) is meaningful i.e., it is true or false for "x". We shall exclude such statements as

"Vanity stands on three legs"

which are meaningless, from the purview of propositions. A propositional function may be always true or always false or sometimes true.

"x is a man" is sometimes true.

"If x is a man, x is mortal" is always true.

"If x is a man, x is immortal" is always false.

## Class-concept and Class

The notion "such that" is quite important in logic. Suppose f(x) is a propositional function, then all the values of x which make f(x) true form a class. Such values are sometimes called the range of f.

For instance, if f(x) is *such that* "x is a citizen of India", then the class of people who satisfy f(x) give us the class which is the range of f(x).

Consider a propositional function f(x); x is a river in India.

"River" is a *class-concept* while the set of all rivers in India gives the class satisfying f(x). We can say that if *a* satisfies f(x) then f(a) is true.

Two functions f(x) and $\phi$(x) are *equivalent* if any value which satisfies f(x) also satisfies $\phi$(x) and *vice versa.*

Thus "x is my brother" and "x is my parents' son other than myself" are equivalent propositions. "My brother" and "My parents' son other than myself" are class-concepts. Though they generate the same class or extension these concepts are not *identical.*

"Man" is a class-concept but "all men in U.K" is a particular class generated by the concept.

"Featherless biped" and "man" are not identical class-concepts but "All featherless bipeds" and "all men" generate the same class or extension viz. the class of all human beings.

A propositional function f(x) is called null when it is false for all values of x. The class or the range it generates is the null class.

## Nothing and the Null Class

The idea of the null class and the very word *nothing* create many problems, when we try to define them extensionally. Consider the function

x is a human *aṣṭānana*

where "aṣṭānana" means one having eight faces. This is false for all values of x. This function generates no class. We shall call such a class-concepts *a null class-concept.* Observe that a *null class concept* can exist though it cannot generate a class.

x is half-man half-tiger

x is a man of height 20 feet

x is a person who can fly.

All the functions above involve null-class concepts. Russell defines the null class as (1) the class of elements that belong to every class or (2) the class which is contained in every class or (3) as the class $\phi$ such that the propositional function "x is a $\phi$" is false for all values of x or the class satisfying any propositional function f(x) which is false for values of x.

Consider another statement

*Nothing* is not nothing

This is a true proposition. The reason is that *nothing* is a denoting concept which itself is not nothing, i.e. it is not what it itself denotes. It simply means that the class-concept *nothing* does not generate a class. But "nothing" *qua* concept has a meaning.

## Zero and the Null Class

Zero has a close relationship with the null class. It is the cardinal number of the null class. You will find it curious that there are infinitely many null class - concepts, but the class they all generate is *the* null set whose cardinal number is zero.

It is interesting to see how the logical zero or the null set can be created tautologically.

E3

Consider the following functions

(a) x is a circular square
(b) x is a blind person who can see an object at a distance of 100 meters.
(c) x is a real number such that
$(x+2)^2 = x^2+4x+3$
(d) x is unmarried and his wife is a doctor.

All the above propositional functions lead to the null class. We do not have to find out what "x" is because each statement is analytically false or self-contradictory. We may call the "nothing" involved in such statements *tautological nothing*, because we do not have to test this "nothing" empirically.

We also encounter in practice sets which may be called null with a high degree of probability. Once I saw a notice displayed in a restaurant, to the effect that free food would be served to those who are above eighty and are accompanied by both their parents. The restaurateur was not familiar with the technical term "null class" but was certainly able to generate one with a sense of humour.

## Object Words

To fully appreciate the meaning of negation and *nothing* we should know something about what is called the hierarchy of languages.

An object-word is a word which has meaning that does not depend upon its occurring in a sentence. We teach children proper and common nouns by pointing out the object or ostensively. Through this method a child learns proper names of close relations as well as class-names such as dog, cat and so forth. He will also learn words indicating actions (walk, jump etc.) and relational words like up, down, between and also adjectives like white, black etc. The object language or primary language is one which solely consists of words defined ostensively. Such language lies at the base of the hierarchy of languages. In the primary language the concepts of "truth" or "falsehood" do not exist. If we teach a child to call a cat, "dog", he will say "dog" when he sees a cat. However, he will have no concept of falsehood or truth which belongs to a higher language.

## Logical Words

Logical words consists of such words as "a", "an", "and", "the", "not", "none", "all", "true", "false" etc. They do not belong to the primary language and cannot be taught ostensively.

Suppose p is a proposition, then "not-p" is equivalent to "p is false". This shows that apart from the rhetorical point of view *not* and *false* are equivalent.

The word "word" does not belong to the primary language. When we speak of the "object-word". We are using the secondary language. If we assume that the logical words belong to the secondary language, the word "logical word" will appear in the tertiary language. If by "tertiary word" we mean the word which appears first in the tertiary language then the word "tertiary word" itself belongs to the higher language i.e. quaternary language and so forth.

While the words "true" and "false" do not belong to the primary language it does not mean that a sentence is neither true nor false in this language. "Adam running" belongs to the primary language since Adam is a proper name and running is an action.

But I may mistake Ibrahim (who is running) for Adam and my statement is false. But the word *false* belongs to a higher language.

It is interesting to see how the logical words "nothing" or "none" behave from the viewpoint of epistemology. We can disprove a proposition involving these words by providing a single instance, but we cannot prove it unless it belongs to logic or mathematics. For example, (a) "No man is immortal. (b) "Nothing is sweeter than sugar."

A single example will disprove the above statements but in order to prove these statements we will have to know in (a) the biography of all men who ever existed or will exist. Similarly to disprove (b) only one instance of food which is sweeter than sugar is necessary. To prove (b) we will have to taste everything that exists or ever existed. This shows how difficult it is to prove a proposition related to "nothing".

## Contradictions in Logic

It is interesting to see how negations and contradictions appear in logic. Consider the following example.

Suppose during an interval between 5 and 5.5p.m. "A" utters only one sentence "I make a false statement". Call this statement 'p'. Is p true or false?

Suppose p is true i.e., A makes a false statement during this interval. Since p was the only statement he made during the interval, p must be false. Conversely suppose p is false, then every statement A makes in the interval must be true. Since p is the only statement he makes, p must be true. Thus if p is true it is false and if it is false it must be true.

This ambiguity can be removed only if we assume a hierarchy of languages. [2]

## Concept Formation

It would be pertinent to briefly discuss the epistemology of the "objectivists" led by Ayn Rand. According to them concept formation occurs in three stages. The first stage is sensation. Since isolated sensations are not retained in memory, the next stage *perception* is the foundation of our knowledge. A percept is a bundle of sensations automatically stored and integrated in a living organism.

The basic components of knowledge are existents. An existent is that which exists. It can be a thing, an attribute or an action. An existent undergoes three stages of development. The first corresponds to the child's awareness of things. Conceptually, this stage gives rise to "entities". At the second stage the child is able to perceive specific or a particular entity which stands out against the rest of his visual field. The entity at this stage has acquired the status of "identity". When at the third stage the child can identify relationships among the various identities he has reached the "conceptual" stage where an identity becomes a "unit". According to Rand, "the ability to regard entities as units is man's distinctive method of cognition, which other living species are unable to follow"[3]

Though we have used the word *concept* before, the child reaches the conceptual stage only at this stage. The concept formation involves the process of "differentiation and integration". To understand this, suppose a child's environment contains many tables and chairs. It integrates the most common characteristics of the tables; shape, flat top on which things are kept, etc. These characteristics are combined into the concept "table". The chairs are differentiated on the basis of another class of common characteristics: seat, back, its use for sitting etc.. This leads to the concept of "chair".

Both tables and chairs can have inessential characteristics. For example, a chair can have different colours, different heights, cushioned seat, etc. These characteristics are called "measurements". Thus in the formation of the concept "chair" these measurements are omitted or dropped.

Concept formation is a process of abstraction and there can

be an abstraction of abstractions which leads to a hierarchy of concepts. For instance as science progressed, the concept "man" became a subdivsision of the broader concept *animal* which in turn led to a still broader concept of living organism. There is also a progress in another direction. "Human being" could be subdivided on the basis of racial characteristics or sex or profession and so differntiation and integration lead to a web of the interconnected concepts at different levels.

## Axioms in Objectivism

While we use logic, induction, memory etc. as the sources of knowledge, we need some axioms to start with, without which the superstructure of knowledge cannot be built. Usually these axioms appear "obvious" and we cannot prove them. The objectivists have three axiomatic concepts relating to existence, identity and consciousness, which are experienced directly. They are present at all stages viz. sensation, perception, concept formation and the formation of higher concepts.

According to the objectivists, "existence exists" and "consciousness is conscious".

The units of "existence" and "identity" are the same: every entity, attribute, event or phenomenon. There is, however, some difference between "existence" and "identity". The former is generic; it distinguishes "is" from "is not" or an "object" form "nothing". "Identity" is a narrower concept which distinguishes between *this* existent and *that* existent.

The units of "consciousness" are every state of awareness that ever existed, exists or will exist.

Existence and Conciseness are metaphysically the most fundamental and omit all measurements of the existents they subsume. Rand calls them "constants" of man's consciousness. She sums up the essence of human cognition as "something *exists* of which I am *conscious.* I must discover its *identity.*"[4]

In regard to the primary concepts, it must be clarified that they appear as concepts to adults, but they are implicit in the awareness of infants and animals. While the infant grows to the conceptual level, animals remain at the perceptual stage.

## Nothing and Nonexistence

According to Rand the concept "nothing" is relative, i.e. it can only be spoken of in relation to something. If I point to the book-shelf and say "there is nothing" I am referring to nonexistence of any book on the shelf I am not suggesting that the shelf is non-existent. If someone tells you that there is nothing in the water-jug, he merely means that there is no water inside, he is not denying that there is air in the jug.

*Nothing* cannot be a primary concept because it cannot be prior to an object. The objectivists severely criticize existentialism which, as we saw in earlier chapters, often talks of "nothing" as an entity. According to the objectivists there is no concept as "nothing" except in the relational sense.

Since according to Rand "Existence exists", there is no concept called nonexistence. Existentialists often treat nonexistence as opposite to existence and nonbeing as opposite to being. According to Rand this is a gross mistake. Existence integrates all existents ignoring their individual characteristics. Nonexistence from the psycho-epistemological viewpoint is therefore devoid of any meaning: it is a non-concept.

29

# Quantity and Magnitude

## Quantity and Number

In earlier chapters, we used the expression "quantitative zero" assuming that we intuitively know what quantity is. The notion of quantity and magnitude have been a source a controversy among philosophers. We shall briefly discuss what is called the *absolute theory of quantity*.

Many scientists and philosophers believed that quantity like number fell in the domain of pure mathematics. It looked as if quantity and number could not be separated. Numbers were essential to indicate quantity. But in fact, quantity is the concept that does not belong to pure mathematics, rather its field is physics. It is true that the use of numbers makes quantitative measurements sophisticated, but comparison of quantities is not dependent on numbers.

You will recall that in Chapter 9 (Relations) we introduced the concept of partial order. There is an allied concept called simply *order* or *strict order*. It is a relation which is asymmetric and transitive. *Less than* (<) is an example of order. For every order relation we have a converse order relation. For example, the converse of "less than" is *greater than* (>) . Before numbers were invented, people used the notion "order" to decide which quantity was greater and which quantity less. For example, if we have three unequal weights A,B,C we could arrange them in order such that (say) A<B<C or C>B>A. Of course human judgement or a device like "balance" would be necessary to arrange the weights in order.

## Absolute Theory of Quantity

Note that "greater than" and "less than" are fundamental notions which are indefinable. In this theory, the elementary notions are 1. magnitude 2. kind of magnitude. 3. quantity.

A magnitude is an indefinable concept. Magnitudes form different classes A,B,C... etc. so that a magnitude belongs to any one of them. The magnitudes belonging to the same class are called *magnitudes of the same kind.* Hence we have magnitudes of pleasure, volume, length and so forth.

Consider the magnitudes of one kind, say, pleasure. All magnitudes of pleasures can be ordered according to their intensity which gives us a non-numerical scale of intensity of pleasure.

It is presumed that magnitudes of the same kind are comparable and arranged in (strict) order. In the absolute theory, quantities are instances of magnitude which are "particularized by spatiotemporal position or (in case of relations which are quantities) by the terms between which the relation holds."[1]

In this theory we do not compare quantities; we compare magnitudes of the same kind. Magnitudes are distinct from their quantities.

We recall the principle of abstraction. Symmetry and transitivity lead to quasi- equivalence classes and all elements in the same class have a common property or common relation with some other element or concept. The magnitudes belonging to the same class have this relationship with quantity. It must be noted that two magnitudes of the same kind cannot coexist in one spatiotemporal place or prevail as relations between the same pair of terms.

We say that magnitudes are the same (and not equal). We

use the word equal for the quantities whose magnitudes are the same.

We may summarize the absolute theory as follows:

There are two indefinables: (1) greater and less which are order relations (2) particular magnitude.

To these indefinables are added indemonstrable propositions.

(1) Every magnitude has the relations to a term which makes the magnitude "of a certain kind."

(2) Of the two magnitudes of the same kind one is less or greater than the other. (We reserve the word equality for quantities when they have the same magnitude) This means the class of the magnitudes of the same kind is totally ordered.

(3) Two magnitudes of the same kind cannot have the same position in space or time. For example the lengths A, B where A>B cannot be at the same place. If they are relations, they cannot both hold between the same terms.

(4) No magnitude is greater than itself.

(5) If A is greater than B, B is less than A and *vice versa.*

(6) If A is greater than B and B greater than C then A is greater than C.

In 5-6 A,B,C are magnitudes of the same kind.

## Relational Magnitudes

Some kinds of magnitudes do not pose any problems. Length, for example, can be completely appreciated as a distinct kind. But a few cases are confusing. Consider colour. If I say this flower is brighter than that, we can perceive brightness as the legitimate kind that can be arranged in order. However, if I say this flower is "more yellow" than that, the case becomes difficult. In this case we will have to decide which is the standard yellow and arrange other flowers A,B,C,D.... in such a way that the flower closest to A is more similar to A.

Suppose our arrangement is

A B D C E ....

where A is the "yellowest" by our standard. As we go away from A to B,D,C... we perceive greater dissimilarity in colour in comparison to A. Actually the variation of colour not only involves a quantitative but also a qualitative component. But we can arrange the flowers in order of similarity with A. This device has an advantage: we can speak of the "distance" between B and A, C and A and so forth. These are in fact relations which we have converted into order in the sense of ordering the objects on the basis of magnitude.

We need not go deep into how we can measure those relations say A to B, A to C, B to C etc. But these distances can be treated as magnitudes comparable with one another. There are also examples of relational magnitudes. From points in space the relations give us distances in space.

E1

Consider the magnitudes of the same kind viz. volume arranged in order:

$a<b<c<d....$

Quantities x, y, z occupy different portions of space, each having the magnitude b. Then the statement "x, y, z have the same magnitude" and "$x = y= z$" are equivalent.

## Measurement

Numbers, as we said earlier, are not essential for measuring quantity, but they afford a sophisticated tool. What we need is a 1-1 correspondence between numbers and magnitude. A simple example is the cardinal number of a set.

1 2 3 ....
Δ ΔΔ ΔΔΔ ......

In the above natural numbers are arranged in order and the objects in classes are also placed in order of less numerous to more numerous.

One-one correspondence establishes the method of numerical measurement. We can say for example that the set ΔΔΔ has the cardinal number three.

For certain measurements, where magnitudes form a "continuum"we may have to use the real numbers.

It should not be supposed that the direct correspondence between the numbers and magnitudes is the only method of measurement. Physical laws are complicated and we may have to use functions which are not simple.

For example, the law relating to radioactive distintigration is given by

$N_t = N_0 e^{-\lambda t}$

where $N_0$ = number of atoms at time t = 0

$N_t$ = number of atoms at time t

λ = disintegration constant or decay constant which is the characteristic of the radioactive element.

A simple calculation will tell you that there is no *total disintegration*. If you put $N_t = 0$, you will require $t = \infty$. Hence we cannot take the "life" as the measure of a given quantity of radioactive substance. Physicists use a related parameter viz. *half-life.* This is the time required to reduce a given quantity to its half value.

If we let $N_t = N_0/2$ above, the equation can be written as

$T = \log_e 2 / \lambda = 0.693/\lambda$

T is called *half-period* or simply period which is inversely proportional to λ.

## Quantity and Zero

We have now to consider the commonsense zero or quantitative zero which is in fact the "zero magnitude". Many theories have been propounded by philosophers and mathematicians in respect of the zero magnitude, and some of them are briefly discussed below.

*1. Immanuel Kant (1724-1804)*

According to Kant, an intensive magnitude while retaining its kind can become zero. But though zero is a definite magnitude, a quantity whose magnitude is zero cannot exist. Thus we can speak of "zero gram", "zero centimeter" etc. but cannot say, "this is the quantity with magnitude zero gram or zero centimeter".

It may be remarked that physicists have retained this tradition. Students are asked not to forget the units of length, velocity, force etc., and even when in a certain instance the magnitude is zero, the units have to be mentioned. This is, of course, helpful when the physicist is concerned with dimensional analysis in which length (L), time (T) and mass (M) are considered basic dimensions and other quantities are represented in terms of these dimensions. For example,

| Quantity | Dimension |
|---|---|
| Area | $L^2$ |
| Volume | $L^3$ |
| Velocity | $LT^{-1}$ |
| Acceleration | $LT^{-2}$ |
| Force | $MLT^{-2}$ |

Using dimensional analysis physicists can arrive at a tentative formula relating to a physical phenomenon containing many parameters. The formula contains some constants which are determined through experiments. What is important is that even when the magnitude is zero, its units or dimensions do not vanish.

Incidentally Kant used the notion of quantitative zero to refute Mendelssohn's proof of the immortality of soul. [2]

*2. Alexius Meinong*

According to Meinong, zero is "the contradictory opposite of each magnitude of its kind". Unfortunately, the words do not convey precise meaning. In logic for example, opposite of a class C is everything which is not contained in C.

3. Zero may be defined as the least magnitude of its kind. Russell thinks that this definition merely characterizes zero whether magnitude is discrete or continuous. It cannot stand as a definition.
4. We may define zero synonymous with *nothing*, with reference to a particular magnitude. This would mean zero should not be followed by any units or dimensions. This would, however, be inconsistent with the physicists' viewpoint.
5. To avoid the conflict Russell suggest a modification of Meinong's views. Zero should be defined as the *denial of the defining concept* of a kind of magnitude; neither the denial of one kind of magnitude nor the denial of magnitudes. According to Russell, a concept which defines a type of magnitude should be assumed to define by negation, a particular magnitude of that kind viz. zero which is less than other magnitudes of that kind.

I think these contradictions can be solved by calling zero magnitude as *generic quantitative zero* which means "no magnitude". However, in a particular context we can speak of zero magnitude *of a kind.* In practice, we often use the word "zero" without context. We must remember that the controversy regarding the interpretation of quantitative zero arises because we are living in the time after the number zero was invented. A savage would have used the word "nothing" if there were no men, no sticks, no volume or whatever the kind. He might have added the *kind* in the way "no men", "no trees". For him "no" simply means an adjective showing the absence. If we introspect, we will find we, too, use the word (quantitative) zero in the generic sense almost synonymous with *nothing.*

30

# Mysticism and Non-science

## Features of Mysticism

It is curious to find that the notion of zero and nothingness exists not only in our daily life, but also in such diametrically opposite departments of knowledge; mysticism and science. What's more, this notion goes hand in hand with the substratum of positive and negative or the pairs of opposites. While this is quite patent in mysticism, scientists too encounter contrariness and relativism, though not as often. This may lead us to draw parallels between mysticism and science and try to establish a universal law encompassing opposites and nothingness. It is, therefore, necessary to understand the characteristics of both, mysticism and science and realize how they differ in respect of epistemology as well as ontology. This will help us in comparing the concept of zero, nothing and opposites used in different fields : mysticism and science. Russell eloquently describes four main characteristics of mysticisim[1]. First, insight and intuition play an important role. A mystic acquires knowledge through a unique experience which is, strictly speaking, indescribable. This knowledge comes as revelation. Although there are stages of progress involved in such disciplines as yoga and tantra the final enlightenment, liberation or superconscious experience is sudden. A belief closely associated with such insight is that reality is different from what appears to the common people. There is, therefore, the search for the Ultimate Reality. It is necessary to mention that such mystical experience is not the same as a belief in mysticism. For instance, I may believe in liberation achieved through *jñānayoga* or the knowledge of Brahman through meditation and introspection. This, however, does not make me a mystic so long as I do not *feel* Brahman. Similarly most of those who assert that the superconscious state can be gained through *rājayoga* have faith in mysticism, they are not mystics.

Second, mysticism tries to view the universe as a whole and usually posits all-pervading consciousness. This approach usually leads a mystic to reconcile the opposites, good-bad, hot-cold etc. and posit either that they are the two sides of the same coin or are illusions of the Reality. Oxymorons and contrary statements characterize those who try to describe mystical phenomena "We step and do not step into the same rivers", "Brahman exists or does not exist", "Ātman is beyond the pairs of opposites" are some examples found in mystical philosophy.

Third, there is the denial of time as reality. This stems from the perception that time is not divisible. In the Western philosophy it appears in Parmenides, Spinoza and Hegel. In the Eastern mysticism we may make a statement to the effect that "time exists and exists not" with similar statements relating to space and almost all things.

Fourth, evil is treated as nonreal. Though good and evil appear in the world, evil is illusory. This is especially necessary if we believe that God is just and good. In the Eastern philosophy, evil does not appear as a specific category to be denied. Almost anything can be denied as well as asserted.

The most important aspect of mysticism is its epistemology which is the personal experience of a mystic which cannot be verbally communicated. The literature in mysticism is usually the creation not by mystics but by those who believe in mysticism. Since the mystical experience is indescribable, even to the mystics contradictions and nothingness are *sine qua non* of the mystical idiom to be used to convey the experience to ordinary people.

## Characteristics of Science

The word "science" can be used in different senses. In the broadest sense it connotes a body of knowledge about nature through observation, experiment and logic. In English it is usually restricted to "natural science" which includes physics, chemistry and biology. Despite the wide difference in the definition of science, the following can be accepted as the features of sciences.[2]

*(1) Empirical Adequacy*

This consists of theoretical models which describes the universal phenomena with accuracy. The model usually consists of (a) an exhaustive list of rules (b) mathematical / statistical formulas correlating different events, and (c) when quantification is not possible, the relationship between the cause and effect.

In physics we can usually have mathematical models. In linguistics when treated as science, we may have to be content with a set of rules with (a few) exceptions to the rules.

A theory can be called scientific only when we can make definite predictions about the future. If the model merely describes the results already obtained it cannot be called "scientific" in the true sense.

The scientist, of course, can not expect cent per cent agreement of the observational data with the predictions of the theory since all scientific knowledge of the external world is only probabilistic. We can expect a very high probability in physics, while in case of social sciences we have to be satisfied with a moderate probability.

*(2) Abstraction*

A scientific theory sometimes introduces entities which should be treated as abstractions or convenient fiction. Points, lines, electrons and other elementary particles, electromagnetic fields, the gravitational field are abstractions in the sense they help us establish scientific or mathematical theories. The physicists is more concerned with events and their interrelations rather than the ultimate reality. We really do not know the ontological status of a point or even an electron or a proton but they can be treated as physical parameters. The scientist has to see that these entities or parameters form a consistent model. Consistency here does not imply agreement with experiments; this aspect is covered by empirical adequacy. What is implied here is internal consistency in the very apparatus we use for describing a theory.

*(3) Provisional Nature*

A scientific theory is always provisional. As the human ability of probing nature improves, the old theory may show deviations or errors. A new theory is needed to take account of the new phenomena discovered. This entails modification of the old theory which still has utility in narrower range of observation. For example, the Newtonian mechanics has been superseded by Einstein's relativity theory. Nevertheless, the older theory can be used in practice except when we deal with velocities close to the velocity of light.

Our observations relating to quantum theory and uncertainty principle which is discussed at some length in Chapter 31 is instructive. At the subatomic level the "quantum world" behaves strangely. For example, "elementary particles" have a dual nature of a particle as well as a wave. The scientists are baffled by the apparent paradox that an electron can be at two places at the same time. While this is startling because our conception of a thing at macrolevel is seriously challenged, we must remember that we do not know about the existential nature of a photon or an electron. People often try to mystify such results suggesting that human ability of understanding is limited and hence we cannot handle science beyond a certain level. Why not accept the dual nature of a single electron? Why should we treat an electron like a table or a chair? We cannot see an electron, we can only perceive its effects. The correct attitude for the physicist would be to search for a revised theory which takes into account the quantum world, retaining old theories relating to objects and waves as good approximations for the macro world.

*(4) Generalization*

As science progresses special laws are integrated into general laws. This is what Einstein calls "stratification of a scientific system"[3] For instance, the planetary behaviour can be explained with Kepler's laws, while the laws relating to falling bodies are governed by Galileo's theory. However, Newton's discovery of the law of gravitation was able to integrate both theories at a higher level.

Epistemologically, mysticism involves personal experience of an individual and it is difficult to compare such experiences undergone by several mystics. Science on the other hand is objective, its results can be tested not only by different humans but also by different instruments. Ontologically, mysticism is interested in finding the ultimate reality behind the appearances. Science can make do with entities and parameters which can be correlated consistently.

## Non-science

It is convenient to divide knowledge into two broad classes; science and non-science. This is important because the epistemology and goals of science are usually different from those of the knowledge which cannot be called science. For this the best test available is Karl Popper's criterion based on his falsificationism theory.

If a statement in principle is falsifiable, it is a scientific statement. If it is not falsifiable, it does not belong to the domain of science, it pertains to non-science.

A few illustrations will elucidate the point.

E1

(a) A person claims that she can walk on water.
This is falsifiable. In fact, such a claim was made by L.S. Rao, a haṭhayogi, in 1966, but he failed to demonstrate his putative power. Such claims are called miracles. If testable, they will belong to the province of science in as much as they can be falsified.

(b) *A* claims that she will be born a tiger after her death. This is not falsifiable and hence does not belong to the domain of science.

(c) *B* claims that he can be at two places at the same. This can be falsified and hence the statement belongs to science.

(d) *C* contends that before the universe was born there was nothing. This is not falsifiable and hence his assertion pertains to non-science.

(e) *D* claims that he is an incarnation of god Viṣṇu. Not being falsifiable this statement does not belong to science.

(f) A rājayogi claims that he reached a superconscious state in his samadhi and he is now liberated.
His claim cannot be falsified in respect of the superconscious state and also "liberation". This is the province of non-science.

(g) The void, whatever its location, is a conscious void.
This is not falsifiable and pertains to non-science.

(h) A person claims that his health has improved ever since he realized Brahman.
Insofar as his health is concerned the statement is testable, but the cause (Brahman) cannot be falsified and pertains to non-science.

(i) Śūnya and infinity are equal. If by "śūnya" and "infinity" we mean the notions in mathematics, the statement can be falsified and hence it is scientific. However, if the words are used in the mystical sense, the statement belongs to non-science.

(j) Brahman is neither void nor non-void. This is clearly a statement belonging to non-science.

# Void in Modern Physics

## Absolute Space and Time

During the last 120 years physics has totally changed our concepts about space and time. It is impossible to do justice to modern physics in one Chapter. Nevertheless, we can briefly describe these advances insofar as they are relevant to our ideas of void and nothingness.

In an earlier Chapter we mentioned that ether was regarded as superfluous. This meant electromagnetic radiation including what we call the visible light has an independent existence of its own. In other words, electric or magnetic fields exist without the help of any medium. Maxwell's equations for propagation of light have a constant "c" which is identified with the velocity of light.

In classical physics both space and time are absolute : time flows from the past to the future with a regularity that is not dependent on anything else. Though Newton had a hunch that space was not absolute, his theory implied the classical premise.

The space the classical physicists thought of was called Euclidean space of three dimensions. One of its properties is that the distance between two points P(x,y,z) and Q(a,b,c) is given by

$$d^2 = (x-a)^2+(y-b)^2+(z-c)^2$$

as we mentioned in Chapter 2. This distance or *interval* is the same or "invariant" for all observers.

Physicists usually write it in the form

(1) $ds^2 = dx^2+dy^2+dz^2$

which refers to extremely small distances : d, |x-a|, |y-b|, |z-c| This is the characteristic of the Euclidean or flat space in three dimensions.

If there are two material bodies with masses $m_1$, $m_2$ separated by distance r, the force, between them according to Newton's law is given by

$F = Gm_1m_2/r^2$

where G is called the universal gravitational constant. Of course, the force experienced by a body is the result of the forces exerted by all masses in the universe. It was believed that this gravitational force was instantaneously acting. A phrase "action at a distance" was used to denote the embarrassing phenomenon of instant action.

## Relativity Theory

All of us know the notion of relative speed. We know that the speed of a train with respect to us appears different when we are standing on the platform and when we are moving in another train. Physicists naturally believed that light would appear to have different velocities depending on who observes it. In 1887 Albert Michelson and Edword Morley to their surprise found that the velocity of light was a constant 186,000 miles per second, whether it was measured in the direction of the earth's rotation or against it. It is seldom realized that the constancy of the velocity of light or electromagnetic waves is the most important discovery which was to appear in Einstein's special relativity equations. Einstein's special relativity deals with empty space without taking into account of material in the universe.

Equation (1) of section 30.1 of the invariant interval mentioned above now becomes

(2) $ds^2 = dx^2 + dy^2 + dz^2 - c^2dt^2$

Here "dt" represents a small time interval. In order to specify an event with respect to two observers we now require four coordinates for each observer : (x,y,z,t) and (x',y',z',t'). It looks strange that an event should appear to occur at different times to different observers. This is because in equation (2) unlike (1) time is entwined with space. The invariant "ds" now contains a time element.

However, this effect is pronounced only when the relative velocity of one observer with respect to another is very large, close to c. This has some interesting consequences. For example, two events appearing simultaneous to one observer may appear to occur at different times to another observer. This entanglement of space and time was anticipated by Hermann Minkowski (1864-1909) who gave the idea of the four-dimensional space-time, three dimensions for space and one dimension for time. Einstein's equations implied that we could no more talk of space and time as two entities but simply as one complex entity, space-time.

One of the consequences of the theory is that mass (m) can be converted into energy (E) and *vice versa* by the equation

$E = mc^2$

under suitable conditions.

The difficulties of defining a void now increase manifold. Epistemologically, if we say that a large portion of space is a void, we will have to prove empirically that every part of this portion has neither a material body nor any kind of energy, a task which is impossible in practice.

Einstein's general relativity deals with the situation where masses or gravitational forces are taken into consideration. The space-time interval. ds in (2) now becomes extremely complicated involving what is called a tensor whose components depend upon mass distribution. The space described by (1) is called flat space or Minkowski space. In presence of matter this space is no more "flat" but becomes "curved"

## Quantum Theory

Max Planck, a German physicist, suggested that electromagnetic radiation is not emitted or absorbed continuously but in discrete "packets" Einstein called them "quanta". The energy (E) given out by quanta depends upon the frequency ($\nu$) of the radiation

$$E = h\nu$$

where h is a constant called *Planck's constant.* The unit of "quantum" determines the minimum energy that is absorbed or emitted. We cannot have energy of, say, half a quantum. This implies that light behaves as if it were a stream of particles.

Electromagnetic radiation has thus a dual personality: certain phenomena, say, like interference can be explained on the basis of the wave theory while some phenomena like emission and absorption need to treat light as the "packets" of energy if not as particles. Incidentally this wave packet of light is called photon.

While in classical physics atoms were considered solid and indestructible, Ernst Rutherford's experiments exploded the myth of the solid atom. Scientists began to believe that there was a nucleus consisting of protons, positively charged particles, and neutrons (electrically neutral.) Around the nucleus were orbiting electrons, negatively charged particles at high velocities, in different orbits or "shells".

In 1923 French physicist de Broglie suggested that not only light but even matter should have a dual nature of wave-particle type. This was confirmed and the phenomenon of interference could be observed in case of a stream of electrons.

To understand the phenomenon of interference, consider two waves (fig 31.1) which interact with each other. For simplicity, we may assume that their amplitudes and wavelengths are the same. The amplitude of a wave is the distance between the crest (or trough) and the mean path of its propagation. The wavelength is the distance between the two consecutive crests (or troughs). If the waves are "in phase", i.e. at any given time their crests have similar positions they tend to reinforce each other and the amplitude of the resulting wave is doubled. Since brightness is proportional to the square of amplitude, it is four times the brightness of the original wave. Fig. 31.1 A shows the interaction of the waves which are "almost" in phase. The resulting wave is the outcome of their superimpostition. If the waves are totally out of phase, i.e. the crests of one fall on the troughs of another, there is cancellation everywhere and the result is the dark band. Fig. 31.1 B shows the waves which are almost out of phase. The resulting wave appears diminished in size.

Consider the experiment shown in Fig. 31.2. D and E are two slits through which the light from source S situated along MO passes. The waves starting from D and E reach the screen at a typical point C. If MC = y, then it can be proved that the conditions for C to have maximum brightness and darkness are given by

$y = n\lambda D/d$ (Bright fringes)

$y = (n+1/2)\,\lambda\, D/d$ (Dark fringes)

$\lambda$ is the wavelength, n = 0, 1, 2, 3......

d = DE and D = OM

On the surface of the screen (perpendicular to the plane of the paper) we should have alternate bright and dark fringes. In the absence of the slits, the screen would appear the brightest at the center M and the brightness would decrease as we move away radially from the center.

A

B

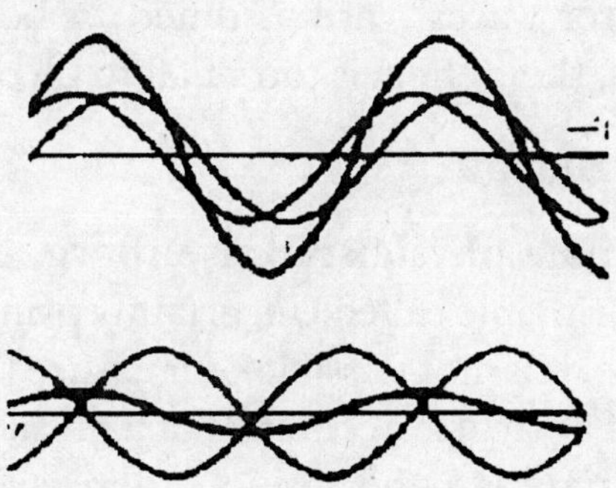

Fig. 31.1

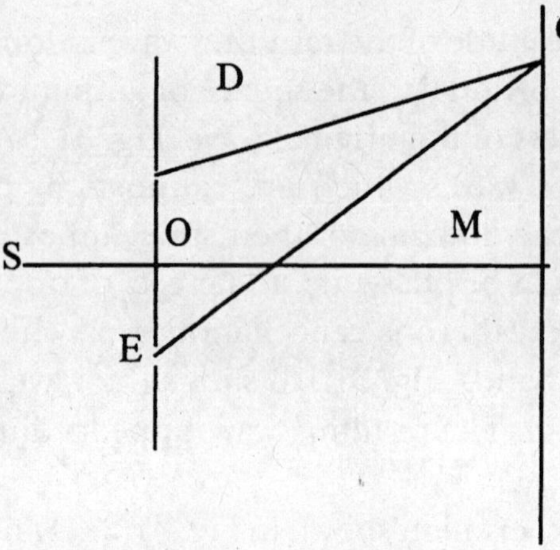


Fig. 31.2

If instead of light a beam of electrons is used, a similar pattern of interference is observed confirming de Broglie's hypothesis. However, what is most astonishing in this case is that interference occurs even when a single electron is sent from S. If a single electron behaves like a wave, it must be at D as well as E at the same time. This is really shocking to us because in the space in which we live, an object cannot be simultaneously at two places. This dual nature of particle-wave however, has significance only at the subatomic level and can be observed in case of elementary particles such as electrons and protons. At the macro level in the world which is perceptible to us, theoretically even if de Broglie's "matter waves" are assumed to be associated with moving objects, their effect is too small to be observed.

## Uncertainty Principle

In 1926 German physicist Heisenberg propounded a revolutionary principle called Uncertainty principle. According to this principle, it is not possible to measure both momentum and position of a particle accurately at a given instant. If we try to be more accurate as to the position, there will be greater error in the measurement of momentum, and *vice versa*. There is an absolute limit on these accuracies. If dx and dp represent the errors in the position and momentum, the principle says, we should always have

$dxdp \geq h/2\pi$

where *h* is the Planck's constant

What's more, this inaccuracy is not on account of human perceptive limits or the limitations of the measuring instruments, but is a natural law closely related to the quantum world in which the particles have a dual particle-wave nature.

A consequence of the dual nature of particles is that, the elementary particles are regarded as "probability waves" and their behaviour becomes a network of probabilities. Moreover, the particles cannot be divorced from the observer. Unlike the classical theory which appears valid at the macro level, the observer and the observed appear to be linked.

Another feature of the quantum world is interesting for us. To us the matter, molecules and atoms appear solid. Actually the fact is that the size of the nucleus with the revolving electrons put together is only a small fraction of the size of the atom. The electrons move at a fantastic speed of 600 miles per second, so that the atom as a whole appears solid. The uncertainty principle also means that the revolving electrons can be imagined as "probability waves". We can neither "locate" the position of the electron, nor can we even say that they are going around the nucleus. You will realize that an atom is more of a void than a plenum, from this angle. However, we do not know what lies in the space between the nucleus and the electrons. Is it really empty?

## Elementary Particles

Electrons, protons and neutrons appeared to be the only elementary particles once. Physicists today know more than 200 elementary particles and their number is increasing. The word "elementary" seems to be a travesty.

There is another aspect at the quantum level that is interesting. For almost every particle, we have an *antiparticle* of the same size but with opposite charge. An electron which is negatively charge has a positive correlate called *positron.* Under suitable conditions one can create pairs of particles and antiparticles out of energy. Conversely, these couples can be annihilated to obtain pure energy. The plethora of particles and antiparticles has upset the previous notion of the building blocks of matter for which the physicists were searching : matter can be converted into energy and *vice versa* and the plurality of "elementary units" is really baffling. Its philosophical implications will be discussed in the next chapter.

It must, however, be mentioned that most of these elementary particles are not stable and last only a fraction of a second.

In modern quantum physics the forces between elementary particles which interact are explained on the basis of exchange of other particles. These mediators are called *virtual particles* : the stronger the force between the particles, the greater is the probability of the exchange. These virtual particles exist only during the exchange period when the uncertainly principle operates. Heavy particles interact only when they are close to each other because greater energy is required to bring about the interaction.

In case of photons (the particles of light) the picture is different. Since their mass is zero, they can exchange virtual photons even when they are at a very long distance (theoretically infinite distance) from each other.

Relativity theory and quantum effects have led many physicists to think entirely in a different way. They contend that an isolated phenomenon cannot be understood unless the whole environment (theoretically the entire universe) is taken into account.

In the next Chapter we shall briefly consider this new philosophy — briefly insofar as it concerns void and nothingness.

You will find that "void" has now become an elusive concept. What we call void usually has electomagnetic fields or energy — the energy may get converted into a pair of a particle and an antiparticle.

# 32

# Science and Mysticism

## Introduction

In recent years there have been attempts to reconcile the Eastern mysticism and modern science. Broadly, there are two groups who have contributed to this process. The first group consists of the Indian intellectuals who revere their ancient culture to such an extent that they deify their ancestors. Using the maxim that the Vedas and the terse Upaniṣadic sentences need to be "properly interpreted" they have come to the conclusion that the Vedic society was not only advanced in philosophy and literature but also in science and technology. If these interpreters are to be believed, the Vedic society knew the structure of atoms, and discovered antimatter and black holes.[1] Their scientists could construct airplanes and advanced weapons, and knew the difference between the Euclidean geometry and Riemannian geometry and possibly were familiar with Einstein's theory of relativity.

The second group consists of the Western intellectuals, many of them scientists, who, shocked and puzzled by revolutionary theories, especially the relativity and quantum theories, have tried to find a solution in Eastern mysticism.

They point out parallels between the Eastern mysticism and modern science. Overwhelmed by the apparent parallels, scientists have often lost sight of the epistemology involved in mysticism and science. Undoubtedly there are similarities but these similarities also exist between ancient Western philosophy and modern science. On the other hand there are Eastern schools of philosophy who do not agree with the dominant school of monism and even differ from the teachings of the Vedas.

We cannot describe in detail what these people think about the link between mysticism and science. We shall briefly deal with those topics which are relevant to śūnya, space, void, and try to appraise the theories related to them.

## The Big Bang Theory

The big bang theory in astrophysics maintains that the universe was infinitesimally small and infinitely dense about 10-15 billion years ago. The theory implies that space, time and the universe can be supposed to have begun at that instant. The theory is based on Edwin Hubble's discovery of the expanding universe. By extrapolation "back in time" scientists have determined the instant when the universe was almost a point of infinite density. Not every scientist accepts this theory. Its serious fault is extrapolation over 10-15 billion years, which gives a mathematical "zero space": from the standpoint of physics, this appears to be a dubious epistemology.

What is more astonishing is that some Indians claim that the big bang theory was known to the Vedic civilization. In his book *Vedanteel Vidnyan,* ("The Vedic Science") Dhananjay Deshpande interprets the Nāsadīya Sūkta which we mentioned in Chapter 16. According to him the Sukta embodies the big bang theory. His interpretation is based on the following arguments.

1. There was neither existence nor non-existence then (RV 10-129-1). This verse clearly suggests the description of the stage before the universe was born.
2. "One breathed without air with its own vibrations"(RV 10-129-2). Deshpande finds breathing without air quite significant since it denotes the state when the universe,

> and hence the air, did not exist. The vibration without air is interpreted as the appropriate description of the cause of the big bang, because without vibration there cannot be an explosion.

There are also other parallels between the Sūkta and the big bang theory. It must however, be mentioned that this Creation Hymn has been interpreted in several ways. The poetry of the distant past appears obscure and interpretation affords us an opportunity to prove almost anything.

The Creation Hymn is undoubtedly profound philosophically, but there is no reason to interpret it as a description of a scientific theory. There is neither internal (intra-Vedas) not external evidence to suggest that the Vedic society was advanced in science or technology. Nevertheless one does not deny the acuity of the mind which describes the prenatal stage as "neither existence nor non-existence". If the Sūkta really refers to the creation of the universe, the hymn has a rare philosophical insight.

## Zero and the Vedas

In Chapter 1 we mentioned that the earliest inscription involving zero is dated 595 CE. It has been claimed by some Indians that the Vedic society was conversant with zero. The most intriguing work is *Vedic Mathematics* by Jagadguru Swāmī Śrī Bhāratī Kṛṣṇa Tīrthajī Mahārāj (1884-1960) who held the title of Śaṅkarācārya of Goavardhana Maṭha, Puri.

The book explains some simple methods of calculations in various areas of mathematics; algebra, geometry and calculus. The book uses zero, implying that the number was known to the Vedic Indians. According to the author, it is based on an appendix (*pariśiṣṭa*) to the Atharvaveda. However, one of his disciples Manjula Trivedi agrees that the sūtras in the book are not in the present recension of the Atharvaveda. According to her the swami reconstructed the formulas on the basis of intuitive revelation from the material scattered here and there in the

Atharvaveda. The swami is believed to have reconstructed the formulas after assiduous research and "tapas" (austerity) for about eight years in the forest surrounding Sringeri. The book does not contain a systematic development of advanced mathematics, but a few shortcuts based on terse sutras are considered. Was his mystical experience responsible for his remarkable feat? We do not know. Two things need to be mentioned. First the swami was a brilliant mathematician and held a masters degree in mathematics from the American College of Sciences, Rochester, New York. Second, there is no external evidence to suggest that Vedic society had the notion of mathematical zero and possessed knowledge of advanced mathematics. In all probability, the formulas were his own creation for which he did not want to take credit.

Such puzzling disclaimers do take place. For example, the great mathematician Srinivas Ramanujan often claimed that the goddess of Namakkal appeared in his dreams and provided him mathematical formulas which he wrote down and verified after he woke in the morning.[2]

## Relativism and Relativity

In Chapter 6 we mentioned anekantavāda and syādavāda which are based on relativism (also called relativity) that have roots in different viewpoints. This is a sound philosophy based on common sense. It also incorporates the principle that opposites appear to coexist in almost every phenomenon. However, some thinkers have tried to hint that these doctrines anticipate Einstein's theory of relativity and also matter-wave duality.

Relativity theory, special or general, does not advocate general relativism. It confines itself to space, time and events. Further, it is based on the premise that the velocity of light is a universal constant *c* - there is nothing relative about c.

Similarly, the uncertainty principle and matter-wave duality applies to the quantum world. What's more, even the uncertainty principle can be quantified. Our problems of the "uncertainty" appear on account of our present state of knowledge of physics. What's important to remember is that both relativity and uncertainty principle relate to definite problems in physics. They do not suggest that "everything is relative" or "nothing is certain". There is no reason to believe that the relativism of ancient India has anything to do with these principles in physics.

## Void and Matter

According to modern physics, there is no real void or emptiness. A. W. Thirring points out, "the field exists always and everywhere; it can never be removed. It is the carrier of all material phenomena. It is the 'void' out of which the proton creates the pi-mesons. Being and fading of particles are merely forms of motion of the field."[3]

Capra argues that since the vacuum is not empty but can create unlimited number of particles which may come into existence and then vanish, it has close parallel to the void of the mysticism of the East - it is a living void. It is what the Indian monists called Brahman and what the Chinese called ch'i.

In other words, according to Capra what the modern scientists call the quantum field, the Eastern mystics called the One.

Capra is right in saying that both the modern physics and the Eastern mysticism contemplate the one Ultimate Reality behind all plurality. However, this parallel is only illusory. Eastern mystics and philosophers have always maintained that the Ultimate Reality is indescribable. The void which Capra mentions is the void of the phenomenal level. The mystics treat "void" merely as a metaphor. According to Dattātreya. "If the Self is devoid of essence and lack of essence, if it is without void and nonvoid, if there is one indivisible all-comprehensive Absolute, how can there be a first, how can there be a last? (AG 6-6)

Self, Brahman or the One is neither void nor nonvoid. How can It be a quantum field? When Chang Tsai says:

"When one knows that Great void is full of ch'i, one realizes there is no such thing as nothingness"[4]

We can not treat Great void as the void of physics and ch'i as a field. Mystics tell us again and again that the One is ineffable and their expression should not be taken literally.

## Space-Time

Capra maintains that the relativity theory unites space and time into one reality "Relativity theory is crucial for the description of the world, and in the relativistic framework the classical concepts are transcended by going to a higher dimension, the four dimensional space-time".

Two arguments can be put forward to counter the concept of space-time unity. First, when we say that "time is the fourth dimension" or that "space is curved in the presence of matter" we really do not know what we are saying. We are only trying to interpret the equations involving space and time. The "fourth dimension" and "the curved surface" can be treated as mere metaphors extended from the three dimensional world. What's more, even in the simplest expression of the flat space,

$ds^2 = ds^2+dy^2+dz^2-c^2dt^2$

(x,y,z) and t do not appear symmetrically. Physicists often describe a system of n particles as a *function-space* of many dimensions. The word "dimension" is used by them for convenience to describe a parameter. The word "space" in such cases becomes a "metaphor". It might be argued that time like space is "relative". There is one time that does not change: we can completely describe the events in the universe with respect to a given observer. The clock stationary with respect to this observer does not show any ambiguities, nor does it have any similarities with space coordinates.

In support of his space-time unity, Capra quotes Lāmā Govindā.

"An experience of higher dimensionality is achieved by integration of experiences of different centers and levels of consciousness. Hence the indescribability of certain experience of meditation on the plane of three dimensional consciousness and within a system of logic which reduces the possibilities of expression by imposing further limits upon the process of thinking."[5]

The world of relativity and that of Lāmā Govindā are incomparable. The former is objective and can observed and measured by all scientists. The relativistic equations are not personal experiences, they have objective implications which do not vary from person to person. Time may be different for different observers who are watching the same event - the relativity equations are not. Lāmā Govindā is trying to describe his personal experience as best he can. His words can be interpreted in scores of ways. If Lāmā Govindā could express his personal mystical experience with precision and without ambiguity he would cease to be a mystic and his statement would be a scientific fact which can be verified by anyone.

Commenting on Govindā's expression Capra says, "when the mystics try to express this experience in words, they are faced with the same problems as the physicists trying to interpret the multidimensional reality of relativistic physics".[6]

There is a fundamental differences between a mystical dilemma and the physicist's embarrassment. When the physicist encounters a phenomenon that does not conform to the classical concept, he is confused, but comes out with solutions such as:

"An electron has a dual nature of particle and wave"

"Energy and matter can be converted into each other"

These are the discoveries that confused the physicist. But the dual nature can be described. We find the dual nature strange because we still do not know the metaphysical status of the electron - we know only its behaviour. In fact, it is doubtful if we can ever find the "ultimate reality" of the electron. For that, we will have to descend to the subatomic level individually, losing in that process our sense of perception. We can only observe and correlate events. We cannot know the ultimate existential status of an entity though for the purpose of physics we may assign it a generic name "electron", "proton", "cat", "man", etc. on the basis of its general properties.

## The Quantum World

The *matter waves* have indeed confused the physicists because they were accustomed to assuming the premise: a thing can only be at one place at a given moment. Though the behaviour of the subatomic particles shockingly violates this principle, we should treat this as a problem in physics and not mysticism. Our perception of a "thing" is based on a solid object which can be identified by human senses. Once we know that at the quantum level a particle behaves also like a wave we should revise our concept of the "thing" at the micro level.

We recall the experiment of interference in Chapter 31. Our dilemma there was how an electron or a proton can be at once at the slits A and B. But knowing that an electron is also a wave, the paradox disappears. This puzzle appears real only to the generation of physicists who have been trained to think at the macro level or according to the classical physics. If an electron can be a wave, there is no reason why it cannot be at A and B simultaneously. The problem with most of us is that while we accept the laws at the quantum level we cannot stop thinking in terms of things or objects which appear to us at the macro level. We unconsciously try to find "one identity" of the electron and also try to determine the real nature or "shape" of the electron. We seldom realize that we cannot understand the existential status of certain entities because of the limitations of our perceptive power. I repeat that we can at best find the correlation between several events, we can never find the ultimate "stuff" of either matter or energy.

In support of his parallels between mysticism and modern science, Capra furnishes the following example.

"Where there is duality, as it were, there one sees another;

there one smells another... But where every thing has become just one's own self, then whereby and whom one would see? Then whereby and whom one would smell then whereby and whom one would taste?"[7]

Two observations are necessary here. First, the quotation reflects the views of the *advaitin* who believes in the single Ultimate Reality which is not the world we find either at the quantum level or at the grosser level. It is unfortunate that we select only one level viz. the subatomic level for drawing parallels with mysticism. Second, those who believe in advaita are not necessarily mystics who experience Brahman. The Majority are intellectuals to whom monism appears a solution that contains symmetry and equality.

It is also necessary to point out that Heisenberg's principle though it involves uncertainty, has been expressed as inequality. It is also true that when we speak of the observer being essentially involved in a quantum phenomenon, we do not mean subjectivism. It is doubtful that the quantum phenomena depends on the nature of the observer or his emotional or intellectual qualities or his convictions.

It also appears that those who highlight the parallel between the quantum world and mysticism are selective. For the mystic, chronology and dimensions mean nothing. He would certainly be surprised that his experience is being compared with the physical phenomena restricted to a certain range of grossness. The mystic as well as the monist does not stop at the quantum level. Can the scientist say what lies below the quantum level? Or can he speak about the phenomena which are beyond the reach of the telescopes developed by humans? The mystic believes that his knowledge of enlightenment encompasses everything that exists, has existed and will exist.

The above arguments do not imply any bias against mystical experiences or Capra's intellectual prowess. Fritjof Capra is a theoretical physicist who has done research in high energy particles in European and American universities. He is also a renowned author of many books. His works, *The Tao of Physics*, *The Turning Point* and *The Hidden Connections* are thought-provoking. He has a holistic approach to the universe and the environment, which stresses the importance of a system as against its constituents. It incorporates all branches of science. It is even possible that he was inspired by the Eastern mysticism. However, we must be circumspect about drawing parallels between mysticism and science, always remembering that the mystic's experiences are unique, personal and indescribable. Further, we cannot be selective and ignore those experiences which are totally inconsistent with science as we know it today.

# Chapter Notes

(Authors cited below are listed in the Bibliography)

## Introduction

*General*

The word *śūnya* is derived from *śūna* which has the root *svi.* The root means "to swell" with the connotation of morbid enlargement. However, it has acquired several meanings such as void, empty, absence and so on. Śūnya has scores of names having different meanings: *randhra, tuccha, rikta* and *kṣudra* indicate nothingness; *ākāśa, antarikṣa, kha, gagana, jaladhara-patha, diva, vyoma* mean infinite expanse of sky; *pūrṇa* indicates fullness; *ananta* means infinite; *balam* and *dravinam* connote strength and force, *bindu* means a point; *chidra* is a hole *asat* means nonexistent, *nagna* implies nude and so on. All these words are used in *Bhūtasankhyā* (word-numbers) for number zero (Chapter 1)

### 1. Zero In Arithmetic

1. An exhaustive list of words used in *Bhūtasankhyā* will be found in K.V. Sharma's paper "Word and Alphabetic Numerical Systems in India", *The Concept of Śūnya* (2003)
2. Ibid., p. 39
3. Ibid., pp.47-48
4. See Ajay Mitra Shastri's "Brāhmī Numerals and Decimal Notation: Nature and Evolution", *The Concepts of Śūnya* p. 73

5. Sreeramula Rajeswara Sarma has discussed this subject at length in his "Śūnya in Piṅgala's Chandaḥsūtra", *The Concept of Śūnya.* See also *General* notes below.
6. See A.M. Shastri's "Brāhmī Numerals and Decimal Notation: Nature and Evolution" *The Concept of Śūnya,* p. 75
7. Ibid, p.75
8. For other inscriptions, see B.N. Mukharjee, "Kharoshṭī Numerals and Early Use of Decimal Notation in Indian Epigraphs", *The Concepts of Śūnya.*
9. See his paper "Zero and the Symbol for Zero in Early Sexagesimal and Decimal Place-Value Systems", *The Concepts of Śūnya.*
10. See *General* notes below.

*General*

**A. Zero in Piṅgala's Chandaḥsūtra**

Piṅgala (ca 400-200 BCE) mentions śūnya and its symbol in *Chandaḥsūtra* in connection with verse and its meters. Sanskrit meters are based on long (*guru*) and short (*laghu*) syllables. *Pratyayas* is a topic which deals with the combinations which give rise to different meters. One of these is related to zero and is called *saṃkhyā.* Piṅgala is concerned with *saṃavṛttas* or meters in which the feet of the verse are identical. Given that a meter consists of *n* syllables, he tries different combinations or arrangements to find out how many possible varieties we can have.

Suppose we are given a meter consisting of 6 syllables in a foot (Gāyatrī, a well-known meter, exemplifies this situation). We know that if there are six places and in each place we can place either a laghu (l) or a guru (g), the number of combinations is $2^6$ i.e. we can theoretically have 64 distinct meters.

Piṅgala arrives at the same answer using his own method which is briefly described below.

| | Operation | (i) | (ii) | (iii) |
|---|---|---|---|---|
| 1. | Write the number of syllables | 6 | | stop |
| 2. | Halve 6 | 3 | 2 | $(2^2\,2)^2$ |
| 3. | 3 cannot be halved. Subtract 1. | 2 | 0 | $2^2\,2$ |
| 4. | Halve 2 | 1 | 2 | $2^2$ |
| 5. | 1 cannot be halved. Subtract 1. | 0 | 0 | 1.2 |
| | | Stop | | Start |

In this case the number is 6(col i). Halve it. Write the quotient (3) below it. Write 2 against it (col ii) because division is possible. The new number 3 again should be halved. Since this is not possible, subtract 1 and write the answer (2) below. Since division was not possible, write zero (śūnya) against 2 (col ii) Repeat the process. Since 2 can be halved, the answer 1 is to be written below it. Against it write 2 because division was possible. You cannot halve 1, hence subtract 1 to get 0 against which you will write 0 because division was not possible. You have to stop when you reach zero in col (i).

Now the process restarts from bottom to top. Against zero in col (ii) write 1 multiplied by 2 in col (iii) Go upwards using the rule to fill col (iii): for nonzero values in col (ii) square the number in the previous row and column (iii); for zero in col (ii) multiply by two the number in the previous row, col (iii). Repeat the procedure till you reach the second row. In the present case the answer is $(2^2 2)^2$ which is the same as $2^6$.

The important conclusion we can draw is that śūnya qua symbol was known to the Indians before the common era began.

Contrary to what S.R. Sarma contends in "Śūnya in Piṅgala's *Chandaḥsūtra*", *The Concept of Śūnya* (2003), Piṅgala's method is not easy. The modern formula ($2^n$) for the number of combinations appears much simpler.

It is also contended that 0 implies absence of operation and is similar to Pāṇini's *lopa.* Quoting Joseph Needham, Sarma also maintains that the existence of the symbol for zero indicates that the place-value system prevailed at that time. However, there does not seem to be sufficient evidence to substantiate the last two claims. Nevertheless, one would say that Piṅgala's system resembles the flow charts used in computer science.

## B. Pāṇinian Zero

Pāṇini is one of the greatest grammarians the world has produced. The technique of "zeroing" (*lopa*) which he employs in his *Aṣṭādhyāyī* uses abstraction in the same way as modern scientists use. Actually he uses the technique at three different levels.

The first *lopa* is purely linguistic. For example, what is termed "zero-grade form" in linguistics is formed by dropping the vowel *e*. Thus in case of the following root

yeug (to join) → yug *cf* yuga

This is governed by Pāṇini's sūtra (1.1.60) *adarśanam lopaḥ* or "non-appearance is *lopa*".

M.D. Pandit in his paper "Reflections on Pāṇinian Zero" *The Concept of Śūnya* discusses the subject at length. Consider two roots *khād* and *ad* (second conjugation) both connoting "to eat". According to Pāṇini the present third person singular appears as

(i) khād+śap+ti
= khād+ta+ti
=khādati

(ii) ad+ti
=ad+śap+ti
=at+ti
=atti

(*śap* disappears according to a specific rule)

You will find that unlike in (i) *a* does not appear in (ii) or *a* is "zeroed". Instead of taking (i) and (ii) as different "types" Pāṇini used the maximal situation to create a single formula in which *a* appears, but is zeroed in (ii)

Thus khādati = khād+a+ti

while atti = ad+0+ti

Pandit also likens the process with a peculiar method used in factorization. For example, $x^4+4$ cannot be factorized in this form. We add and subtract $4x^2$ to get

$x^4+4$

$=x^4+4x^2+4-4x^2$

$=(x^2+2)^2-4x^2$

$=(x^2+2+2x)(x^2+2-2x)$

In the present case, to bring *atti* to the level of *khādati* we add and subtract *a* in

atti = ad+a+ti-a

The second and third zeroing is purely technical. The second use involves what Pāṇini calls *It-Saṃjñā* (*It* appellation). "It" is the name of the sound or group of sounds which is defined as such in his sūtras 1.3.2 to 1.3.8. The sūtra immediately following these "It" sūtras explains the *raison d'etre* of "It": *tasyo lopaḥ* which means that "It" sound so defined in the seven sūtras becomes zero.

For example, when applied to the termination *ṣyañ* in sūtra 4.1.78, *ṣ* and *ñ* are successively elided, and we get *ya* which remains unchanged since none of the "It" sūtras affect it.

The third method of zeroing is concerned with *anuvṛtti* which roughly means "pursuing" or "carrying over". This method applies to the very apparatus of the sūtras in Pāṇini's Aṣṭādhyāyī: it pertains to their arrangement and interpretation, and employs the principle of economy. The technique is also known as *alpākṣaratva* or "having fewer letters"

The first of the *It* sūtra is *upadeśe ac anunāsika it.* The subsequent sūtras do not have the words *upadeśe it,* but in the second, third and the fourth these are to be added. In other words there is an implied "ditto" (*anuvṛtti*) of *upadeśe it.* We may say that they are "zeroed". Similarly the fifth sūtra requires anuvṛtti of *upadeśe it* and also that of *ādiḥ* from the fourth sūtra. In the sixth and seventh, four terms are zeroed; *upadeśe it, ādiḥ* and *pratyayasya* (from fifth sūtra). To give one illustration, the second *It* sūtra is *halantyam* which will have to be read as *upadeśe halantyam it* in which the zeroed elements *upadeśe* and *it* are reinstated.

The economy brought about by this technique can be appreciated from the following example: the anuvṛtti of *dhātoḥ* in sūtra 3.1.91 is applicable to a whole *adhyāya* (3rd) and the anuvṛtti of the word *prātipadikāt* of sūtra 4.1.1 covers no less than 1990 sūtras.

You will find a detailed technical discussion on Pāṇini's techniques in Pandit's paper cited above.

A similar process of zeroing the ditto is found in *padapāṭha* of the Rigveda. The padapāṭha is obtained from the original *saṃhitāpāṭha* by rearrangement of the words and is memorized by some people. This is a mnemonic device to countercheck that the original samhitāpāṭha is not distorted. Those who constructed padapāṭha were called *padapāṭhakāras* who faced the problem of re-writing certain verses which were repeated. As a time-saving device, they used a technique called *galita* or *galanta* ("dropped down"). Instead of rewriting the repeated portion, the zero sign or the word "galita" was written at the appropriate place. Of course, when someone wanted the correct form one had to reinstate the portion that was zeroed.

You can find many parallels closely resembling Pāṇinian zeros in other fields.

In mathematics the equation

$x^2+y^2+z^2 = 49$

represents a sphere with center at the origin (0,0,0) and radius 7. Let $z = 0$. We get

$x^2+y^2 = 49$

This is the equation of the Great Circle or the section of the sphere made by the horizontal plane $z=0$ passing through the origin. The second equation

(1) *per se* represents any circle with center at the origin and radius 7.

(2) when added to $z=0$, represents the Great Circle mentioned above.

(3) coupled with $z = a$, represents a similar circle on a plane $z = a$ with the origin (0,0,a) and radius 7.

(4) coupled with $ax+by+cz = d$, which is a plane whose orientation depends on constants *a,b,c* and *d,* represents a circle of the same radius in this plane.

Depending upon the context, (i) the "zeroed" z would have to be reinstated if you want a sphere or (ii) the equation of the plane will have to be added to get the equation of the circle in a plane.

A case similar to Pāṇini's third zero effecting economy appears in case of legal language. Those who are familiar with several legal Acts will recall that a certain section, say, *A* is applicable to cases b,c,d, etc. In the list b,c,d, *A is* not repeated. Economy is also achieved by using the clauses "unless otherwise stated", "subject to the conditions" or "provisos". Depending on the context the "zeroed" clauses have to be assumed to exist though they are not repeated.

Another parallel from the theory of relativity may be mentioned. In the *general theory,* in the presence of matter, a space-time interval ds between two very close events is represented by

$ds^2 = dx^2+dy^2+dz^2-c^2dt^2+X$.... (1)

The events are separated by dx, dy, dz (distance coordinates) and dt (time coordinate), and c is the velocity of light which is constant for all observers. According to Einstein's theory "ds" is invariant or the same for all observers. X is a group of terms involving dx,dy,dz and dt. The above space-time is called "curved". When there is no presence of matter, X can be zeroed, and we get a "flat" space-time

$ds^2= dx^2+dy^2+dz^2-c^2dt^2$...... (2)

in which $ds^2$ is similar to the distance $ds^2= dx^2+dy^2+dz^2$ between two points separated by dx,dy,dz in the three dimensional Euclidean space. Equation (2) is the case of special relativity and the space-time is also called Euclidean.

Relativity can be taught in two ways: (1) the special theory (equation 1) is introduced first to the beginners, while the general theory is taught later only to advanced students (2) The general theory (equation 1) is introduced at the outset. Equation 2 is subsequently derived by zeroing X in equation 1. When the first method is used, a student often gets some misconceptions which can be avoided if we use the second method, in which we start with the maximal situation and then shift to the less complicated conditions by zeroing X. This is comparable with the Pāṇinian approach of *lopa.*

## C. Śūnya-gaṇita

It is interesting to see how the concept of zero in arithmetic was handled by the earlier Indian mathematicians.

Brahmagupta's discussion of *śūnya-gaṇita* (mathematics of zero) in his *Brāhmasphuṭa-Siddhānta* (7th century CE) shows his clear understanding of positive numbers (p), negative numbers (n) and their connection with zero.

A few formulas in modern notations may be mentioned.

p+0=p, n+0=n, p+(-p)=0 and 0+0=0

p-0=p, n-0=n, 0-0=0

0xn=0, 0xp=0,0x0=0

He was wrong in assuming 0/0=0. He calls p/0 or n/o as *taccheda*

Śrīdhara's *Triśatikā* (ca 750 CE) correctly mentions the commutative property ax0=0=0xa

Mahāvīra (9th century CE) correctly mentions the additive and multiplicative properties of zero in *Gaṇitasaṅgraha* but gives a wrong formula x/0=x

Śrīpati (11th century CE) also correctly expressed addition and multiplication by zero and even considered powers of zero: $0^2=0, 0^3=0$ and so on. Unfortunately his perception of division by zero was wrong. He thought that x/0 = 0 and 0/0=0

However, in his later astronomical work Siddhānta-Śekhara he revised his opinion. He writes x/0 = *khahara.*

This last term has been used by several mathematicians subsequently.

Bhāskara II (ca 12th century CE) stated the same rule. He had a deeper insight and thought that khahara was infinity (*ananta rāśih*). He even maintained in his *Bījagaṇita* (Algebra) that

khahara ± x = khahara

where x is any finite number. In modern language this would appear as $\infty \pm x = \infty$

However, Bhāskara also stated a rule which was an exception to

ax0=0. He thought that (ax0)/0 = a. In effect, he was using the law of cancellation ay/y = a which, we know, is not valid when y = 0.

Kṛṣṇa (ca 1600 CE) wrote a commentary on Bhāskara's *Bījagaṇita* in which he summarizes the views of Indian mathematicians. Zero according to him is neither positive nor negative. He also explains why x/0 or khahara is infinite (*ananta*). His argument is the same as was explained in chapter 1. He refuted the contention of another mathematician Ganesa (ca 1560 CE) that there are different khaharas such as 4/0 or 8/0. Thus according to him x/0 = y/0. His empirical "proof" relating to the shadow of a gnomon will be found in R.C. Gupta's "Zero in the Mathematical System of India", *The Concept of Śūnya (2003)*.

**2. Commonsense Zero and Relative Zero.**

1. See Cohen (1969)

**3. The Null Class**

1. See Cohen (1969), p.2

**4. The Void and Science**

1. Russell (1999), p. 86
2. Quoted in Russell (1999), p.87
3. Russell (1999), p. 87

**5. The Void in Darśanas**

1. The details of these divisions will be found in Tigunait (1983), chapter 3.

**7. Zero and the Grammar of Numerals**

1. See Clawson (2004), chapter 5, for a detailed discussion on different systems.

**8. The Variable Zero**

1. Modern mathematicians use the term series for summations such as $x_1+x_2+....x_n...$ However, I have retained the old word since it is extermely convenient and because we shall not encounter summations.
2. See, for example, Russell (1993), p.119.

**10. The Commonsense Zero**

1. Russell (1993), p. 27
2. *American Journal of Mathematics*, Oct 1902, quoted in Russell (1992), p.119

**11. The Natural Numbers Without Zero**

1. The proofs of the results involve the use of Recursion Theorems which have been omitted here. See Cohen (1969), pp. 19-20

**16 Superconsciousness Beyond Void**

1. Swahananda (1956), p.68
2. Aurobindo ( 1970 ), pp. 89.90
3. Ibid. p. 143
4. These different states are described in the *Māṇḍukya* ( 2 - 7 )
5. Śaṅkara on the *Māṇḍukya* . See Gambhirananda ( 2000 ), p.32
6. Om or Aum is sometimes believed to have 3 1/2 mātrās, The last half mātrā is not audible
7. See, for example, Deussen (1980), p.922
8. See, O'Flaherty (2000), p.23. Other things related to "Creation " will be found in pp. 29-40. For other interpretations, see Burde (2004), chapter 6 and 15.
9. Sarvananda ( - ), p. 138

10-11. Ibid. p.138

12. Aurobindo ( 1970 ), pp. 26-27
13. Ibid.pp. 28-29

**17. Buddhism and Śūnyavāda**

1. Smith (1991), p.109
2. Tigunait (1983), p.52
3. Burtt, *Teachings*. Quoted in Smith (1986), pp.11.3-11.4. The dialogue is not verbatim.

## *General*

The concept of Śūnyatā has several facets and can be discussed on different planes. Nāgārjuna contemplated three motivational contexts in respect of love and compassion: (i) love and compassion that emerges from the similarity between one's self and other selves (*sattva-ālambana*) (ii) that which is motivated by similarity of psychophysical elements *(skandhas)* that constitute human existence (*dharma-ālambana*) (iii) absence of motivational context. The first context holds good for common people, the second is relevant in case of the spiritually advanced such as the *Bodhisattva* ("threshold Buddhas") The third or the absence of motivation is the characteristic of the Buddhas who have a true insight of ultimate emptiness or *Śūnyatā*:

To understand the concept of śūnyatā it is necessary to know about the dual negation in Buddhism. First, the self was negated (*anātman*) because a human being is a mere aggregate of several components - ātman is a mere name. Mahāyāna introduced the second negation and repudiated even the existence of psychophysical elements. The first insight is called *dharma-svabhāva* and the second *dharma-niḥsvabhāva.* The second insight leads to the Buddha's non-motivational love and compassion; and is called *dharma-śunyatā.*

The concept of *śūnyatā* in logic is quite interesting. In the western logic the three important laws are the law of identity, the law of the excluded middle and the law of contradiction. These laws appear to be violated in the dialectics of Mādhyamika. Nāgārjuna has addressed this problem to resolve the apparent contradiction.

When we light a candle, darkness to some extent disappears. This leads to some logical contradictions. Light and darkness have their self-identity (*svabhāva*). Their opposite identities should preclude them to come together. Nevertheless we find the phenomenon of their juxtaposition or interpenetration. Nāgārjuna suggested that the concept of self-identity should be replaced by functional interdependence (*parasparāpekṣatā*): the two contrary entities are simultaneously identical and different i.e. *niḥsvabhāva* which implies śūnyatā. According to Ichimura (2001) p. 242, in the dialectical context we have to accept two principles. First, (1) mutual accommodation (interpenetration of light and darkness) is possible in the dialectical context: light and darkness are simultaneously identical and different (2) such "ultimate factual reference ought to be regarded as *dual natured* which transcends logical and linguistic convention." In fact the advocates of this view feel that when we go from the plane of logic to the dialectical level, the conventional logic breaks down.

In a wider sense Buddhist doctrine accepts the system of four-fold truth-value, called *catuṣkoṭi*:

Something is A

Something is not A

Something is both A and not A

Something is neither A nor not A

However, the last two statements are considered inapplicable at the logico-linguistic level.

Those scientists who tend to mystify the world of quantum mechanics seem to find a solution in *catuṣkoṭi*. However, whether Nāgārjuna would have concurred with their views is debatable. The scientists who study quantum mechanics and relativity theory themselves use the physical and mathematical apparatus (for observation) which does not transcend the world of logic or linguistics.

**18. Fullness in Emptiness**

1. Krishnamurti (1985), p.12.
2. Osho (2003), p.67
3. Ibid., p. 70

4. Rajaneesh (1979), p.109

**19. Taoism and Zen**

1. Smith (1991), p.198
2. Capra (1993), p.120
3. Smith (1991), p.129
4. These poems will be found in Smith (1991), p.129
5. Smith (1991), p.137
6. Ibid. p. 137
7. Ibid. p. 139

**20. Śūnya and Void In Tantra**

1. Woodroffe (1997), p.429

*General*

## A. Tantra

Tantra literature is replete with innumerable interpretations of śūnya. Since śunya can mean "nothing" on the one hand and "infinite" on the other, the paradox lends itself to a plethora of concepts.

According to one tradition there are six śūnyas, but they are to be rejected and the seventh śūnya is to be accepted. The first six are relative, the seventh is absolute, the Supreme Reality.

*Mahānaya Prakāśa* conceives śūnya as the conscious void, it is not negation or *abhāva* of Vaiśeṣika. Hence though void it should be regarded as *aśūnya* (nonzero).

According to one text, the source of the universe is *a* which is precisely śūnya, but appears as the first letter (akāra) in Sanskrit alphabet. At the same time the very śūnya represents the dissolution of the universe.

According to Śākta tradition the term śūnya is used to indicate the subtle aspect of Śakti, Supreme Mother. In *Devī Upaniṣad* when Mother is asked who she is she replies that she is both void and nonvoid. In *Sāradātilaka* Rāghava Bhaṭṭa describes Goddess as without form and subtle. *Empty* in this connection means that she is unmanifested, as she is united with Śiva.

In *Devyatharvaśīrṣa* Goddess is described as "supraconscious in the knowledge and energy of emptiness in the voids".

Another text *Mahākālasamḥitā* says that śūnya is Brahmāṇḍa (the universe) and also mentions "fifty śūnyas and five voids" as the abode of Goddess Tārā. *Mahānirvāṇa Tantra* describes goddess Kālī as the devourer of Time which she reduces to Śūnya. The fifty śūnyas mentioned above are interpreted as fifty letters of the alphabet and five voids (śūnya) as five elements (mahābhūtas) destroyed by Goddess.

Goddess Śrī is usually associated with creative cosmic energy while Kāli and Tārā symbolize destruction. In consonance with their nature they can be associated with śūnya in its creative aspect (potential of infinity) or the aspect of annihilation.

In a nutshell, tantra regards śūnya as a mystical entity in which extreme opposites merge.

## B. Śūnya and Temples

The fact that the bindu or śūnya is a potential creator has ramifications in several areas of religion and mysticism.

The advaita Vedānta believes in monism or in all - pervading Brahman. The practice of polytheism is usually reconciled with this philosophy by positing that though Brahman is devoid of parts (*niṣkala*), formless (*nirākāra*), and *nirguṇa* (without attributes), at a certain level he appears as Iśvara. The images of different gods are nothing but illusory manifestations of Brahman. Thus the *liṅga* symbolizes Śiva or Brahman while images (*pratimá*) of gods represent the manifestations of Brahman on a lower plane.

The nucleus of the sanctum (*garbhagṛha*) of a temple is treated as the zero-point. It is from this *śūnya* that all emanations arise. It is interesting to observe that the liṅga symbolizing the Supreme Śiva (Brahman) occupies this *śūnya-bindu* or the center of the *garbhagṛha.* This potential infinity or the center is kept vacant if the liṅga is absent. Other icons are placed at a distance from the center. The highest point (*śikhara*) lies exactly above the center of the garbhagrha. This point or the finial is conceived as a visual correlate of the *bindu.* Devangana Desai describes the relevance of śūnya in temple art at length in a paper, "Śūnya in the Context of Temple Art", *The Concept of Śūnya.*

**21. Being and Nonbeing**

1. Quoted in Peterfreund ( 1968 ), p.5
2. M.Nahm, *Selections from early Greek Philosophy,* quoted in Peterfreund ( 1968 ), p.65
3. Quoted in Peterfreund (1968), p.81
4. A fuller discussion on the manifesto will be found in Peterfreund (1968)

**23. Consciousness and Nothingness**

1. Introduction by Hazel E. Barnes to Sartre ( 1966 ), p. xv
2. Ibid., xviii
3. Sartre ( 1966), p.29
4. Sartre (1966), p.56
5. Sartre (1966), Introduction, p. xxvii
6. Sartre ( 1966 ), p.419

**24. Nonbeing and Anxiety**

1. Tillich in *The Courage to Be,* quoted in Perterfreund (1968), p.207
2. Tillich quoted in Peterfreund (1968), p.216

**25. Conflict and Contradictions**

1. A detailed discussion on interpretation and hermeneutics will be found in Burde ( 2004 ), Chapter 6.
2. Cornfords' translation, quoted in Russell (1999), p.93
3. Quoted in Russell (1999), p.93
4. Russell (1999), p.93

**26. Cynicism and Skepticism**

1. Quoted in Russell (1999), p.241
2. Ibid., p., 243

3. Ibid., p.244
4. Ibid., p.245
5. Durant ( 1953 ), p.97

**27. Space and Time**

1. Russell (1992), chapter 51
2. Ibid., p.350
3. Ibid., pp.472-473

**28. Epistemology**

1. Russell (1992), p.3 or 73
2. Russell (1992), p.62 N The paradox can also be explained as follows: The truth or falsehood of the statement can be ascertained only when we know what the *statement* is in " I make a false statement " The word statement refers to an extraneous utterings already made.
3. Rand (1990), p.6
4. Ibid., p.59

**29. Quantity and Magnitude**

1. Russell (1992), p.165
2. Russell (1992), p.184

**30. Mysticism and Non-Science**

1. Russell (1994), chapter 2.
2. Einstein (1979), p.227 from his speech "Principles of Research"

**32. Science and Mysticism**

1. See, for example, Deshpande (2001)
2. See Salmon (1963), p.10
3. Walter Thirring, quoted in Capra, (1993), p.246
4. Quoted in Capra (1993), p.247
5. Quoted in Capra (1993), p.163-164
6. Capra (1993), p.163
7. Quoted from Upniṣads, Capra (1993), p.154

# Bibliography

Acharya, S.S. (2001). *Rig Veda, Vols. I – IV.* Sanskriti Sansthan, Bareli.

(1998). *Sāma Veda.* Sanskriti Sansthan, Bareli.

(2001). *Yajur Veda.* Sanskriti Sansthan, Bareli.

(1998). *Atharva Veda, Vols. I – II.* Sanskriti Sansthan, Bareli.

Aurobindo, Sri (1970). *The Life Divine.* Sri Aurobindo Ashram, Pondicherry.

Bapat, K.M. (—). *Gorakshanath Yoga.* Raghuvanshi Prakashan, Pune.

Basham, A.L. (2001). *The Wonder That Was India.* Rupa & Co., New Delhi.

Berne, Eric (1968). *Games People Play.* Penguin, Middlesex.

Bose, A.C. (1970). *The Call Of The Vedas.* Bharatiya Vidya Bhavan, Mumbai.

Burton, David (1989). *Elementary Number Theory.* UBS, New Delhi.

Burde, Jayant (2004). *Rituals, Mantras and Science: An Integral Perspective.* Motilal Banarsidass, Delhi.

Capra, Fritjof (1983). *The Turning Point.* Flamingo, London.

(1993). *The Tao Of Physics.* Flamingo, London.

Chidbhavananda, Swami (1965). *The Bhagvad Gītā.* Sri Ramakrishna Tapovanan, Tirupparaitturai.

Clawson, Calvin C. (2004). *The Mathematical Traveller.* Viva, New Delhi.

Cohen, Leon W., Gertrude Ehrlich (1969). *The Structure of the Real Number System.* Affiliated East-West, New Delhi.

Deshpande, Dhanajay (2001). *Vedanteel Vidnyan.* Popular Prakashan, Mumbai.

Deussen, Paul (1980). *Sixty Upanishads of the Veda, Vol. II.* Motilal Banarsidass, Delhi.

Durant, Will (1953). *The story of Philosophy.* Pocket Books, New York.

Einstein, Albert (1979). *Ideas and Opinions.* Rupa & Co., Calcutta.

Gambhirananda, Swami (1989). *Māṇdukya Upanishad.* Advaita Ashram, Calcutta.

Hawking, Stepen W. (1989). *A Brief History Of Time.* Bantam, N.Y.

Ichimura, Shohei (2001). *Buddhist Critical Spirituality: Prajna and Sunyata.* Motilal Banarsidass, Delhi

Iyengar, B. K. S. (1992). *Light On Yoga.* HarperCollins, New Delhi.

Krishnamurti, J., David Bohm (1985). *The Ending of Time.* Krishnamurti Foundation, Chennai

Narayan, Shanti (1961). *A Text Book Of Modern Abstract Algebra.* S. Chand & Co., New Delhi.

O' Flaherty, Wendy Doniger (2000). *The Rig Veda.* Penguin, New Delhi.

Osho (2003). *The Fullness of Emptiness.* Sterling, New Delhi.

Penrose, Roger (1991). *The Emperor's New Mind.* Penguin, N. Y.

Peterfreund, Sheldon P., Theodre C. Denise (1968). *Contemporary Philosophy and Its Origins* East-West, New Delhi.

Rajaneesh, Bhagwan Shree (1979). *The Beginning of the Beginning.* Vikas, New Delhi.

Rajaraman (1999). *The Fundamentals of Computer.* Prentice-Hall, New Delhi.

Rand, Ayan (1984). *Philosophy: Who Needs It.* Signet (Penguin), N.Y.

(1990). *Introduction to Objective Epistemology.* Meridian (Penguin), N.Y.

Russell, Bertrand (1988). *Logic and Knowledge.* Routledge, London. (N.Y.)

(1948). *Human Knowledge.* Routledge, London.

(1992). *The Principles of Mathematics.* Routledge, London.

(1995). *An Inquiry into Meaning and Truth.* Routledge, London, (N.Y.)

(1993). *Introduction to Mathematical Philosophy.* Routledge, London.

(1994). *Mysticism and Logic.* Routledge, London.

(1995). *The Analysis of Mind.* Routledge, London.

(1994). *Philosophical Essays.* Routledge, London.

(1999). *History of Western Philosophy.* Routledge, N.Y.

Salmon, Weseley C. *Logic.* Prentice-Hall, New Jersey

Śaṅkarācārya (108), Śrīyogesvarānandatīrtha (1996). *Mantra-śāstra.* Keshav Bhikaji Dhavale, Mumbai.

Śaṅkarācārya (1978). *Ātmabodha.* Sri Ramakrisna Math, Madras.

Śaṅkarācārya, Bhārātī Kṛṣṇa Tīrthajī Mahārāja (1992). *Vedic Mathematics.* Motilal Banarsidass, Delhi.

Sartre, Jean-Paul (1966). *Being and Nothingness.* Pocket Books, N.Y.

Sasine, Jayvijay (1999). *Kundalinichya Shodhat.* Vedanta Publishers, Mumbai.

Simmons, G.F. (1963). *Introduction to Topology and Modern Analysis.* McGraw Hill, N.Y. (Kogakusha Tokyo).

Smith, Huston (1991). *The World's Religions,* HarperCollins, New Delhi.

Staal, Frits (1996). *Ritual and Mantras: Rules Without Meaning.* Motilal Banarsidass, Delhi.

Svanandasarasvati (—). *Patañjala Yogavidyā.* Raghuvanshi Prakashan, Pune.

Swami Ashokananda (1995). *Avadhuta Gītā Of Dattātreya.* Sri Ramakrishna Math, Madras.

Swahananda, Swami (1956). *Chāndogya Upanishad,* Sri Ramakrishna Math, Madras.

*The Concept of Śūnya.* (2003). A.K. Bag, S.R. Sharma (Eds.), IGNCA, Aryan Books International, New Delhi.

Tigunait, Pandit Rajmani (1983). *Seven Systems of Indian Philosophy.* The Himalayan International Institute of Yoga Science and Philosophy of the U.S.A., Honesdale.

(1996). *The Power of Mantra & The Mystery of Initiation.* The Himalayan International Institute of Yoga Science and Philosophy of the U.S.A., Honesdale.

(1999). *Tantra Unveiled.* The Himalayan International Institute of Yoga Science and Philosophy of the U.S.A., Honesdale.

Tyagisananda, Swami (—). *Svetasvatara Upanishad.* Sri Ramakrishna Math, Madras.

Woodroffe, John (1997). *The Serpent Power.* Ganesha & Co., Madras.

# Index